STUDENT DISCIPLINE
STRATEGIES

SUNY Series, Educational Leadership

Daniel L. Duke, Editor

STUDENT DISCIPLINE
STRATEGIES

Research and Practice

Edited by
Oliver C. Moles

State University of New York Press

DISCLAIMER

The content of this publication does not necessarily reflect the views or policies of the U.S. Department of Education nor does mention of trace names, commercial products, or organizations imply endorsement by the U.S. Government. The papers by persons who are not federal employees were funded under Contract No. 400-86-0055-III by the U.S. Department of Education, Office of Educational Research and Improvement.

Published by
State University of New York Press, Albany

® 1990 State University of New York

For information, address State University of New York
Press, State University Plaza, Albany, NY 12246

Library of Congress Cataloging-in-Publication Data

Student discipline strategies : research and practice / [editor],
    Oliver C. Moles.
        p.   cm.—(SUNY series in educational leadership)
    Bibliography: p.
    Includes index.
    ISBN 0-7914-0192-8.—ISBN 0-7914-0193-6 (pbk.)
    1. School   discipline—United   States—Case   studies.   2. Classroom
management—United States—Case studies. 3. Community and school—
—United States—Case studies. I. Moles, Oliver C. (Oliver Clinton),
1934-   . II. Series.
LB3012.S88   1990
371.1'024—dc20   89-4578
                                                                     CIP

10 9 8 7 6 5 4 3 2 1

CONTENTS

LIST OF FIGURES
AND TABLES

FIGURES

TABLES

FOREWORD

Attend any conference of school principals and observe the most popular meetings; invariably they focus upon student behavior.

This phenomenon defines the scope of the discipline problem. It is serious; it is pervasive; and it seldom improves despite the energies committed to controlling misbehavior in school.

Nor have school administrators relied upon themselves for solutions. For thirty years, they have looked to psychologists and sociologists for advice. Few general principles, however, apply in practice. Handling student discipline is still primarily a cottage industry. What works in one school does not necessarily work in another. Controlling misbehavior remains an idiosyncratic business depending upon the particular characteristics of students, family, teachers, and community.

Of this mix, family values are perhaps the dominant element. Witness the low rate of misbehavior among new Asians raised with Confucian regard for teachers and for learning. But the expectations of the school also play a central role in discipline. Clear rules, made with student participation and enforced firmly and fairly, do preempt many serious student discipline problems.

A stream of cultural and political traditions contribute to America's reputation for growing frisky adolescents—our suspicion of authority, our focus upon individualism, our spirit of independence. We are a difficult breed to brand.

A little irreverence goes a long way toward destroying the learning climate in a classroom. Teachers, after all, do not enter the profession to correct kids. Nor do they appreciate the classroom tension generated by uncertainties about student conduct.

Consequently, our national tolerance has been tested to the limit, and some changes are in order. Secondary students possess no intrinsic privilege to express their First Amendment rights by disrupting the education of their classmates. Teachers are not destined by God to play cat and mouse with troublemakers. School property is not a public canvas upon which to draw obscene graffiti.

How does America get things moving in the right direction? As this publication makes clear, student discipline is a many-layered thing. The causes and the solutions lie in strata, ranging from the individual classroom through school and community and state to national public opinion. Schools that control discipline problems act as a conductor to all these players, making certain to develop a harmony of acceptable levels of behavior while defining appropriate sanctions. All institutions require sanctions, schools no less than others.

But even this symphony can be troublesome because the time and energies required to control misbehavior often cause a drain on the central mission of the school—to teach and to learn.

Today, student misbehavior costs Americans too much in misdirected energy and the loss of too many superior teachers who simply quit to maintain their self-respect.

Unfortunately, we possess no magic bullet. But we must focus on the problem with renewed vigor. This excellent publication provides a useful platform. The reader, in searching for solutions among its pages, must not look for a magic bullet, for none exists. Rather, the reader must hope to better understand the wide variety of prevention and intervention strategies which now exist, and then direct that insight to cost-effective programs that reduce the discipline problems faced by our schools to levels equal to the schools of other nations.

Scott D. Thomson

ACKNOWLEDGMENTS

This work could not have come to fruition without the diligent and creative efforts of many persons. The conference from which these papers spring was suggested by Ronald P. Preston, former Deputy Assistant Secretary for Policy and Planning in the Office of Educational Research and Improvement (OERI), U. S. Department of Education. Chester E. Finn, Jr., former Assistant Secretary for OERI, suggested persons who became important conference participants and contributors to this volume.

Amy L. Schwartz helped plan the meeting. She, Keith Baker, and Joan Greer, all formerly of the U.S. Department of Education, ably led discussion groups during the conference which elucidated various issues regarding student discipline strategies. Other participants not represented here, but whose ideas enriched these papers, include Greg Bowman, Peter Blauvelt, Ivan Gluckman, Mildred Hannaham, Elaine Nolton, James Rapp, William Rudolph, Kevin Ryan, and Charlotte Stokes.

Refining the mass of material from the conference to this digestible form would not have been possible without the perceptive and constructive comments of anonymous reviewers commissioned by OERI and the publisher. My special thanks go to Dorothy James and Frances Clark, who cheerfully and carefully typed numerous versions of my material for this book. A final word of gratitude for her support, encouragement, and keen analysis throughout this project goes to my wife, Pat.

O.C.M.

___ GENERAL INTRODUCTION

Oliver C. Moles

This collection of research reviews and model programs emphasizes the influence of the community environment of schools, the social organization of schools and classrooms, and the processes of staff-student interaction on the behavior of students in schools. These areas are treated by a diverse set of scholars in order to show the various ways that they bear on issues of student discipline.

A unique feature of this volume is its examination of discipline strategies at multiple levels: in the classroom, in the school, and in the resources and opportunities of school-community relationships. Each higher level becomes the environment within which strategies at lower levels take place. This organization of material will make it easier for readers to locate material of direct interest.

Yet another feature is the broad range of student ages and grade levels considered: strategies applicable to both elementary and secondary school situations are discussed. The sociologists, psychologists, educators, and other contributors deal with student discipline problems in depth and offer important insights to guide teachers, administrators, and program developers.

The main sections of this book are devoted to the three levels or settings for the development and implementation of student discipline strategies. Following this introduction, the section on school strategies discusses properties of schools as social organizations, research on specific school programs, and model schools and training programs that have improved student discipline. The second sec-

---

Note: The editor's contributions to this volume do not necessarily represent the positions or policies of the U.S. Department of Education, and no official endorsement or concurrence is intended or should be inferred.

1

tion, on classroom strategies, focuses primarily on classroom organization and management issues, and also reviews various policies and practices that may influence student discipline and character development. The final section, on school-community relationships, spans topics from court decisions and police cooperation to university-based school team training and a proposed form of community service for offenders.

Several topics in this introduction may help orient the reader to this volume. First is a discussion of the nature, extent, and academic effects of student misbehavior. This raises several questions. Is the problem serious enough to warrant concern with strategies of amelioration? Does misbehavior affect student learning? Second, discipline strategies themselves are considered—their defining properties, some common types of strategies, and their uses. This leads to a section on the special features of this collection. Finally come brief comments on the origin of these papers, and some concluding thoughts about the uses of this volume and the development of discipline strategies. Overviews of each paper, and comments on how the papers fit together and into the larger fields of research and practice, can be found at the beginning of the sections on school, classroom, and school-community strategies.

STUDENT MISBEHAVIOR

Student misconduct and how to promote better discipline in schools are serious concerns not only of educators and the public, but also of students. National studies indicate that up to a quarter of students in secondary schools fear for their safety, with more students fearful in junior high than in senior high schools (Gallup, 1985; Wayne and Rubel, 1982). School staff are also apprehensive. In a national survey of public school teachers, 11 percent in urban schools mentioned fear of student reprisal as a major limitation on teachers' ability to maintain order in their schools, whereas only small proportions of teachers feared student reprisals in suburban or rural areas (3 percent and 5 percent, respectively). Almost a third (29 percent) of all teachers nationwide said they seriously considered leaving teaching because of student misbehavior (Center for Education Statistics, 1987).

In another national survey, secondary school principals reported an average of 10 suspensions during a school year for every one hundred students, with again more in urban (18.8) than in suburban

(10.9) or rural areas (6.6). Smaller schools and those with fewer low-income students had fewer suspensions (Center for Education Statistics, 1986). In addition, many large school districts now employ a school security force.

Less serious but more widespread forms of disruptive behavior are also reported in the previously mentioned national survey of teachers (Center for Education Statistics, 1987). In just the previous week, over half of all teachers had a student talk back to them (55 percent), pass a note or whisper (85 percent), or show up late for class (82 percent)—behaviors which disrupt the normal flow of teaching. Student behavior was seen to interfere with teaching at least to a moderate extent by 35 to 42 percent of teachers at different grade levels.

Persistent concern has also been expressed by the public. When asked what were the biggest problems facing their local schools, respondents to Gallup polls have cited discipline first almost every year back to the early 1970s. In 1986-88 discipline was second to use of drugs, itself a discipline-related problem (Gallup and Elam, 1988). When the public was asked to interpret *discipline*, over half said obeying rules and regulations (Gallup, 1982). Hence, the public has a broad view of discipline, and does not think exclusively of serious incidents such as vandalism, violence, and theft.

The public's broad view of discipline is also adopted in this book. Discipline problems may range from crimes in school committed by students or intruders, such as robbery and drug dealing, to lack of respectful behavior toward teachers and classmates. The spectrum from crimes to disrespect is discussed in the chapters of this volume. Although disciplinary code infractions are much more common, both infractions and crimes represent disobeying rules and regulations. The essential difference, as Rubel's chapter points out, is that crimes refer to the breaking of laws, even though some school administrators treat incidents like theft and assault as disciplinary problems rather than as crimes. But even the meaning of *good discipline* is open to different interpretations, as Wynne's chapter immediately makes clear, and there is a question of which rules of conduct beyond the laws should govern student behavior.

This issue cannot be decided here. It is fair to assume that rules, regulations, and even laws, let alone customs, will vary from place to place and from time to time. This suggests that what is a discipline problem in one school or classroom may not necessarily be a problem in another, and that the analyst should first understand the teacher's, school's, or school district's rules before trying to understand student deviations from them. Having only a few disciplinary incidents could reflect a permissive environment, or it could mean a tightly controlled or even a self-disciplined student body.

It is deceptive to use disciplinary referrals, suspensions, or other system responses as indicators of the level of misbehavior, since some may go undetected or unreported, and administrators may choose not to punish some misbehaving students as severely as others. A better method of determining the level of certain offenses is to ask the victims themselves. This method was adopted in the Safe School Study of 1976 (National Institute of Education, 1978). From that national sample survey, it was determined that in a typical month 12 percent of public secondary school teachers had property worth over a dollar stolen from them at school. The same was true for 11 percent of their students. In addition, 1.3 percent of the students and 0.5 percent of the teachers reported being attacked at school in a month. The rate for junior high school students was about twice that for senior high students (2.1 percent vs. 1 percent). About half of 1 percent of both students and teachers were robbed in school in a typical month.

Amid this somewhat bleak picture, there is some encouraging word about serious forms of student misbehavior. Using annual surveys of teachers and students, it has been possible to observe trends of theft, assault, and other crimes in schools from the early 1970s to the mid-1980s. Except for an increase in attacks on teachers in the late 1970s, all other indicators have remained level or declined. Thefts against students showed a marked and continuous drop (Moles, 1987).

These and other data lead to the conclusion that there has been some decrease in serious disciplinary incidents from the 1970s to the 1980s (Baker, 1985; Moles, 1987). Although many public school teachers (44 percent) have recently reported more disruptive classroom behavior in their schools than five years before (Center for Education Statistics, 1987), this difference may be due in large part to faulty memory of events that far in the past. More precise information would be obtained by using a shorter recall period (National Institute of Education, 1978). Still, it would seem that many schools, particularly junior highs and schools in urban areas, confront unacceptably large amounts of disruptive behavior. The problem is far from solved.

MISBEHAVIOR AND ACHIEVEMENT

It should be clear from the foregoing discussion that student misbehavior affects the learning environment of schools. Various kinds of minor disruptive behavior occur frequently. A large proportion of teachers at all grade levels believe student misbehavior interferes with their teaching. Even more, over half think it interferes with effective student learning (Center for Education Statistics, 1987). In fact, a major tenet of the effective schools movement, based on much research, is that a safe and orderly school is necessary before learning can take place (Edmonds, 1979). The situation seems far removed from that ideal for too many schools and teachers.

Student misbehavior also discourages teachers at a time when the country is trying desperately to upgrade the quality of education, including the retention and development of highly capable teachers. Almost a third of public school teachers have considered leaving teaching because of student misbehavior (Center for Education Statistics, 1987). Among those who had actually quit in the five years before 1986, 15 percent complained in one large-scale survey of discipline problems (Metropolitan Life survey, 1986). Thus teacher turnover and the loss of good teachers due to concern for student discipline also hampers the schools' educational mission.

Individual victims are also fearful, as noted already. For both teachers and students this may lead to avoiding situations and absence from the classroom. One might also question the level of academic performance among student offenders. The correlation between juvenile delinquency and student achievement is well established, although the direction of causation has been the subject of much theory and dispute. A recent national study of high school students indicates that misbehavior predicts a drop in grades and achievement test scores, but that low grades also lead to greater misbehavior (Myers et al., 1987). Thus causation seems to work in both directions, at least for older students. The common practice of removing students from the classroom and suspending them for serious misbehavior no doubt contributes to their lower achievement because they miss periods of instruction, and their motivation for school work diminishes.

By its effects on teachers, the school learning environment, and individual students, misbehavior can have a profound influence on student achievement. It should be clear that an improvement in student behavior could reap large benefits for learning.

DISCIPLINE STRATEGIES

These papers explore various strategies educators might use to maintain order and bring about student compliance with school rules and regulations. They do not systematically analyze the causes of student misbehavior. These may involve, among other factors, personal dispositions, perceptions of the future, social background, family life, and peer group influences the student brings to school (Gottfredson, 1987; Johnson, 1979). To understand them in any detail is beyond the scope of this volume. But the organization of schools and classrooms, and the interactions between students and staff, can ameliorate or exacerbate student propensities toward misbehavior, and it is these manipulable features of schooling that are the subject of these papers.

Thinking of strategies as careful plans or methods to deal with student discipline problems, it is clear that strategies can vary immensely in specificity, scope, complexity, target students and behaviors, and a host of other dimensions. What strategies have in common by this view is a stated and systematic course of action based on a thoughtful analysis of existing conditions. Those conditions might include the specific kinds of misbehavior of concern, student social characteristics, school organization, climate and operation, and the larger community environment. Each condition can be important in shaping an appropriate strategy.

This broad view of strategies leads to the point made in several papers that there is no one best strategy, and that successful strategies in one context cannot be expected to work automatically in another. Local conditions may simply dictate a different approach, although some approaches may be preferable to others.

Strategies may be classified in different ways, such as prevention versus intervention. In his chapter, Rubel employs a nice distinction between prevention strategies and two kinds of interventions: response to chronic problems and control of acute ones. Most principles of classroom management, as explicated in Doyle's paper, would emphasize prevention, whereas some of the packaged teacher-training programs, such as Assertive Discipline, discussed in Emmer and Aussiker's paper, would stress intervention strategies as well as prevention.

Another set of distinctions is between direct strategies designed to curb specific misbehaviors, indirect strategies aimed at presumed underlying student problems such as low achievement, and nonstudent strategies concerned with school and classroom conditions thought to affect student conduct, such as improving teacher effectiveness.

In addition, strategies vary in terms of who designs and implements them. The chapter by Dunn describes the training of school teams which include teachers, administrators, support staff, school board members, representatives of community agencies, and parents.

They develop unique action plans for their own school situations. Furtwengler's chapter carries this further to describe how students can be integrated into the planning and action process. These program developers and others recognize the power of involving participants in the process of organizational change to gain their commitment.

Finally, it should be noted that none of the writers in this volume recommends suspension or expulsion of students as a general strategy for dealing with discipline problems. There are few well-designed studies of suspension, as Toby and Scrupski note. Suspension has been overused in the past, sometimes giving truants the free time they want, and applied more often against minority students than against others (Garibaldi, 1979). Although removing students can relieve the school of troublemakers, it shortchanges them educationally and only shifts the problem to the community, and sometimes the police.

The lack of support for suspension and expulsion does not mean that there is no role for punishment in strategies to reduce student misbehavior. On the contrary, one of the best-established research findings is the link between firm, fairly administered, and consistent discipline and lower levels of discipline problems in schools (Metz, 1978; Gottfredson and Gottfredson, 1985; National Institute of Education, 1978). Knowing that misbehavior will not be tolerated and that no special exception will be granted seems an effective deterrent. Punitive responses have a place among discipline strategies, and they are discussed in the papers by Doyle, Emmer and Aussiker, Wynne, and Toby and Scrupski.

But some of these authors and others raise the question of whether punishment should be considered the central means of solving discipline problems. Punishment increases resentment, does not emphasize desired behavior, and must be applied consistently (Slavin, 1986). Purkey concludes from the scant historical evidence that the punitive approach has proven ineffective, and that fundamental changes in the structure of schools will be necessary before student behavior is likely to change. For Purkey and others, this would mean altering the social organization and the culture of schools to make them more conducive to teaching and learning. The norms of such a school would include order, discipline, and serious attention to the work of schools by students and teachers.

Thus, a number of different kinds of strategies are presented in the chapters of this volume, and sometimes argued with intensity. The strategies can be classified by classroom, school, and school-community level, by emphasis on prevention or intervention, and by whether they focus on changing the student or the organization, to reiterate some of the main distinctions identified. Keeping these distinctions in mind should help the reader sort out the strategies of most interest and application in specific circumstances.

FEATURES OF THIS COLLECTION

This volume presents an unusual mixture of approaches to student discipline problems. It contains reviews of recent research, programs, and program evaluations in various domains by noted scholars. These appear first in each section. A few model programs are also described by persons in key positions—their originators or directors. There are advantages to both approaches. Research offers rigorous and systematic analysis of discipline strategies and their effects, and the reviews synthesize these findings. But many strategies are relatively new, unique, or complex, and may prove difficult to study systematically. Educators and policy makers must make decisions with the best information available at the time. Detailed accounts of promising practices by perceptive and innovative practitioners such as these represent another strand of information useful for such decisions.

It should be noted, however, that this volume differs from other books on student discipline strategies. Many of them were written as advice for the teacher or administrator based on the best experience of seasoned practitioners. Others have been based on distillation of goals and activities of "exemplary" programs (e.g., Wayson et al., 1982). Still others have been organized around school programs for disruptive students (e.g., Safer, 1982). Although some have referred regularly to the research literature, as a group they are not organized first to synthesize the available research and then to draw implications for practice. Systematic research may yield different conclusions than one obtains from "best practice," as the analysis of popular teacher-training programs by Emmer and Aussiker suggests.

A different set of books on discipline strategies is based on behavior modification principles. This approach is not emphasized in this volume, although behavior modification principles are used in several of the chapters. As Doyle points out, there is considerable controversy surrounding this approach and its practicality for classroom teachers. Token economies prove complex, ignoring undesirable behavior may become unrealistic, and rewards for desired behavior can undermine intrinsic motivation. Doyle and other chapter authors cite more promising newer applications which teach students social skills, coping strategies and participation skills, and self-monitoring and self-control strategies.

An obvious feature of this collection is the grouping of chapters by setting—classroom, school, and school-community relationships. This grouping facilitates access to the discussions of strategies of most interest to teachers, principals, school system administrators, program developers, school policy makers, and others. The overview which introduces each section will alert readers to areas of special interest.

In the school strategies section, the research chapters discuss organizational properties, including leadership, school culture, specific school programs, and means of organizational development. The model school programs chapters describe a public high school in a low-income area which has turned around, and a training program to improve student discipline through involving students and teachers in all phases of the change process. These chapters form a context for a consideration of the organizational, instructional and interpersonal processes within the classroom in the next section.

The three chapters in the section on classroom strategies focus primarily on classroom organization and management: research-based principles and techniques, studies of popular packaged training approaches, and a review of various policies and practices that may influence student discipline and character development. The final section on school-community strategies encompasses a wide variety of topics. These include research reviews on the influence of court decisions on school discipline policies, and school cooperation with the police. They also include model program descriptions of university-based training of school teams, a community service program, and various programs in one system to deal with different kinds of discipline problems. In the collection as a whole, both elementary and secondary schools are discussed, with more attention to the elementary level in the section on classroom strategies, particularly Doyle's chapter.

The nested arrangement of classrooms within schools and schools within community contexts means that each higher level serves as an environment for lower-level settings. Not all influence flows downward, however, and the initiative taken by staff and schools to obtain team training is a case in point. The community environment can serve several functions. It can be the locus of resources for schools and their personnel, as in the case of cooperation with the police, school team building by outside developers, or the alternative schools described by Sang. It can be the setting for school activities, as in the coerced community service proposal of Toby and Scrupski. The community environment can also provide parameters or constraints on school actions, as Lufler's discussion of the role of legal commentators illustrates. The same concepts of resources, constraints, and settings can be applied to the school as an environment for classroom activities.

DEVELOPMENT OF THE PAPERS

The papers in this volume were first presented at a conference on student discipline strategies sponsored by the Office of Educational Research and Improvement in the U.S. Department of Education. The editor organized this research agenda-building conference held in Washington, D.C., in November 1986. He earlier worked on the Safe School Study (National Institute of Education, 1978), and headed an NIE group which sponsored various studies on discipline-related issues. The conference brought together a wide range of researchers, educators, and program administrators to present and discuss papers on ways to ameliorate student discipline problems in elementary and secondary schools.

The papers in this collection have been revised, some of them extensively, since the conference. The research review papers represent the best evidence approach to summarizing and synthesizing research findings. The findings selected depend on the reviewer's judgment of the strongest studies available, including unpublished works. To ensure sound judgment to the greatest extent possible, paper writers were chosen for their depth of relevant professional experience and for their reputation as thoughtful, objective analysts.

This approach differs from meta-analysis, wherein all relevant studies with a sufficient degree of methodological rigor are used to calculate the average strength of the effects of interventions or conditions (Glass, 1977). The wide range of discipline strategies considered in these papers would have been quite unwieldy, and also thin in many places, if turned into a series of quantitative summaries. Moreover, meta-analysis has been criticized for combining studies of uneven quality and different emphases (Slavin, 1984).

Given the current state of knowledge on student discipline strategies, it seemed prudent to rely on the best evidence identified by recognized scholars. As a check on the adequacy of this approach, each research and practice paper was reviewed by three to five other experts, and their recommendations were considered in writing the final version of the papers which appear here. The scope of each paper is described at the beginning of its section.

CONCLUDING COMMENTS

This collection should be useful to social scientists and educational researchers who study school organization and improvement, school-community linkages, classroom environments, staff-student interaction, and the nature and extent of student discipline problems. A number of ideas for further research are presented in various papers.

These papers should be equally useful to educators and those in training who need to understand how specific and manipulable features of schools, classrooms, and their surrounding environments affect the course of student behavior and prospects for sustained improvement in the discipline climate in schools. The information in these papers provides many practical ideas, as well as some cautions, for trying new approaches to make schools more orderly learning environments for all students.

Many student discipline strategies, and issues in the development and application of such strategies, are presented within these pages. But which strategies are best? The answer is bound to vary by local needs and circumstances. After weighing these conditions, one might try a strategy for a sufficient period, and evaluate its utility with well-designed research. In this way, the answer will come from local experience guided by the best available evidence from other settings.

One test is to see whether the strategy can change student behavior on a sustained basis without the commitment of excessive resources. Staff time and energy, retraining, equipment, and facilities costs are part of this equation. So is the need to demonstrate that change is real and enduring. For more recalcitrant and serious discipline problems, a larger commitment of resources would be warranted.

The ideal situation is for students to become self-disciplined, following rules and regulations without the need for surveillance, so that fewer school resources are necessary. To move toward this state, organizational studies point to the need to involve a wide range of staff and students themselves in the development and implementation of school rules and school improvement programs. (See, for example, the chapters by Furtwengler and by Gottfredson.) Other principles underlying discipline strategies could be extracted, and many good ones are set forth by these authors. But among the most important, a genuine and continued involvement of students and staff would appear necessary to win their cooperation toward reducing discipline problems.

PART I
School Strategies

INTRODUCTION:
School Strategies Section

This first set of chapters deals with school-level strategies. Student discipline is often a schoolwide concern, and much misbehavior happens in hallways and other open areas. Thus the whole school is an important focus of attention, both as a social organization and as a setting for misbehavior.

In the lead chapter, Daniel Duke examines the contribution of school leadership and key organizational elements of schools to maintaining student discipline. He presents a model of how these are linked together, and reviews several sources of information: studies of school effectiveness, reanalyses of large data sets, survey and case study research, and studies of alternative schools. He also examines over a dozen district-sponsored evaluations of local discipline programs. Duke then relates the research on organizational elements and leadership to the needs of practitioners, discussing points of agreement as well as disparate findings. He asserts that no single organizational strategy is best for all schools, but that the implementation of effective changes is very dependent on the quality of school leadership.

In the next chapter, on developing effective organizations, Denise Gottfredson discusses attempts to reduce disruptive behavior by changing school practices in ways guided by research. The first part of her paper describes a collaborative project between researchers and practitioners to design, implement, and assess school practices to reduce disorder, based on an organizational development approach called Program Development Evaluation. This project led to changes in various areas, particularly classroom management and instruction. Other approaches with high-risk youth—a pull-out program, an alternative class, and an alternative school—are also described, along with evidence about the efficacy of each strategy. Gottfredson sees as essential for any change a solidly grounded and well-understood theory about the causes of the problems, and adapting strategies to local circumstances.

The programs described by Duke which work to improve student achievement, such as alternative schools, help to reduce the disparity between students' academic goals and their actual achievements. As such, these indirect strategies are linked to the strain theory of deviant behavior (Merton, 1938; Cohen, 1955; Cloward and Ohlin, 1960). This theory proposes that adolescents become delinquent and disruptive in reaction to experiencing or anticipating failure. School failure is frustrating both in the present and for what it portends for one's future. This situation can lead students to violate rules so as to get what they want, as in cheating, or to express unconventional and unacceptable but attainable values.

In his chapter, Stewart Purkey argues that there is no one best solution to discipline problems. He advocates forms of organizational restructuring that facilitate cultural change and improve the quality of life in schools as a means to create lasting change. Noting that student misbehavior is not a new phenomenon, he argues that the application of harsh punishments has not cured discipline problems and may even be counter-productive, and that a systemic approach is more appropriate than resorting to any specific disciplinary method. Finally, Purkey suggests ways of creating a school culture supportive of teaching and learning that will lead students to accept and comply with school rules. He argues that special attention must be paid to the nature of the curriculum, and the form of instruction if students are to become fully engaged with their work in school.

Moving to school strategies actually applied in various school districts, Willis Furtwengler and Denise Gottfredson show how organizational development processes can improve student discipline, even in schools with sizeable problems. The process Furtwengler calls Reaching Success Through Involvement (RSI) focuses on changing the culture of the school and its productivity. This is done by involving the whole educational community, including students, in solving problems, implementing solutions, and monitoring effectiveness. Furtwengler traces the development of RSI over some years, and describes its basic framework and activities at the school level. He provides examples and research findings on how discipline has improved, and the aspects of school culture which might need to be changed.

This kind of strategy is designed to increase the social bonding of students to the school as students and staff work closely together. Students become more bonded to the school when their attachment to adults and peers, commitment to conventional goals, involvement in constructive activities, and belief in the validity of social norms is strengthened (Hirschi, 1969). Organizational development efforts like those described by Furtwengler and Gottfredson have the potential to increase social bonding. All school culture strategies would, if effective, change student norms to increase commitment and belief in the school. As staff show more concern for students individually, students care about their approval and develop social and emotional ties to them. The processes of social bonding can be found in various strategies discussed in this volume.

In the final chapter on school strategies, Victor Herbert describes his experiences as principal of Samuel Gompers Vocational-Technical High School in the Bronx. He came into a school ridden with drugs, fights, low achievement, and poor attendance. Five years later the school had turned around on all fronts. In the process, the curriculum changed, the school became co-ed, the faculty improved, and student recruitment and support were strengthened. How this happened, Herbert dramatically portrays in terms of specific goals and actions taken during the first year and at subsequent stages.

These chapters on school strategies share a concern with school leadership. Duke identifies seven critical leadership functions, and others expand on the concept of leadership. For Gottfredson this involves seeking the advice of those who would have to implement new practices. For Furtwengler, both faculty and students are formally integrated into the planning and action stages. Purkey adds that the qualities of leadership may be different and more authoritarian for an out-of-control school than for one without severe discipline problems (see also Schwartz, 1988).

Herbert's chapter shows the principal in action, intuitively following practices well supported by the research. Trying to catch redhanded those who tripped alarms demonstrates the principle of "management by walking around" at a fast pace. Clearly enunciating a code of conduct is essential for students to feel that discipline policies are fair, an attribute essential to order in schools (see chapters by Gottfredson and Duke).

More generally, the effort to increase Gompers high school faculty and student participation in school improvement is exactly the kind of approach to school leadership advocated in the research review chapters of this section. However, changes at Gompers did not happen overnight, and the promise of quick fixes anywhere appears illusory. Others have noted that first attempts seldom work, and real changes may take years to accomplish, as they did here (see Klausmeier, 1985; and chapter by Furtwengler).

A second theme is an emphasis on organizational development, or organizational self-improvement in communication, trust, participation, problem solving, and dealing with conflicts. It usually involves an outside change agent and the use of behavioral science techniques to assemble data on organizational functioning. The application and impact of organizational development in schools has been carefully reviewed (Fullan, Miles, and Taylor, 1980). Gottfredson's and Furtwengler's chapters are good examples of organizational development in action.

Purkey argues that changing the organization of schools will be more productive than treating the "symptoms of the problem," the misbehavior. Duke has identified basic elements in a sociological analysis of organizational structure, and Herbert describes a variety of structural changes at Gompers. Gottfredson and Furtwengler argue for organizational development as a way of changing the school culture or climate to build cooperation and to strengthen the problem-solving process.

The school culture is a prominent focus of change efforts in organizational development. It is the prevailing pattern of activities and interactions, and of shared norms, attitudes, and values. Where there is a cultural press for order and safety, the school climate is more supportive of student learning. From the research, Duke identifies pervasive caring for students and staff collegiality as characteristics of school culture that promote student discipline. Furtwengler sees school culture as "the way we do things around here," and his school improvement approach explicitly focuses on changing the school culture.

Some would argue that the principal is central to changing the school culture (e.g. Sarason, 1971). But the "loosely coupled" nature of teaching (Weick, 1976), which is beyond the principal's immediate supervision, suggests that trying to increase school effectiveness by imposing policies from above may be much less productive than building staff consensus on desired norms and goals. Staff need to "own" new discipline goals and strategies in order to act autonomously to promote them (Purkey and Smith, 1983).

Taken together, the chapters in this section illuminate a rich array of both broad-based and specific organizational strategies available to school district administrators and program developers.

1

School Organization, Leadership, and Student Behavior

Daniel L. Duke

A perennial concern for educators, student behavior has been examined and addressed from a variety of perspectives. Some have dealt with behavior problems clinically, investigating the origins of dysfunctional student conduct and developing highly personalized treatments. Some have adopted instructional approaches in which students are taught how to behave appropriately and teachers are encouraged to regard good instructional practice as the first line of defense against misconduct. Some have sought to control student behavior through cooperative action involving school authorities, parents, community agencies, government programs, juvenile justice offices, and the like. Some have invested energy in providing organizational structures to reduce the likelihood of inappropriate student behavior. This chapter takes an in-depth look at the last set of approaches, which henceforth will be referred to as "organizational approaches to student behavior," and the leadership functions needed to implement and maintain them.

The first objective entails a review of research studies that attempt to link elements of school organizational structure with student behavior. The elements that will be addressed include the following:

- School goals—Desired outcomes targeted for special emphasis by school personnel.
- Control structure—The mechanisms by which schools ensure that organizational goals are pursued. Mechanisms include evaluation, supervision, rewards, and sanctions.

19

- Complexity—The degree of specialization and technical expertise required to achieve school goals.
- Centralization—The extent to which school decision making is open to participation by individuals other than school officials.
- Formalization—The extent to which the behavior of students and/or teachers is constrained by rules and regulations.
- Stratification—The distribution of status and privilege within schools.

In addition to these six basic elements of organizational structure, school climate and size will be investigated. Although not a structural element per se, school climate—or school culture, as some prefer—embodies norms, expectations, and collective aspirations that are closely related to aspects of school organization. Similarly, school size—in terms of the numbers of students and employees—frequently influences the nature of school organization.

Following the review of research on school organization and student behavior, the focus shifts to leadership. Assuming that schools can be structured in ways that minimize the likelihood of inappropriate student behavior, how should school leaders proceed to create and maintain orderly environments in which teaching and learning can occur? The model which emerges from this investigation of school organization and student behavior presumes that school leaders' primary influence on student behavior is exercised indirectly through efforts to shape and define elements of school organization and climate. This model is depicted in Figure 1.1.

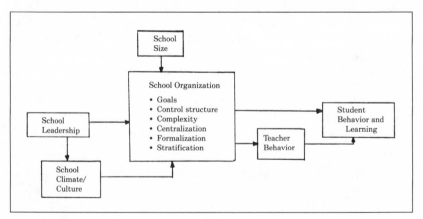

Figure 1.1 A Model of School Leadership, School Organization, and Student Behavior

RESEARCH ON LEADERSHIP, SCHOOL ORGANIZATION, AND STUDENT BEHAVIOR

Compared with clinical and instructional approaches to student behavior, organizational approaches have not been researched extensively. The only comprehensive review of organizational research related to student behavior was conducted by the author and a colleague in 1983 (Duke and Seidman). The present review covers research studies since 1983 along with important prior investigations. Studies were identified through a comprehensive ERIC search, solicitations of school district research directors, and consultation with leading authorities in the field of school discipline. To facilitate the review, studies will be organized according to focus and methodology. Categories include school effectiveness studies, reanalysis of large data sets, survey and case study research, research on alternative schools, and district-sponsored evaluation studies of local discipline programs.

School Effectiveness Studies

Undertaken to challenge the conventional wisdom that schools explain very little of the variation in student achievement, the so-called school effectiveness studies compared the characteristics of schools with relatively high and relatively low levels of student achievement. The schools tended to be urban elementary schools serving large numbers of disadvantaged students. In the wake of these studies came prescriptive syntheses, cautionary reviews, and documented efforts to implement school effectiveness findings.

School effectiveness research is pertinent to the concerns of this chapter because an orderly environment has emerged from syntheses of findings as a consistent characteristic of schools with relatively high levels of student achievement (Duke, 1982; Stedman, 1985). Furthermore, many other factors associated with high student achievement represent aspects of school organization, thereby raising the possibility that orderly environment and school organization are closely related.

Effective schools tend to be characterized by such organizational factors as frequent and systematic evaluation of students, goals linked to the acquisition of basic skills, and clear rules for student conduct (Stedman, 1985). The cultures of effective schools encompass norms of collegiality among staff members and pervasive caring for students (Anderson, 1985). Student stratification is minimized as a result of efforts to utilize fluid ability grouping strategies (Stedman, 1985).

Syntheses of findings from school effectiveness research invariably have led to prescriptions for practitioners. These prescriptions consist of a variety of strategies, suggesting that improving schools is not a simple matter of one or two changes. Hundreds of school districts in the mid-1980s have rushed to implement school effectiveness recommendations, prompting a second wave of research and research reviews. The reviews have been much more cautionary in tone than the initial prescriptive syntheses. Questions have been raised about the extent to which generalizations concerning school improvement can be made from studies of urban elementary schools. Cuban (1983) warned that the criteria for determining whether schools are effective—namely, student performance on standardized tests of basic skills—were too narrow. Stedman (1985) noted that researchers did not use systematic procedures to observe schools, but relied on the impressions of observers who knew, in advance, which schools were effective and ineffective.

Despite the warning, school administrators saw in the school effectiveness findings practical guidelines for school improvement. Although researchers might debate the quality of data, educators still had to make daily decisions about the operation of schools. The latter could not afford to wait for the perfect school effectiveness study to be conducted. Local school effectiveness projects therefore continued to proliferate, followed by studies of implementation efforts. In one of the most detailed investigations, Purkey (1984) examined one urban district's efforts to incorporate thirteen elements of effective schools research in six high schools. For present purposes, what is intriguing about Purkey's research is not that the project failed, but that attention tended to be focused primarily on student discipline, building security, and attendance. School improvement goals concerning academic achievement, student recognition, and the like failed to command the time and energy of school personnel. Purkey attributed this unofficial narrowing of project goals to inadequate district policies and the naive belief that resolving discipline-related concerns alone would produce student achievement gains.

One study with more encouraging findings involved efforts to implement school effectiveness strategies in two troubled Baltimore, Maryland, junior high schools (Gottfredson, 1986b). One Effective Schools Project was successful and led to decreased school disorder, enhanced school climate, and increased social development and perceived relevance of school. A study of the school improvement process suggests that the introduction of new classroom management and instructional strategies may require supporting organizational development, including systematic training for supervisors as well as teachers and a commitment by organization officials to minimize staff turnover. The failure of the second Effective Schools Project was attributed, in part, to a change in school leadership midway through the intervention and the subsequent unwillingness of staff members to regard the project as more than a pilot effort.

A similarly comprehensive intervention, also under the auspices of the Center for Social Organization of Schools, took place over a three-year period in Charleston County, South Carolina, public schools (Gottfredson, 1986a). Aimed at reducing delinquency and increasing student attachment to school, Project PATHE ("Positive Action Through Holistic Education") consisted of organizational innovations (planning and troubleshooting teams, policy revision, curriculum development, and staff development), instructional innovations, career exploration activities, and special student services.

Since it was impossible to create a true control group, it is not known whether changes identified by researchers were attributable to Project PATHE. The study does indicate, however, that disruption decreased and student attachment to school increased in project schools. Particular schools reported fewer suspensions, greater belief in school rules, decreased victimization, and less drug involvement. What the Charleston County and Baltimore studies seem to suggest is that the creation of more orderly and productive learning environments is a function of comprehensive school improvement rather than isolated innovations. Since student behavior is the result of numerous factors and conditions, no single strategy is likely to produce widespread changes in school climate.

Reanalyses

The availability of several large data bases has provided rich opportunities for researchers interested in student behavior and school organization.

In 1976 McPartland and McDill reanalyzed data collected a decade earlier from nine hundred principals by James Coleman and his associates. They found that school size was positively correlated to reports of the extent and seriousness of student misconduct. Although the relationship was small in terms of the total variance explained, it was statistically significant. Further, the reanalysis controlled for student ability level, racial composition, and socioeconomic status. The researchers concluded that "all behavior is more visible in smaller schools and naturally subject to greater control" (p. 19).

A second finding related to school organization concerned student involvement in school decision making. A measurable positive impact on attitudes opposing violence and vandalism was found in schools where students played a role in deciding such things as school rules. This finding is supported by studies of alternative schools, where student involvement tends to be extensive. Research on alternative schools will be discussed later in this chapter.

The Safe School Study, commissioned by Congress and conducted by the National Institute of Education, has proved to be one of the most fertile grounds for reanalysis. It consisted of three components: (1) a mail survey of principals in several thousand public elementary and secondary schools, (2) an intensive study of 642 public junior and senior high schools in which thousands of students and teachers completed questionnaires, and (3) case studies of ten schools (National Institute of Education, 1978).

Wu et al. (1982) used Safe School Study data to look at the relationship between suspensions and the way schools organize and operate disciplinary activities (control structure). They recognized that schools differ in the degree to which discretionary authority is delegated to teachers in disciplinary matters. Using teacher responses from the Safe School Study, the researchers found that a high rate of suspension was positively correlated with a high degree of perceived administrative centralization of discipline. They went on to indicate that a high rate of suspension was not a desirable outcome or an indication of effective control structure.

To demonstrate the undesirability of a high suspension rate, the researchers constructed a Good Governance Scale made up primarily of student perceptions of school disciplinary practices. Well-governed schools were schools that did not suspend frequently. Students in these schools perceived their principals to be firm and fair. High suspension rates appeared to be indications that less severe control mechanisms had failed.

The Gottfredsons (1979, 1985) reanalyzed part of the Safe School data and found that student victimizations in six hundred schools were related to (1) teacher confusion over how school policies were determined (coordination), and (2) the fairness and clarity of school rules as perceived by students. Lower levels of victimization were associated with effective communications, both between administrators and teachers and between teachers and students. The Gottfredsons challenged a finding of McPartland and McDill (1976) when they reported that teacher preference for student involvement in school decision making was related to larger numbers of reported victimizations. Both studies were cross-sectional in nature and thus pose problems of cause and effect.

A major objective of the Gottfredsons' work was to identify organizational characteristics that help explain differences among schools in amounts of personal (teacher and student) victimization, disorder, and disruption. Characteristics found to be correlated with some form of discipline problem included school size, coordination, teacher resources, leadership, and formalization. The Gottfredsons recommend the following organizational strategies for reducing discipline problems:

- Create schools of smaller size, where "teachers have extensive responsibility for and contact with a limited number of students" and "where steps are taken to ensure adequate resources for instruction" (p. 171)
- Consider breaking down large schools into smaller components, such as schools-within-schools (p. 172)
- Encourage a high degree of cooperation between teachers and administrators (p. 173)
- Clarify rules, consequences for breaking rules, and disciplinary policies so that confusion is minimized (p. 173)
- Encourage school leadership that is firm and visible (p. 173)

A third target for reanalysis has been the High School and Beyond study (Peng, Fetters, and Kolstad, 1981). Data were gathered from thirty thousand sophomores and a similar number of seniors in 1980, with a follow-up questionnaire having been administered to both sets in 1982. Initial data analysis yielded the most extensive profile of the American high school student ever produced.

Several reanalyses of the High School and Beyond study have focused on school dropouts. Since dropping out and discipline problems are often related, these reanalyses are pertinent to the present study. Prior to leaving school, dropouts frequently become frustrated and resentful, thereby contributing to school disorder. The organizational conditions that contribute to early school departure also may influence unproductive student behavior in school. Wehlage and Rutter (1986), for example, found that "marginal students" from the High School and Beyond study tended to perceive the effectiveness of school discipline as relatively poor. Students were even more negative about the fairness of discipline. In addition, they felt that teachers were not particularly interested in them. Natriello, Pallas, and McDill (1986) concluded from the data that smaller schools were more likely to be responsive to the needs of "marginal students." One clear message from these and other studies has been that organizational strategies for reducing the number of school dropouts also are likely to foster a climate more conducive to productive student behavior. Little support can be found for strategies that would reduce school size by making life uncomfortable for certain groups of students.

Survey and Case Study Research

Although the capacity for generalization from large data bases cannot be matched by small-scale surveys and case studies, the latter often produce valuable insights into the relationships between organizational characteristics and student behavior.

Hollingsworth, Lufler, and Clune (1984) used an interdisciplinary approach to examine discipline in five public secondary schools in a midsize Wisconsin city during the 1977-78 school year. Methods used to collect data included extensive non-participant observation, interviewing, surveys, and document review. Data analysis was focused on describing how control structure was linked to other elements of school organization. No systematic effort was made to draw causal inferences.

The researchers found little consensus regarding the desired goals and practices of school discipline. Enforcement of rules was "very decentralized," with teachers differing widely in perceptions of misbehavior, orientations toward punishment, and desire to be involved in discipline. Students and teachers alike believed that high-achieving students were favored when disciplinary issues arose. The sanctions used by school personnel were not imposed systematically, nor did they appear to be very effective. On the other hand, the researchers noted that variations in classroom management among teachers did not create problems. Little justification for uniform classroom management practices could be found.

Cheryl Perry (1980) conducted interviews and administered questionnaires in twelve California high schools in order to identify organizational and community-based correlates of student behavior problems. Student behavior problems were defined in terms of attendance, disciplinary referrals, and perceptions of the principal. Schools were divided into those with relatively few and those with relatively many behavior problems. High degrees of absenteeism were correlated with the existence of a school-sanctioned smoking area, programs to deal with drug use, and student uncertainty about consequences for rule breaking. The number of disciplinary referrals was positively correlated with the percentage of students in vocational education (stratification), the existence of a school-sanctioned smoking area, consistent rule enforcement by administrators, and student uncertainty about consequences for rule breaking. Principal judgment of the seriousness of behavior problems was positively correlated with the existence of a school-sanctioned smoking area, consistent rule enforcement by administrators, and the percentage of teachers who determined classroom rules.

As in much of the previous research, it is difficult to separate cause and effect in Perry's findings. For example, did school-sanctioned smoking areas contribute to behavior problems by providing opportunities for students to congregate under poorly supervised conditions or did smoking areas result from administrative acknowledgement that smoking by students could not be prevented? Perry's research nonetheless is noteworthy because it raises the possibility that consistent rule enforcement and teacher firmness, under certain conditions, actually may contribute to student behavior problems.

Whereas Perry spent a relatively brief time gathering data in twelve schools, Metz (1978) took over a year to conduct a field study of two desegregated junior high schools. She sought to understand the ways that schools as organizations addressed the "twin tasks of pursuing effectiveness and maintaining civility, safety, and order" (p. IX). Because students in the two schools behaved quite differently, despite being matched racially and socioeconomically, Metz was able to make some causal inferences. She identified differences in faculty culture and leadership as prime contributors to differences in behaviors at the two schools.

At Hamilton, the school with a higher level of disorder, there was no commonly accepted set of behavioral norms and expectations among faculty members. Teachers disagreed on almost everything, from how to approach children to goals for disciplinary practices. The faculty at Chauncey, the less troubled junior high, shared a common understanding of school discipline. They expected to have to work to maintain order, and they did not waste time finding people to blame for behavior problems. Students at Hamilton quickly perceived that their misconduct would not be dealt with consistently, whereas their counterparts at Chauncey confronted teacher unanimity about how disobedience would be handled.

Metz's study is important because it indicated that classroom management should not be considered apart from school discipline. What happens in the corridors has a direct effect on behavior in classrooms. A similar point had been made earlier by Cusick (1973), in a participant-observer study of student culture in a high school. Cusick also found that the overarching commitment to order by administrators and teachers seemed to interfere with efforts to achieve academic goals and respond to student concerns.

A decade later Cusick (1983) conducted case studies of three integrated high schools—two urban and one suburban. His basic finding was that the organizational structure of secondary schools accounted for much of the general pattern of student behavior. The key element of school structure was a commitment to the goal of equal opportunity—or what Cusick termed the "egalitarian ideal." Were it not for this commitment, Cusick maintained that schools simply could dismiss unruly and unmotivated students, thereby reducing the need for a pervasive control structure. To have abandoned the egalitarian ideal, however, would be to threaten the very legitimacy of public schooling as an institution. The character of American high schools is shaped, Cusick argued, by the fact that they must make every effort to serve the needs of the disadvantaged and the uncooperative. As a result, such organizational functions as teacher evaluation, scheduling, and student activities came to be dominated by a concern for order. This concern is elevated to the level of obsession when racial tension among students is a possibility.

Crawford, Miskel, and Johnson (1980) and Duke and Meckel (1980) also conducted studies of racially mixed urban secondary schools, but their concerns differed from Cusick's. The former tried to account for the success of a school improvement project, whereas the latter investigated factors contributing to the persistent failure of school discipline strategies.

Faced with high rates of withdrawal, suspension, and academic failure among black students, a first-year high school principal worked with university researchers to develop an intervention program (Crawford, Miskel, and Johnson, 1980). The program consisted of various organizational strategies, including faculty agreement on a set of basic school goals, peer counseling, an independent study center, career education opportunities, and development of a school cadre. Data on implementation efforts and outcomes were collected over a three-year period. Data analyses revealed that the rate of minority withdrawals, suspensions, and failures decreased following the intervention.

Although the researchers were reluctant to generalize from a single case, they were prompted to speculate on the key role of leadership in the project's success. Besides ensuring that school goals were always on the faculty's agenda, the principal coordinated the collection and analysis of survey data from students and dealt with unanticipated problems which threatened the intervention. An additional factor in the project's success was the training received by staff members. As a result of an extensive staff development effort, teachers were able to deal with the increased complexity occasioned by new responsibilities (for example, student advisement and career counseling).

Duke and Meckel (1980) addressed a somewhat different concern. While involved in a large school improvement project, they noted that various efforts by school authorities to deal with truancy, class cutting, and other attendance problems failed to have a lasting impact. Over the course of one school year they gathered data in a high school and a junior high school, noting the effects on absenteeism of such strategies as a new detention room, an independent study program for chronic truants, use of plainclothes police personnel, and a midyear amnesty arrangement. As each new strategy was tried, absenteeism would decline for a brief period of time and then return to previous levels or higher.

In their attempt to explain the apparent failure of these strategies, the researchers identified several organizational factors. One problem was increased complexity, as represented by the proliferation of special roles associated with school discipline. Coordination became more difficult as the task of handling student attendance was spread among attendance clerks, school administrators, special security personnel, counselors, community liaisons, and detention supervisors. A second problem involved overreliance on sanctions to produce improved attendance. School personnel failed to recognize the benefits of more positive strategies, such as increased student involvement and rewards for good attendance. Some of the sanctions upon which they relied—such as suspension—hardly seemed appropriate for students whose problem was truancy. A third obstacle concerned how attendance policies were developed. Rarely were students and teachers consulted by school administrators prior to introducing a new policy. In many cases, new policies were unknown to large numbers of each group. In other cases, policies were regarded as meaningless or misguided.

In an effort to understand the school factors affecting rates of suspension, Bickel and Qualls (1980) selected four high-suspension and four low-suspension secondary schools in the Jefferson County (Kentucky) School District. Classroom observations were conducted, and questionnaires were administered to students and staff members. Data analyses indicated that several organizational factors discriminated between the low- and high-suspension schools. Regarding leadership, administrators in low-suspension schools were more visible in and around the school. Their presence had a positive impact on staff morale and student behavior. Low-suspension schools appeared to be more positive environments, characterized by greater concern for human relations and mutual respect between faculty and students. The study is flawed, however, by the fact that observers knew that the schools differed in suspension rates *before* observational data were collected.

Fiqueira-McDonough (1986) conducted case studies of two suburban high schools in the same community in order to understand the relationship between school characteristics, discipline problems, and gender. Both schools were characterized by a high degree of academic success, a low dropout rate, and similar expenditures per student. Self-report data were obtained from a random sample of tenth graders at nine schools. From this set, a subsample of 350 students attending two suburban high schools was selected. The two schools differed markedly, however, in the frequency of minor disciplinary offenses.

In trying to account for this difference, the researcher noted that the less troubled school was characterized by greater student attachment to the school. The more troubled school was described as a more competitive environment, with academic achievement—as measured by grades—serving as the paramount goal. The singular focus on a narrow notion of academic success ensured that the experiences of many students would be unsatisfactory, a consequence that could have contributed directly to misbehavior. The less troubled school, with its more diverse opportunities for success and greater regard for the nonacademic and vocational interests of students, provided a setting in which a larger proportion of students could feel that their needs were accommodated.

Research on Alternatives

The studies referred to so far have focused on conventional public schools. Since the mid-sixties, however, alternative schools have been available in many locations for students unable to function effectively in conventional settings. Alternative schools vary widely in purpose, makeup, structure, and curriculum, but they share a common desire for an identity separate from that of conventional public schools. A small body of research on these alternatives exists and provides an opportunity to examine the impact on student behavior of different organizational structures.

In 1977-78, Duke and Perry (1978) sought to determine whether student behavior was as great a problem in a sample of eighteen California alternative high schools as it was reported to be in neighboring regular high schools. On-site observations and interviews with students and teachers revealed that student behavior was rarely a major concern in alternative schools. This finding came as a surprise, since many students in these alternative schools had been forced to leave regular schools because of discipline problems. The researchers identified a variety of possible explanations for the general orderliness of the alternative schools.

The small size (average enrollment was 111 students) of the alternative schools was one factor. With fewer teachers, students were less likely to confront conflicting expectations. Smallness also meant that teachers could more easily recognize and interact with a larger percentage of students. Another factor was the absence of stratification among students. With fewer students, it was less easy for cliques and ingroups to develop. Classes were not organized into homogeneous groups, nor were there separate "tracks." Additional factors included a low degree of formalization (few rules and procedures), greater tolerance for certain behaviors (tardiness, smoking), substantial student involvement in school decision making, emphasis on consequences rather than punishment, and ample opportunities for conflict resolution. Students indicated that they appreciated being treated like adults.

Gold and Mann (1984) investigated three alternative high schools to determine how effectively they dealt with delinquent and disruptive students. Students attending these schools were compared to students at the conventional schools from which the former group had come. Although the behavior of both groups improved over the course of the study, the researchers concluded that the alternative schools were more effective in using social and psychological processes to reduce discipline problems. The alternative schools tended to have the greatest positive impact on students who were neither overly anxious nor depressed.

In trying to account for the success of the alternative schools, Gold and Mann noted that students praised the flexibility of these schools. Teachers in the alternative schools were perceived as taking account of the fears, moods, and needs of individual students. This finding supports a relatively low degree of formalization, since an abundance of rules and procedures tends to limit the capacity of teachers to respond to individual differences.

The principals in the three alternative schools refrained from playing the role of disciplinarian. Leadership that symbolizes firmness and order may work with most students, but those who are referred to alternative schools often have experienced difficulty dealing with authority. For them, principals with a nonconfrontative style may be more effective.

A problem with most studies of alternative schools is the lack of a control group. Because the New Haven alternative school studied by Trickett et al. (1985) had more student applicants than openings, a control group could be constituted from the nonadmitted applicants who remained in conventional high schools. Modeled after Philadelphia's Parkway Program, the New Haven High School in the Community offered students individualized learning experiences with experts in the city. The school was divided into two autonomous units, each with approximately 150 students and ten staff. The per pupil cost during the two years of the study was equal to or lower than that for students in conventional New Haven high schools.

When compared with controls, alternative school students reported greater general satisfaction with school and more cordial relations between teachers and students. Controls perceived that they had less influence over school policies. Students at the High School in the Community regarded persons of other races and belief systems with less prejudice than did controls. Furthermore, achievement, as measured by the Sequential Tests of Educational Progress (Educational Testing Service), was comparable for both groups.

District-Sponsored Research

A final type of research related to student behavior involves evaluation studies sponsored by local school districts. Districts frequently allocate considerable resources to efforts to improve student behavior. As a consequence, they often are expected to determine whether resources have been used responsibly. In order to review the results of district-sponsored research, requests were mailed to the directors of 108 district research and evaluation units.[1] A total of thirteen studies from twelve districts were found to involve organizational strategies or variables. Given the political environment in which district-sponsored research typically is conducted, it is likely that many of these evaluations tend to portray results in as positive a manner as possible. Caution should be used in interpreting these studies. Table 1.1 presents an overview of the district-sponsored studies.

Studies conducted in Akron, Atlanta, Baltimore, Jefferson County (Louisville, Ky.), Memphis, and Winston-Salem/Forsythe County dealt with several components of school control structure, including in-school suspension, Saturday school, and after-school detention. These sanctions generally were perceived to reduce behavior problems. Atlanta and Austin also reported positive impacts on student self-control, and Akron noted that student grades were perceived to improve. Winston-Salem/Forsythe County found, however, that student attitudes did not improve appreciably. Only Akron, Austin, and Baltimore analyzed actual disciplinary referrals. The other studies relied on student, teacher, and parent perceptions.

Table 1.1

Summary of Recent District-Sponsored Studies of School Discipline

DISTRICT	ORGANIZATIONAL VARIABLE	METHODS	FINDINGS
Akron Public Schools	Saturday detention	Review of referrals; staff questionnaires	5,050 student days of suspension were "saved" in 1986. Staff perceived that grades of participating students improved.
Atlanta Public Schools	After-school detention; In-school suspension	Review of referrals; teacher and student questionnaires	Detention and in-school suspension perceived by majority of teachers and students to reduce repeat offenses and encourage self-control.
Austin Independent School District	School-Community Guidance Center	Review of referrals; analysis of student outcome data	Student attendance and school performance improved after enrollment in SCGC, but number of absences still exceeded acceptable number.

Table 1.1 *(cont'd)*

DISTRICT	ORGANIZATIONAL VARIABLE	METHODS	FINDINGS
	Project ASSIST (crisis classroom)	Review of referrals; teacher questionnaire; principal interview	Number of disciplinary actions was reduced; most teachers perceived that student self-control improved.
Baltimore County Public Schools	Time-out room (in-school suspension) at one high school	Review of referrals over four years; teacher and student questionnaires	Suspension rate did not change appreciably, but 96% of teachers and 69% of students felt behavior improved after referral.
District of Columbia Public Schools	Youth Awareness Program	Review of referrals; various data collection forms; student outcome data	Student attitudes toward specific subjects improved.
Jefferson County (Louisville, Ky.) Public Schools	Uniform Code of Student Conduct (UCSC)	Interviews of school administrators and random selection of teachers and students in twelve randomly selected secondary schools	Data indicated that school discipline plan conformed to the UCSC and were being implemented consistently. No data on student conduct were collected.
	In-school suspension (In-School Adjustment Program)	Teacher and student interviews; observations of in-school suspension facilities	Most teachers felt that in-school suspension contributed to improve behavior by students in general and by suspended students in particular.

Table 1.1 *(cont'd)*

DISTRICT	ORGANIZATIONAL VARIABLE	METHODS	FINDINGS
Memphis City (Tenn.) Schools	In-school suspension	Student, staff, and parent questionnaires at three high schools	76% of parents indicated their children had been helped by in-school suspension. 55% of homeroom teachers perceived that student behavior improved as a result of program.
Montgomery County (Md.) Public Schools	School discipline plan and discipline committee	Survey of staff at randomly selected schools	98% of schools report having a school discipline plan and discipline committee. School staff report having sufficient authority to maintain discipline. Effective elements of discipline plans include detention, referral to principal, parental contact, out-of-school suspension, and in-school suspension.
Oklahoma City (Okla.) Public Schools	Discipline plans (based on Assertive Discipline)	Public hearings; questionnaires to all district teachers, bus drivers, and administrators	Continued use of Assertive Discipline was indicated. All schools should have a written school discipline plan.

Table 1.1 *(cont'd)*

DISTRICT	ORGANIZATIONAL VARIABLE	METHODS	FINDINGS
			Every teacher should have a classroom management plan annually approved by the principal.
			District should provide Assertive Discipline training to all new teachers, substitutes, and bus drivers.
Winston-Salem/ Forsythe County (N.C.) Schools	In-school suspension; Classrooms for Development and Change	Questionnaires given to students, parents, and school staff	Student attitudes were not positively affected. Parents valued the instructional benefits of in-school suspension.
			Staff members preferred in-school suspension. Total number of out-of-school suspensions declined.

Montgomery County, Maryland, and Oklahoma City studies investigated the desirability of school discipline plans. Such plans represent a formalization of policies related to appropriate student behavior and the consequences of misconduct. Both studies supported the continued use of school discipline plans. In neither case, however, were data gathered prior to the implementation of school discipline plans or from control schools. A study by Jefferson County (Ky.) Public Schools found that school discipline plans for middle schools and high schools were being implemented in accordance with the leadership's

Uniform Code of Student Conduct. Data were not systematically gathered, however, on the impact of these plans on student behavior.

Austin and the District of Columbia evaluated special programs designed to deal with discipline-related concerns. Austin found that a residential center providing counseling and tutoring to court-adjudicated students produced modest results in terms of attendance and academic performance. The main benefit of the School-Community Guidance Center may have been to discourage "at-risk" youngsters from dropping out of school. The District of Columbia study gave high marks to its Youth Awareness Program, a multifaceted effort to provide students with information and counseling related to drugs, sexuality, and other adolescent concerns. The behavior of participants was perceived by some school personnel and parents to have improved as a result of the intervention.

PROMISING ORGANIZATIONAL STRATEGIES

Having reviewed a variety of studies in which efforts have been made to link organizational characteristics of schools to student behavior, it is now necessary to consider the relevance of this body of data for practitioners. Although some of the research would not meet the most rigorous standards of good empirical investigation, it is still better in most cases than no research at all. Practitioners are required to deal with problems on a daily basis, whether or not there is high-quality data available.

Table 1.2 summarizes the major findings of the preceding studies in terms of the primary elements of school organization described at the beginning of the chapter. The first of these elements is school goals. Orderly school environments have been linked to a schoolwide commitment to appropriate student behavior and to a diversity of school goals reflecting the varied interests of different groups of students. Several researchers warn, however, that school discipline can become an end in itself, rather than a means to productive learning. The goal of good behavior is necessary, but not sufficient to ensure academic growth. One study pointed out that too narrow a definition of academic growth also can be counterproductive, since it limits the number of students whose needs can be well served by the school.

Research on the impact of the school control structure reflects some diversity of opinion. Several researchers, having discovered that rules and consequences are applied inconsistently, urge educators to become more consistent disciplinarians. One researcher found, though, that consistent discipline is associated with a high degree of perceived misconduct. Disagreement exists over the effectiveness of certain sanctions, particularly suspension. District-sponsored research tends to support the use of in-school suspension and detention.

Table 1.2

Summary of Studies of School Organization and Student Behavior

ORGANIZATIONAL VARIABLE	STUDY	FINDINGS
School Goals	Various "school effectiveness" studies	An "academic focus" is associated with an orderly school environment.
	Cusick (1973)	School commitment to maintenance of order interferes with academic and other goals.
	Cusick (1983)	School commitment to equal opportunity forces schools to concentrate on maintaining order.
	Fiqueira-McDonough (1986)	Diverse school goals that acknowledge a wide range of student academic and non-academic needs are associated with lower frequency of discipline problems.
Control Structure	Wehlage and Rutter (1986)	School discipline perceived by marginal students to be ineffective and unfair.
	Perry (1980)	Consistent rule enforcement by administrators correlated with high degree of perceived behavior problems.

Table 1.2 *(cont'd)*

ORGANIZATIONAL VARIABLE	STUDY	FINDINGS
	Duke and Meckel (1980)	Suspending students with attendance problems fails to have a positive impact. Detention also is an ineffective sanction.
	Hollingsworth, Lufler, and Clune (1984)	Sanctions for misbehavior are not applied systematically, and they do not appear to be very effective.
	Duke and Perry (1978)	Relatively orderly alternative schools stress consequences rather than punishment.
	Studies by Atlanta, Austin, Baltimore, Jefferson County, Memphis, Winston-Salem/ForsytheCounty	In-school suspension and student detention can be effective sanctions and can lead to reduced behavior problems, improved self-control, and higher grades.
Complexity	Crawford, Miskel, and Johnson (1980)	Staff development helps school personnel deal with new roles involved in a program to assist minority students.
	Duke and Meckel (1980)	Proliferation of disciplinary specialists increases coordination problems and reduces accountability
Centralization	Wu et al. (1982)	High degree of administrative centralization of discipline is correlated with high rate of suspension.

Table 1.2 *(cont'd)*

ORGANIZATIONAL VARIABLE	STUDY	FINDINGS
	McPartland and McDill (1976)	Student involvement in school decision making is positively related to attitudes opposing violence and vandalism.
	Gottfredson and Daiger (1979)	Teacher preference for student involvement in decision making is associated with higher levels of victimization.
	Perry (1980)	Teacher determination of class rules is correlated with high degree of perceived behavior problems.
	Duke and Meckel (1980)	Lack of student and teacher involvement in making attendance policies is related to failure of strategies to reduce absenteeism.
	Hollingsworth, Lufler, and Clune (1984)	Lack of uniformity in classroom management practices among teachers was not found to be a problem.
	Duke and Perry (1978)	Relatively orderly alternative schools involve students in decision making and conflict resolution.
Formalization	Gottfredson and Daiger (1979)	Student victimizations are related to teacher confusion over school policies and student uncertainty regarding rules.

Table 1.2 *(cont'd)*

ORGANIZATIONAL VARIABLE	STUDY	FINDINGS
	Perry (1980)	Student uncertainty about consequences for rule breaking are correlated with absenteeism and disciplinary referrals.
	Duke and Perry (1978)	Relatively orderly alternative schools have few formal rules.
	Gold and Mann (1984)	Alternative schools are perceived by students to be more flexible and responsive to individual differences.
	Studies by Montgomery County (Md.) and Oklahoma City school systems	School discipline plans are perceived to contribute to orderly schools.
Stratification	Perry (1980)	High percentage of students in vocational education is correlated with large number of disciplinary referrals.
	Duke and Perry (1978)	Relatively orderly alternative schools have few student cliques and virtually no homogeneously grouped classes or "tracks."
Culture and Climate	Anderson (1985)	Effective schools are more likely to be characterized by pervasive caring for students and collegiality among staff members.

Table 1.2 *(cont'd)*

ORGANIZATIONAL VARIABLE	STUDY	FINDINGS
	Gottfredson (1986a, 1986b)	Improved school climate is linked to staff training in classroom management and cooperative learning, curriculum development, community support, parental involvement, and stable leadership.
	Wehlage and Rutter (1986)	Marginal students perceive that teachers are not interested in them.
	Metz (1978)	Faculty culture—including expectations for students and norms for discipline—influences student behavior.
	Bickel and Qualls (1980)	Positive school climate is associated with lower rate of suspensions.
	Trickett et al. (1985)	Alternative high school is associated with greater student satisfaction with school, greater perceived influence over policies, and lower levels of prejudice.
School Size	Gottfredson and Gottfredson (1985)	Small school size is correlated with lower rate of victimization.
	McPartland and McDill (1976)	School size is positively correlated with reports of serious discipline problems.

Table 1.2 *(cont'd)*

ORGANIZATIONAL VARIABLE	STUDY	FINDINGS
	Duke and Perry (1978)	Small size of alternative schools permits teachers to get to know students and minimizes likelihood of conflicting expectations.

Part of the confusion generated by conflicting findings could be cleared up if researchers agreed on a common conception of effective discipline. At present, some think of effectiveness in terms of creating conditions under which students who wish to learn can do so. Others judge discipline to be effective when the behavior of those who disobey rules improves. Is the purpose of school control structure to minimize the likelihood of irresponsible behavior or to maximize the likelihood of responsible behavior? The organizational strategies required to achieve one goal can differ markedly from those required to achieve the other.

Researchers acknowledge that school discipline is becoming more technical and complex. Various studies support the need for staff development to keep educators apprised of new strategies for handling behavior problems. One study warned, however, that the spread of specialists is not necessarily the antidote to growing complexity. More specialists can mean more coordination problems. The willingness of teachers and administrators to play active roles in discipline may be undermined by the proliferation of discipline-related support staff.

Numerous studies looked at the relationship of centralization to student behavior. A high degree of actual or perceived behavior problems is linked to apparently contradictory conditions: (1) centralized disciplinary decision making by school administrators, (2) teacher determination of classroom rules, (3) student involvement in decision making, and (4) lack of student and teacher involvement in decision making. Researchers do not always distinguish clearly between types of disciplinary decisions, thereby making the results of this research even less illuminating. Studies are needed of schools where students and/or teachers help determine school rules, classroom rules, consequences for misconduct, disciplinary procedures, and the guilt or innocence of accused rule breakers. Is student or teacher involvement appropriate for certain types of decisions but not others? What is the impact of parental involvement in disciplinary decision making?

Research on formalization supports the conclusion that student and teacher uncertainty regarding rules and policies contributes to behavior problems. There is evidence in district-sponsored studies that school discipline plans and classroom management plans help eliminate uncertainty. The experience of alternative schools, however, indicates that long lists of rules and elaborate disciplinary procedures may not be necessary to maintain order, at least in settings where teacher-student relations are open and positive and school size is small.

The relationship between student stratification and behavior has yet to be investigated systematically. One study found that disciplinary referrals were positively related to the percentages of students in vocational tracks. A study of alternative schools with relatively minor behavior problems revealed an absence of student cliques and a homogeneous grouping of students.

School culture and climate are identified by various studies as key factors in the maintenance of order. Among the important aspects of culture and climate are pervasive caring for students and staff collegiality. Small school size was found to contribute to orderly, caring environments.

In summary, what is known about the organization of orderly schools is that they are characterized by a commitment to appropriate student behavior and clear behavioral expectations for students. Rules, sanctions, and procedures are discussed, debated, and frequently formalized into school discipline and classroom management plans. To balance this emphasis on formal procedure, the climate in these organizations conveys concern for students as individuals. This concern manifests itself in a variety of ways, including efforts to involve students in school decision making, school goals that recognize multiple forms of student achievement, and a deemphasis on homogeneous grouping.

The research to date transmits one additional message to practitioners—orderly organizations involve more than rules and punishments. Determining the exact configuration of organizational mechanisms most likely to foster appropriate student behavior is likely to depend on a variety of factors, such as level (elementary or secondary), locale, and student body makeup. No single organizational strategy seems capable of producing safe, orderly, productive environments for all schools or even for a particular school.

THE VITAL ROLE OF LEADERSHIP

It is one thing to identify the organizational characteristics of orderly schools and quite another to transform a troubled school into one in which students behave appropriately and learn what they are expected to learn. This latter task is the challenge facing many contemporary school leaders. Various studies reviewed in this chapter strongly suggest that the implementation of organizational characteristics conducive to learning is highly dependent on the quality of school leadership (Bickel and Qualls, 1980; Gold and Mann, 1984; Gottfredson, 1986b; Metz, 1978). School effectiveness studies, in particular, stress the vital role played by school principals in shaping productive schools. In closing, then, it is necessary to ask *how* school leaders are to go about the task of creating orderly schools.

Elsewhere the author has conducted an extensive review and analysis of research on effective school leadership (Duke, 1987). Seven critical leadership functions were identified:

- Teacher supervision and development
- Teacher evaluation
- Instructional management and support
- Resource management
- Quality control
- Coordination
- Troubleshooting

Supervision represents administrative efforts to monitor teacher performance, whereas teacher evaluation is the process by which the acceptability of teacher performance is determined (Duke, 1987, p. 104). These two functions, when performed ably, allow school leaders to hold teachers accountable for school goals and policies. In the event that particular teachers experience difficulties, school leaders may be called upon to provide opportunities for teacher professional development. Should these efforts fail, school leaders may be compelled to take disciplinary action. Teacher professional development also provides a means for helping teachers deal with increased complexity, represented by new policies, technological change, and growing student diversity.

Instructional management and support encompass (1) the development, implementation, and enforcement of policies and procedures for dealing with predictable or recurring instructional concerns and (2) all efforts designed to establish and maintain school climates conducive to student and teacher growth (Duke, 1987, pp. 182-200). These functions require school leaders to see that policies are in place to ensure the attainment of school goals. Such policies may range from rules governing student conduct to regulations governing student grouping for instructional purposes. The creation of safe and productive school climates may involve keeping school facilities clean and inviting, encouraging teachers to be accessible to students, and recognizing students for achievement (Rutter et al., 1979, pp. 195-196).

Resource management necessitates allocating and monitoring the use of school resources to ensure the accomplishment of school goals (Duke, 1987, pp. 204-216). The primary resources with which school leaders work are personnel, time, and learning materials. They must see that these resources are utilized equitably, thereby minimizing the negative impact of stratification on opportunities for student success.

The quality control function calls for determining the extent to which school goals are being achieved (Duke, 1987, pp. 219-234). Assuming that a central goal of schools is to provide a safe environment in which students can learn, school leaders regularly must gather and analyze data on student behavior and the effectiveness of disciplinary policies. Since students who are not learning up to expectations frequently grow frustrated and exhibit inappropriate behavior, school leaders also must monitor student achievement and encourage corrective action, if they are to promote order.

The final two functions—coordination and troubleshooting—cut across all the others (Duke, 1987, pp. 236-255). Coordination encompasses activities designed to reduce the need for organizational control through better communications and internal integration. It is of little value, for example, to develop school goals and expectations pertaining to student behavior if students, staff, and parents are unaware of or unclear about them. Involving these individuals in the process by which goals and expectations are determined is one means by which school leadleaders can enhance coordination and increase the likelihood of compliance.

Troubleshooting entails processes and procedures designed to anticipate and minimize the impact of problems that threaten to interfere with the accomplishment of school goals. "Management by walking around" is one of the most valuable sources of troubleshooting data for school leaders. The greater their visibility and the more accessible they are to students and staff, the more likely school leaders are to hear of concerns before they grow into major problems. The fulfillment of supervisory and quality control functions often provides important troubleshooting information.

The seven functions of school leadership provide a framework to assist administrators in thinking about the implementation of organizational structures that help reduce the likelihood of student behavior problems. It is imperative that contemporary school leaders appreciate the role of school organization in the etiology of student misconduct.

2

Developing Effective Organizations to Reduce School Disorder

Denise C. Gottfredson

School disruption and concerns about lack of discipline among school-aged youths have long been among the most pressing problems facing schools (Bahner, 1980; National Commission on Excellence in Education, 1983). Disruptive behavior is an obstacle to learning. It robs instructional time not only for the disruptive students, but also for the nonoffending youths as the teacher interrupts the learning process to handle the disruption.

What contributes to school disruption? An analysis of national data from over six hundred secondary schools (Gottfredson and Gottfredson, 1985) showed that schools with discipline problems are schools where the rules are not clear, fair, and firmly enforced; schools that use ambiguous responses to student behavior—by lowering grades in response to misconduct, for example; schools where teachers and administrators do not know what the rules are or do not agree on responses to student misconduct; schools that ignore misconduct; and schools where students do not believe in the rules. Large schools, schools that lack resources needed for teaching, schools with

The research reported in this paper was funded by the National Institute of Education and the Office of Juvenile Justice and Delinquency Prevention and was performed at the Center for Social Organization of Schools at the Johns Hopkins University. The author gratefully acknowledges the assistance of Gary Gottfredson, Lois Hybl, Oliver Moles, and Amy Schwartz in the preparation of this manuscript.

poor teacher-administration cooperation or with inactive administrations, and schools where teachers tend to have punitive attitudes also experience more disruption than other schools. These school characteristics are related to school disruption even when characteristics of the community—urbanicity, racial composition, socioeconomic status, and level of crime—are held constant.

In addition to these school-level correlates of disorder, a number of individual-level correlates of disorderly behavior have been identified. Individuals at high risk for engaging in unsocialized behavior display less academic competence, have limited career and educational objectives, dislike school, have more delinquent friends, and have lower levels of belief in conventional social rules than do more conforming youths (Empey, 1982; Gottfredson, 1981; Hirschi, 1969). Understanding the characteristics of misbehaving students can help focus efforts aimed at reducing disorder.

The research on correlates of disorderly schools and disruptive youth implies that there is much schools can do to reduce disorder. The combined sets of correlates help focus attention on specific risk factors for disorder. These risk factors converge in suggesting the need for clear, fair, and consistent rule enforcement that is implemented in a way that promotes liking for school and belief in the validity of the rules among delinquency-prone youths. The research suggests the need for educational strategies that promote academic success among low achievers and that motivate these youths to attend school on a more regular basis. The research suggests the need for strategies that encourage attachments to prosocial others—both teachers and peers. And the research suggests the need to strengthen schools as organizations—to increase communication, consensus, and cohesion.

This paper summarizes work attempting to reduce school disruption and disorderly behavior by altering school practices in ways suggested by research. The first section describes a collaborative effort between researchers and practitioners to design, implement, evaluate, and refine school practices aimed at reducing school disorder. The next section describes focused attempts to reduce school disorder among high-risk youths using three different approaches—a pull-out program, an alternative class, and an alternative school. The final section discusses implications for practice.

ORGANIZATIONAL DEVELOPMENT IN SCHOOLS

The last decade has taught us important lessons about the process of creating beneficial change in schools. Attempts to "install" effective practices identified by research have been far less successful than expected. These attempts have usually resulted in incomplete, inadequate, or sporadic implementation (Berman and McLaughlin, 1978; Gottfredson, Gottfredson and Cook, 1983; Grant and Capell, 1983; Hall and Loucks, 1977; Johnson, Bird, and Little, 1979; Sarason, 1971). Indeed, Sarason (1971) has characterized many educational innovations as "nonevents" and Miles (1981) has described innovations as "ornaments" when goals and success criteria are vague.

Studies on improvement efforts have provided insight into schools' failures to effectively adopt effective practices. This research was summarized in Corcoran (1985). Some characteristics of school improvement efforts that have impeded innovation are the assumptions that technological advances can be transported from school to school and district to district with little or no alteration to fit each environment and that effective implementation of new practices can result from "one-shot" training sessions. Teachers are often expected to return to their schools and implement new ideas or practices with little or no support. Unclear school missions, reward structures, and role definitions also impede effective implementation. For example, teachers may be rewarded for maintaining order in their classrooms, even when the increase in orderliness is gained at the expense of limiting opportunities for learning.

Yet another source of implementation failure is the top-down approach to decision making and planning that fails to seek the advice of the primary implementers of the new practices in designing the intervention. This practice generally results in flawed program plans and alienated staff.

Bringing about beneficial change in schools requires an organizational development (OD) approach to school change. This kind of approach focuses attention on the school as an organization—it examines the organizational culture and climate, and it seeks to improve the systems and procedures used by the organization. It usually focuses on improving communication, building trust and cooperation, enhancing the organization's problem-solving and decision-making capabilities, and strengthening its planning processes.

Program Development Evaluation (PDE; Gottfredson, 1984; Gottfredson et al., 1984) is an organizational development method intended to help schools and other organizations define problems and set organizational goals, specify theories of action on which to base the school improvement program, define measurable objectives based on the theory, select interventions with a high likelihood of achieving these objectives, identify and plan to overcome the obstacles to the implementation of the interventions selected, and develop detailed implementation standards to serve as blueprints for the interventions. Using the method, educators and researchers work together to evaluate their programs and use the resulting information to further improve the programs. Planning and program development become part of the everyday routine in the school, creating a spiral of improvement.

The PDE method makes the following assumptions about organizational change:

1. Projects guided by explicit theories that can be translated into action will be most effective.

2. Projects will be implemented with most enthusiasm, be strongest, and contribute most to knowledge of school improvement if the theory on which the project is based is regarded as sensible by project implementers and accords with evidence from previous research and evaluation.

3. Effective implementation of an intervention or innovation is more likely if blueprints for the intervention are available and if implementation is guided by data about the extent to which project activities accord with the blueprint.

4. Effective adoption of an innovation is more likely when explicit plans for adoption are available and when these plans are likely to overcome obstacles to organizational change.

5. Projects will become more effective in the presence of "evaluation pressure." Evaluation pressure takes many forms, some of which are pressure to focus on theory, and to heed relevant information from previous research and evaluation and from current data about program strength, fidelity, and effectiveness.

6. Organizations that internalize these principles will be more effective than those that simply comply with them (Gottfredson, 1984, pp. 1101-1102).

The method translates each of the above assumptions into concrete steps that school personnel can take to increase the likelihood of strong implementation and effective adoption of new practices. The method is rational. It assumes that the effectiveness of organizations will increase as rational behavior increases. It recognizes that schools often work as loosely coupled systems (Weick, 1982) using *ad hoc* management methods, but it assumes that loose coupling often inhibits school effectiveness. The PDE method attempts to tighten management by developing explicit standards for performance, communicating these standards, assessing compliance or noncompliance with the standards, and adjusting interventions when necessary.

We have used the PDE method in several studies in a variety of school settings, some of which will be described in the following pages. These studies yielded useful knowledge about the conditions necessary for effective implementation of the PDE method to enhance organizational effectiveness. The following section describes one of these tests—The Effective Schools Project—in which the PDE method was used to structure a collaborative effort by researchers and school personnel to implement change in a demoralized urban public school.

THE EFFECTIVE SCHOOLS PROJECT[1]

The Participating Schools

Two junior high schools were selected by central administrators of the Baltimore City Public School system to collaborate with researchers at the Johns Hopkins University to improve their schools using the PDE method. The schools were selected because they (1) had experienced considerable disorder in the recent past, (2) were believed to be in need of help, (3) were expected to be receptive to the project, and (4) were expected to remain stable in terms of their student, teacher, and administrator populations for the three-year period beginning in fall 1982.

One of the two schools never implemented a strong program. The original principal, who did not support the program, was replaced at the beginning of the second year along with two of the three assistant principals. The new administrative staff did not fully support the program. Attempts to build commitment to the project failed, and although some minor changes in the school were implemented, the staff never fully backed the program. Readers interested in what was implemented in the school and in a more detailed account of the obstacles to implementation should refer to Gottfredson (1986a). This report concluded that organizational development methods will not work without administrative backing. The remainder of this report focuses on the second school, in which attempts to plan, implement, and evaluate strategies to reduce disorder were successful.

First, a word about the community context of the school is in order. Gottfredson (1987a) showed census data describing the school's community characteristics. The school is located in an impoverished inner-city neighborhood. The school district is predominantly minority, and has a high percentage of female-headed households, persons in low-status occupations, and families below the poverty level. The community falls well below the national average on these measures of socioeconomic status, placing the school at especially high risk for school disorder.

Measures of the school environment and the behavior and attitudes of teachers and students in the school taken during the first year of the project (a planning year) indicated severe problems. Teachers regarded the school as unsafe and their classrooms as disorderly. They reported that they were victimized frequently, were dissatisfied with their jobs, and that morale was low. They also had a low opinion of the effectiveness of the school administration. Students' reports of school safety were also below average, and a scale measuring the level of punitive action taken against students indicated that the school was characterized by extremely high levels of punishment. This picture of poor discipline in the school is corroborated by disciplinary removal records showing that, during the three years prior to the intervention, an average of 39 percent of the student population was suspended from school each year at least once in response to disciplinary infractions. Many students were sent home more than once, so that for every one hundred students in the school, seventy-two removals from school were recorded in the average year. The school assessment also showed that students felt more alienated, did not frequently receive rewards or recognition for their work in school, felt that they were treated disrespectfully by the school staff, and engaged in somewhat more delinquent activities than schoolchildren in similar schools.

The Improvement Process

The principal, after being oriented to the program, selected a school improvement team composed of teachers, a guidance counselor, administrators, a social worker, a school psychologist, and a parent liaison worker. The team was oriented to the project and trained in the PDE method, and spent the 1982-83 school year planning for implementation the following fall.

The planning included specification of program goals, consideration and prioritization of major sources of the schools' problems, and specification of program objectives directed at the primary sources of the problems. Measures were developed for every goal and objective, and surveys were designed to assess progress toward these goals and objectives. The planning team administered surveys to all teachers and students in their school to obtain baseline information and to provide information for refining program plans. It also developed plans for program components targeted at each objective, oriented the entire school staff, and generated considerable staff enthusiasm for the project.

Eight program components were developed as part of the project, and standards for both the intensity and fidelity of the components were established. During the two intervention years that followed, these standards were monitored on an ongoing basis using various sources of information about implementation, including teacher logs, teacher observations, interviews with school staff, questionnaires completed by school staff, and reports of program implementers. The school improvement team met formally once a month to review the status of each component and to modify plans to strengthen the program.

The following paragraphs describe the two strongest program components. These components received the most attention from the implementers throughout the implementation period and were implemented with the most integrity.

Classroom Management Innovations. Two classroom management techniques—Assertive Discipline (Canter and Canter, 1976) and Reality Therapy (Glasser, 1969)—were used. The techniques are intended to promote a calm, orderly classroom atmosphere. Assertive Discipline teaches teachers to (1) set clear, consistent limits and specify consequences for students; (2) provide uniform follow-through; and (3) offer students warmth, support, and rewards for appropriate behavior. Reality Therapy also stresses clear rules and consistent application of consequences, but it places more emphasis on getting the student to make a commitment to change his or her behavior. Structured classroom meetings encourage students to present their views on a topic without fear of being ridiculed by other students or the teacher. The meetings are designed to promote positive interactions in the classroom and to increase attachments to others. They are also expected to promote introspection about values and attitudes.

All participating teachers were trained to use both techniques. Implementation surveys and observations showed that by the end of the second year, 73 percent of the trained teachers were using the Reality Therapy techniques and 79 percent were using Assertive Discipline techniques. The average teacher held classroom meetings with three different classes, and held between two and three meetings with each class each semester. This translated into an average of seven meetings per student in the last semester.

The project staff emphasized positive reinforcement of appropriate behavior in their implementation of Assertive Discipline. Rewards were given to the classes with the best and the most improved attendance and behavior, and the winning classes were announced and displayed on a prominent bulletin board. The nine most troublesome classes were targeted for an intensive positive reinforcement program. The nineteen teachers involved received training in basic principles and specific strategies of positive reinforcement. They were told that rewards should always be contingent on the students' behavior, that students must always be aware of exactly how they could earn rewards, and that tokens should be coupled with social reinforcers such as teacher praise. The teachers developed positive reinforcement plans that specified which behaviors would be rewarded, how frequently, and with how many tokens. They awarded points throughout each week according to their plan and recorded the points won on a chart visible to the students. Tokens were dispensed weekly, and students were able to redeem them for food treats, school supplies, admission into a game room, and special events, including parties and trips.

Teachers implemented the Assertive Discipline techniques with considerable fidelity. A technical report for the project (Gottfredson, 1986a) showed that the frequency of traditional responses to misbehavior (sending the student to the office and detention) declined, and the use of alternative responses (parent conferences, removal of privileges, and behavior contracts) increased. The most striking improvement was in the use of positive reinforcements. The percentage of teachers reporting that they usually used awards, special privileges, material rewards, and positive notification of parents increased by between 15 and 25 percent (depending on the particular positive response).

Classroom Instructional Innovation. Student Team Learning (STL; Slavin, 1980) techniques were used to change the classroom climate from a social to an academic one and to increase student motivation to master academic material. The STL techniques provide incentives for students to learn academic material by establishing competitions for team reward or recognition. Teams are composed of four or five students of differing ability. The team members study together and coach one another in preparation for classwide tournaments or individual tests. Points are awarded to teams on the basis of their members' improvement over their own past performance or on the basis of their performance in a tournament in which students compete against individuals of similar ability levels.

Teacher observations and logs implied that STL was implemented with considerable strength and fidelity. All participating teachers were trained, and 78 percent tried at least one of the STL methods. About one-third of the trained teachers tried more than one of the methods. By the end of the second year, 58 percent of the teachers were using the technique consistently, that is, for at least six lessons during the semester. This level of implementation is much higher than the typical level of implementation achieved when training is provided but no organizational development assistance is given (John Hollifield, personal communication). Observation data confirmed that, for the most part, the techniques were implemented as recommended in the STL manual.

Other Interventions. Other interventions included an intervention designed to inform the students' parents about classroom behavior frequently and consistently, a parent volunteer program designed to increase involvement of parents in school activities, a community support program designed to increase community support and advocacy for the school, and an extracurricular activities program directed at increasing students' attachment to school, sense of school pride, and the extent to which they were rewarded for nonacademic talents. A school discipline review and revision component succeeded in establishing a standard set of school rules, consequences for breaking school rules, and a disciplinary referral system to be used by all school staff members. And a career exploration intervention took students on career-related field trips, provided instruction on career-related topics, and exposed students to positive community role models who volunteered to inform students about the skills required to obtain and perform jobs in their fields.

Outcomes

The data and methods used to evaluate the effectiveness of the project were described in detail in Gottfredson (1986a). Briefly, data from school records on attendance and disciplinary responses and teacher and student survey measures of organizational health, school disorder, and student attitudes and experiences targeted by the program were used to measure change over the three-year project period. The surveys were based on the Effective School Battery (Gottfredson, 1985) but were supplemented with items necessary to assess all goals and objectives. Change in the school that successfully implemented a program was compared with change in the school that did not. Also, the school planning team's decision to pilot most innovations in one "unit"—a grade level physically located in a separate wing of the building—allowed comparisons of outcomes for students in the experimental unit with measures of comparable students from the previous cohort: that is, data collected from the experimental eighth graders at the end of the 1984-85 school year were compared with data collected from the previous eighth grade cohort at the end of the 1983-84 school year.[2]

The intervention school improved dramatically on measures of organizational health. Teacher Morale rose from the 7th percentile on the Effective School Battery norms to the 40th percentile (p ‹.01), teacher reports of innovation rose from the 38th to the 63rd (p ‹.05), and teachers' perceptions of the school administration rose from the 3rd to the 31st percentile (p ‹.01). Two of the three measures of disorder (classroom orderliness and student delinquent behavior) showed significant improvement, and these positive outcomes were accompanied by significant increases in students' sense of belonging in the school (p ‹.01) and in their reports of rewards in school (p ‹.01). School discipline records showed that fewer students were suspended for disciplinary infractions over the course of the project.[3]

The comparison of the experimental and nonexperimental cohorts yielded similar results. On all measures taken from the student survey, the experimental students answered more often in the desired direction. Significant differences were found in areas directly targeted by the program: student sense of belonging (p ‹.01) and their reports of rewards (p ‹.01). Other nonsignificant differences between the two cohorts favored the treatment: experimental students were less rebellious (p = .18), more attached to school (p = .11), and reported more positive peer associations (p = .20).

Measures of disciplinary action taken against students revealed that experimental students were referred to the office much more frequently than were nonexperimental students. This increase in referrals to the office was due to the increased pressure for consistent rule enforcement in the experimental unit. The increase in office referrals was not accompanied by an increase in the more serious responses involving removal from school. Instead, the experimental students were suspended significantly less often than the prior cohort. This decline in suspensions could not be attributed to the program implemented in the experimental unit because schoolwide suspensions declined in the 1984-85 school year. These results, based on measures of *responses* to student behavior, illustrate the danger of interpreting results based on such measures as if they measured student *behavior.* Measures of administrative response are highly sensitive to changes in policies and practices and do not adequately measure student behavior.

Conclusion

The Effective Schools Project was a study of what happens to the students and staff in a demoralized inner-city school when it becomes engaged in a collaborative undertaking with researchers to examine its problems, propose solutions, and implement those solutions. It was not a rigorous test of the PDE method, and it was not a rigorous test of any of the specific interventions attempted. It was a case study.

We can conclude that some combination of innovations implemented in this Baltimore junior high school—including changing the school and classroom environment to increase predictability in the responses of teachers and administrators to disciplinary infractions, increasing rewards for appropriate behavior, and increasing prosocial peer and teacher support—probably increased students' sense of belonging in school and reduced disruptive behavior.

The implementing organization also became healthier during the experience. We expected to see the most dramatic effects in our measures of teachers' feelings of efficacy and the levels of trust, communication, and cooperation among the administrators and staff. We expected that as these indicators of organizational health improved, so would indicators of the strength and fidelity of implementation. We expected that, as implementation of plausible program components was strengthened, we would begin to see change in the targeted student outcomes. These expectations were met.

The modest improvements reported here demonstrate the potential of an organizational development approach in schools to bring about positive change even in the most disadvantaged and demoralized schools. More rigorous tests are needed to determine the essential ingredients of the approach.

SPECIFIC STRATEGIES FOR AT-RISK YOUTH[4]

The foregoing section described an organizational development approach to reducing school disorder. The approach calls for focusing improvement efforts on those factors that research implies are the primary causes of disruption. These risk factors include school- and classroom-level characteristics as well as a number of characteristics and experiences that place certain individuals at especially high risk for disorderly behavior. Effective strategies for reducing disruptive behavior, especially in secondary schools, should focus on increasing academic competence, broadening career and educational objectives, increasing liking for school, decreasing involvements with delinquent companions, and increasing belief in conventional social rules for individual students, in addition to focusing on school-level risk factors.

The remaining pages briefly summarize evidence about the efficacy of specific strategies which focus on one or more individual risk factors to reduce disorder among high-risk individuals. Three examples from the School Action Effectiveness Study (Gottfredson, Gottfredson and Cook, 1983), the national evaluation of the Office for Juvenile Justice and Delinquency Prevention's Alternative Education initiative (OJJDP, 1980), are helpful for pinpointing the effect of interventions designed to enhance the schooling experience for youths identified as at risk for delinquent behavior, drug abuse, school failure, and other undesirable outcomes.

The first was a "pull-out" program that offered counseling and tutoring to students identified as at risk for academic failure. A second was a year-long alternative English and social studies class that used innovative teaching strategies. The third was an alternative school that drew students who were not succeeding in the public school system into a small, orderly environment featuring individualized instruction and a token economy system. A summary of evaluation results will follow the description of the three models.

The first model was the direct service component of project PATHE (Gottfredson, 1986b). Approximately ten percent of the students in each school were identified on the basis of school records and teacher referrals as in need of special services for either academic or conduct problems, or both. Specialists reviewed each target student's school records, interviewed the student and sometimes his or her teachers and parents, and developed treatment plans specifying behavioral treatment objectives. Academic and counseling services consistent with these objectives were prescribed, and progress toward the objectives was frequently monitored. Students were scheduled to meet with program specialists about three times a month to receive tutoring and counseling services, and they were deliberately included in schoolwide project activities such as the student leadership team and extracurricular activities. Implementation records showed that the actual contact with specialists varied from school to school. In one school the average target student met with the specialist only 7.5 times during the 1982-83 year; in another, about 33 times. The average across all schools was about twice per month.

The second program (Gottfredson and Cook, 1986) altered the curriculum and teaching strategies in alternative English and social studies classes to increase commitment to school by making school more relevant to students. The curriculum was highly structured, including lessons on coping with authority, responsibility, and family problems. Teachers relied heavily on nontraditional teaching methods to promote student participation. Audiovisual presentations, field trips, guest speakers, role-playing, and simulations were frequently used.

The scheduling of the classes was novel. A two-hour block was set aside for combined English and social studies instruction. This extended-time block allowed for fieldwork activities, community volunteer work, and class trips.

The class was taught by a team of teachers and aides who were trained to use heterogeneous student learning teams for tutoring and support, individualized learning plans, and frequent rewards both for group and individual progress.

The third program model (Gottfredson, 1986c) was a small alternative school—only about one hundred students were enrolled in the school at any one time. The academic component of the program focused on basic skills acquisition. Students were placed in an intensive basic skills class until they mastered basic skills. Participation in desirable elective courses and in the prestigious "professional/ vocational track" was made contingent upon mastering basic skills. Standards in the academic classes were high. Students were expected to be able to meet the graduation requirements for the county upon completion of grade twelve in the alternative school.

The professional/vocational track consisted of highly structured apprenticeship experiences in community businesses. Eligible students spent as much as half of their day in career training classes and in volunteer work. Those students placed in apprenticeship positions were held to high performance standards: supervisors rated the students daily and communicated the ratings to school counselors. Students kept daily logs of their work experiences.

Discipline was managed with a token economy system. Students earned tokens for meeting agreed-upon behavior and academic objectives. The tokens were exchanged for material goods.

All three programs were successful at increasing academic performance for the participating students. Program participants, when compared with similar control students, learned more academic material. The measures of academic performance varied from project to project. Credits earned, persistence in school, attendance, grades, and standardized achievement test scores were affected. But only the alternative English and social studies class reduced other important risk factors of delinquent behavior: negative peer influence, disattachment from school, and punishing experiences in school. Students in the alternative classes also reported significantly less drug use and serious delinquent involvements than the control group.

The PATHE "pull-out" program appears to have been too weak and not sufficiently focused on theoretical risk factors for disruptive behavior to have been expected to reduce disruptive behavior. Although the design called for equal emphasis on academics and "affective needs," most of what occurred was tutoring. The alternative school was intensive, but it suffered from overcontrol. Students' behavior was under control in the school and they learned more. The atmosphere was calm and orderly. But the controlled atmosphere was gained at the expense of students' attachment to school. The students in the alternative school became significantly less attached to school, and their level of delinquent behavior increased. The atmosphere appears to have been overly controlled, offering few opportunities for youths to develop attachments to prosocial others.

The alternative English and social studies class intervention was at the same time intensive and comprehensive. It increased student participation not only in activities aimed at increasing academic success, but also at broadening the base of social control. Students were actively involved in their own education and in their schools and communities. They became more committed to and attached to school, and reported higher levels of involvement in school activities and less involvement with delinquent peers. Their delinquent behavior declined significantly.

In summary, the results of these evaluations of specific strategies to reduce disruptive behavior among high-risk youths suggest that it is possible to alter the schooling experience for high-risk youths in ways that reduce their level of disruptive behavior. But not every strategy works. Two well-defined and well-implemented programs failed to reduce delinquent behavior even though they succeeded at increasing academic performance. Reducing serious problem behavior among youths who have already developed a pattern of problem behavior may require attention to nonacademic factors such as the influence of peers and prosocial attachments as well as to academic experiences.

IMPLICATIONS FOR PRACTICE

The results imply that organizational development in schools can increase the likelihood of strong implementation of new practices and that specific strategies targeted at risk factors implied by research are effective for reducing school disorder. The results also imply that some well-intentioned and well-implemented practices are not effective for reducing disorderly behavior.

The studies reviewed did not permit an examination of the relative effects of the different components included in each school improvement effort. Such studies are critical if we are to understand *why* some efforts succeed and others fail. My personal experience in working with schools and districts as they attempt self-renewal implies that the most effective elements include program design that is guided by theory and evidence about the causes of the problem the organization is attempting to resolve, sensitivity to particular constraints within the implementing organization, and a long-range perspective.

Theory guidance is critical. In this context, a "theory" is a well-specified idea about the causes of the problem the organization is attempting to solve. The theory should be consistent with the results of prior research and evaluation, and it should be clearly understood by the program implementers so that it can guide implementation decisions. We have found it useful to engage school personnel in a discussion about their perceptions of the sources of the problem, and to invite the participation of individuals who have knowledge of the research in the area. This researcher-practitioner exchange is useful because it allows the practitioners to retain ownership of the program while encouraging them to consider seriously only those ideas showing most promise.

Sensitivity to the differences across implementing organizations is also essential. Although the sources of misbehavior and school disorder may be similar in different environments, the obstacles to implementing new practices directed at those common sources are likely to differ widely from school to school. Strategies for implementing new practices which fail to consider specific local obstacles are bound to fail. We have found it helpful to engage implementers in an open and honest discussion of the organizational force field (Lewin, 1951) for the purpose of anticipating obstacles to progress. Only by openly confronting potential roadblocks can strategies for overcoming them be developed and implemented.

Finally, school personnel must take a long-range perspective. Many attempts to bring about lasting improvements fail because they are embedded in unrealistic expectations about how much change can be expected how soon. Real change may take many years, and first tries seldom work (Fullan, Miles, and Taylor, 1980;

Klausmeier, 1985). Although the political arena may continue to publicize instances of "turned-around" schools, most schools are remarkably stable organizations, and if they have problems, these problems are likely to persist until they embark upon a persistent and long-term effort to improve conditions. Schools must develop their own internal structures for improvement. We have found that teams of school personnel can substantially improve their schools over time when they are guided by an explicit structure for developing, implementing, evaluating, and refining school practices. When school staff adopt such a structure, unrealistic expectations and low morale give way to an experimenting attitude and a belief that every failure brings new knowledge about what does and does not work. This change in school climate increases the likelihood that refined future practices will be effective.

3

A Cultural-Change Approach to School Discipline

Stewart C. Purkey

In recent years, the issue of school discipline and order has been much on the national mind. Scholarly studies (e.g., National Institute of Education, 1978), public opinion polls (e.g., Gallup, 1985), and articles in the popular press (e.g., Bowen, 1988) are testimony to a continuing and widespread concern about disruptive behavior, the safety of students and teachers alike, and the prevalence of various forms of substance abuse in public schools, especially secondary schools.

Whether the public schools are actually dangerously out of control, however, is highly debatable. For example, a study of secondary school teachers revealed that 60 percent "report that student misbehavior, drug or alcohol abuse does *not* interfere with their teaching" (emphasis added) whereas only about 25 percent "work in schools they regard as seriously flawed in . . . learning environment, and amount of substance abuse or misbehavior" (Purkey and Rutter, 1987, p. 379). Nevertheless, if discipline is thought insufficient for teaching and learning to occur by even one-quarter of the secondary school teachers, it is a significant national and educational problem. The question then becomes, what is to be done about establishing and maintaining discipline and order in those schools, whatever their number, where student misbehavior is an obstacle to realizing educational goals?

This paper considers possible answers to that question. The response advocated herein is predicated upon forms of organizational restructuring that facilitate cultural change and that should result in a more profound and lasting means of creating order and discipline by improving the overall quality of institutional life within schools. In particular, this approach is urged over "big brother/big stick" methods which rely on control and punishment.

THE ENDURING NATURE OF MISBEHAVIOR

Historians say that disorder and violence have been features of schools for centuries. For example, schoolchildren in seventeenth century France were often armed, feared by their schoolmates and ordinary citizens alike (Aries, 1962), and in English public schools, between 1775 and 1836, "mutinies, strikes and violence were so frequent—and sometimes so severe—that the masters had to call upon the military for assistance" (Newman, 1980, p. 7; see also Aries, 1962, pp. 315- 328).

Here at home, the level of discipline within schools and schools' contribution to social discipline have been persistent educational issues for over two hundred years (see, for example, Katz, 1968; Nasaw, 1979). This continuing concern with order and discipline has been accompanied by an equally historic effort to discover the best means by which students' behavior in schools can be controlled, their character improved, and their behavior outside of school channeled in prosocial directions.

Toward these ends, a number of solutions have been put forward. These range from advocating the adoption of Plato's recommendations in *The Republic* that the literature read by students be censored to ensure that students only encounter morally correct models of thinking and behavior, to the widespread use of corporal punishment. (For example, during the mid-1800s, Horace Mann reported observing 328 separate floggings in one week in a school of only 250 students—cited in Newman,. 1980). Other proposals have included the life adjustment curricula and social engineering theories of the progressive reformers in the mid-twentieth century United States, and current calls for schools to "get tough" with students, end all vestiges of permissiveness, and expel those students (assuming judicial noninterference) who are habitual troublemakers (see, for example, Toby, 1980).

The historical nature of school disorder does not necessarily mean that the search for discipline in schools is likely to be endlessly frustrating, even though a final answer seems to have eluded educators for several hundred years. As current work, including other chapters in this volume, makes clear, research has provided a variety of promising school-level strategies that can reduce student misbehavior, increase appropriate behavior, or accomplish both.

What this history does suggest, however, and this is a reasonable starting point for an attempt to understand what might be done to improve student discipline, are the following points. First, unless successful discipline methods were simply abandoned, it is reasonable to assume that approaches unable to guarantee proper behavior in the past (e.g., the reliance upon corporal punishment and harsh, punitive discipline indicated by Mann's comments) are unlikely to do so in the present; that is, if the severe and frequent beatings in the school observed by Horace Mann did not bring the students into line, there is little reason to think such tactics would work any better in the modern era.

Second, the enduring nature of misbehavior in schools raises the possibility that the problem is not a technical one that can be efficiently managed or solved in isolation from other aspects of the school. Instead, persistent misbehavior may be more accurately understood as a systemic problem related to the institutional nature of schools as they have been structured (uniform, often relatively impersonal batch processing of students, who are separated from adult community life), to the social conditions in which schools operate at any historical moment (the nature of race relations, labor market needs and hence employment opportunities), and to the developmental characteristics (emotional, social, cognitive) of school-age youth.

Third, given the above, school discipline is more likely to be genuinely improved by comprehensive approaches rather than by disciplinary methods that treat only the symptoms of the problem (the misbehavior itself) while leaving untouched the underlying causes. Since social conditions and child and adolescent development are largely beyond the school's control, educators must focus on those school-level changes that can lead to new forms of student work and human relations within schools and that will result in greater engagement by students (and staff) in the schools' mission.

ORGANIZATIONAL CHANGE AS A STARTING POINT

Ultimately, this may require fundamentally restructuring schools, and completely revamping methods of teaching and learning. In the meantime, less drastic organizational changes have the potential to lower the oppositional behavior of students and create humane, positive learning and working environments.

Put in slightly different terms, such an approach assumes that changes at the organizational level can alter people's subjective experiences and ultimately their beliefs and behaviors. For example, in a theoretical discussion of school-level factors that contribute to student alienation (as reflected in behaviors ranging from absenteeism to low-quality schoolwork to vandalism), Newmann (1981) proposes altering organizational features that research has linked to the degree of alienation in a variety of institutional and social settings. These changes include reducing school size, flattening the degree of hierarchy in role relations, increasing staff and student participation in decision making, providing opportunities for academic work by students that is cooperative, fostering organizational goal clarity, and so forth. He argues that such "objective" changes in the school's structure will positively affect individuals' perceptions of the school and their relationship to it.

Similarly, O'Toole (1981), who is primarily concerned with increasing productivity and innovation in private- and public-sector organizations, states that "changing personalities or behavior to achieve effective organizational change" is a "near-impossible task" (p. 117). He suggests that attention be focused on the "organization context" in which people work, that is, the structure of relationships and the ideology of the organization. By changing these organizational variables, one can encourage new behaviors and discourge inappropriate behaviors. For example, redesigning organizations to permit and reward diversity of task, encourage participation in decision making, and allow for the occupational choice and mobility of members is an organizational strategy that, according to O'Toole, can result in greater commitment by members to their organization's goals and processes.

Neither Newmann nor O'Toole suggests that people be released from taking responsibility for their actions. Both, however, argue (and O'Toole documents) that organizational structures can be built that promote positive behaviors and that facilitate people's willingness and ability to assume responsibility for what they do within the organization. Indeed, organizational change (particularly new forms of management) aimed at developing productive workplace cultures (discussed in more detail below) is precisely the means currently advocated in the private sector for changing the behavior of workers and revitalizing American industry and business (see, for example, Deming, 1982; Kanter, 1983; O'Toole, 1981; Peters and Waterman, 1982).

Applied to schools, this organizational approach assumes that it is far easier to change organizational structure than it is to "fix" the people within schools. More importantly, perhaps, an organizational approach attacks the sources, for most students, of oppositional behavior and thereby increases school authorities' ability (time, energy, resources) to respond appropriately to the relatively few students in most schools whose misbehavior is so serious as to demand exceptional disciplinary treatment.

If it is true, then, that factors at the level of the organization are critical to student discipline, it remains to be determined which factors or levers are likely to prove most powerful. In what follows, I will first offer a general observation stimulated by the literature reviewed elsewhere in this volume (see especially, Duke) and then will comment on an approach that incorporates much of what I find persuasive in that research.

THE ABSENCE OF A ONE-BEST METHOD

To begin, there seems to be a noticeable lack of hard data that could be used to select any one particular school-level strategy for student discipline over another, possibly because such data are not available. Without knowing the size of the effect of using schoolwide discipline codes compared with involving students in school decision making, for example, it is rather difficult for practitioners to know where to put already scarce resources. What seems to be lacking is evidence that with similar populations, in schools operating within essentially the same community context, a particular treatment reduces student misbehavior by x-amount compared with other treatments and with some control group. Although this fact does not make the area of discipline research unique in the field of education, it does suggest the need for caution at this time.

Moreover, the presented data do not permit making causal connections between specific strategies and student behavior, especially changes in student behavior. For example, there seems to be a clear relationship between school leadership and orderly student behavior. In one analysis of the High School and Beyond data, researchers found that less disorder was reported by teachers in whose schools the principal was perceived as "strong" in terms of getting resources for the school, buffering teachers from outside interference, setting priorities and making sure plans were carried out, having and communicating a vision of the school, and letting staff members know what was expected of them (Newmann, Rutter, and Smith, 1985). However, the dynamics of that relationship between leadership and discipline are not clear (see Duke, this volume; also, Manasse, 1985).

Not only could there be intervening or alternative, unrecognized variables producing orderly student behavior, but there is no conclusive evidence that the characteristics of leadership in schools with effective discipline are the same as those necessary to instill discipline in disorderly schools. Hypothetically, out-of-control schools may respond to authoritarian, even autocratic forms of leadership, whereas schools where discipline no longer assumes center stage may do best under leaders whose behavior is more democratic in orientation.

If, then, the school-level data do not yet support either a one-best strategy or causal connections between specific strategies and changes in student behavior, what can be done? As others have argued, while research continues, educators must, nevertheless, concretely act to improve discipline in schools where its absence is interfering with teaching and learning. In any event, that educators will initiate improvement projects without waiting for definitive research results has been demonstrated repeatedly, most recently by the fact that approximately one-third of all high school principals nationwide report having begun an effective schools project, seemingly unconcerned by or unaware of significant criticisms about the quality of that research (Purkey, Rutter, and Newmann, 1986).

THE IMPORTANCE OF COMMON PURPOSE

Another way of looking at the lack of a one-best strategy, however, is that *within limits*, including those suggested by the research reviewed elsewhere in this volume, it may not matter which strategy a school adopts. Put another way, no single method can be said to work across all schools, but a variety of strategies can probably be successful in any given school. Note that this statement emphatically does not mean that anything goes, merely that there are a number of possible options and that there is probably enough information at hand to provide useful maps of how to get where educators want to go.

Consistent enforcement of clear rules by teachers and administrators (Metz, 1978), involving students in rulesetting (McPartland and McDill, 1976), and smaller schools or within-school units (Gottfredson and Gofffredson, 1985) all appear to be valid mechanisms for directly or indirectly improving discipline. What seems to be critical, however, is *how* to get a school's staff to focus their attention on the issue and to work together toward a clear and internally consistent set of goals relative to establishing order. Again within limits, the problem is less "what works" than "How do we implement what works?" If staff members value order and discipline, come to a common understanding of what they want to accomplish and how, and consistently channel their energy in that direction, it is likely that they will be successful, assuming that the strategy they select is logically connected to student behavior and that factors external to the school are not overwhelmingly influential. (See Rutter et al., 1979, whose descriptions of effective British secondary schools illustrate the importance of agreement on goals and consistent enforcement of rules; see also Purkey and Smith, 1985).

Unfortunately, it is here that the available research is most unsatisfactory. Although successful change projects seem to share certain characteristics (see Huberman and Miles, 1984), there is an imprecise understanding of the nature of the change process across school sites. More to the point, there does not appear to be a single factor that, in all settings, will necessarily result in staff agreement and focused activity. Nevertheless, drawing from the literature on educational change and innovation, a prima facie case can be made that the following are necessary, though probably not sufficient, for forging a commonality of purpose among a school's staff around an issue like discipline:

1. Leadership, from the principal or other staff members, which is aimed not at solving the problem but at getting staff to work together to identify and devise solutions to the perceived problem (see, for example, Barth, 1980; Gersten, Carnine, and Green, 1982; Hall et al., 1983; Hargrove et al., 1981)

2. The acknowledgment by a majority of staff members that there is a problem and that, regardless of the cause or possible solution(s), the problem, in general terms, is lack of discipline (or poor skills in reading or whatever)

3. The involvement of all those to be affected by whatever changes are proposed in the decision-making process (see, for example, Berman and McLaughlin, 1977; Elmore, 1978; Fullan, 1985)

4. The support of the district's central office expressed in both concrete and symbolic terms (see, for example, David and Peterson, 1984; Pink, 1986; Purkey and Smith, 1985)

5. Resources, especially technical assistance, release time, and ongoing staff development, perhaps in direct proportion to the magnitude of the change sought (see, for example, Berman

and McLaughlin, 1977; Huberman and Miles, 1984; Purkey and Smith, 1985)

6. Enough time for major changes in staff behavior or beliefs (two to three years) but not so much time (i.e., not open-ended) that there is no pressure to make a change (see, for example, Miles, Farrar, and Neufeld, 1983; Purkey, 1985)

However, having argued that the problem of establishing order in schools lies in getting staff (and students) to work cooperatively toward a valued common goal (which, to some extent, makes this a generic problem of organizational change), it remains to be determined whether, nevertheless, one means still might be more desirable than another, and if so, why. To simply view the problem as one of translating theory into practice or replicating models is the epitome of the technocratic approach criticized earlier.

SCHOOL CULTURE AND STUDENT DISCIPLINE

In thinking about school discipline, it is vital that its purpose be clearly understood. As others have noted (e.g., Duke, in this volume), school discipline is not to be desired for itself, but is necessary to the success of the school's mission. (One wonders, however, if this perspective is shared by all. For instance, those who argue that a primary purpose of schooling is to instill respect for authority and obedience to societal norms might be inclined to question the assumption that discipline is merely a means and not an end.) Beyond the importance of not confusing ends and means, it is also important to make a distinction between disciplined schools and disciplined students (see Gaddy, 1986). Although docility and conforming to school rules can undoubtedly be coerced by a variety of sophisticated control mechanisms, the development of the sort of self-discipline that is likely to transfer to nonschool situations seems to require giving students opportunities for choice and for assuming responsibility for the functioning and maintenance of the school (see, for example, Newmann, 1981; Sprinthall and Mosher, 1978). Indeed, there is little convincing evidence that repressive control or harsh punishment diminishes student misbehavior, and some evidence that it can actually exacerbate student resistance (e.g., Gottfredson, 1986; Kulka et al., 1982; Rutter, 1980).

What this discussion suggests, therefore, is that strategies seeking to directly influence student behavior, especially those that are excessively preoccupied with discouraging inappropriate conduct, could prove counterproductive in the long run. Even if order is restored to schools (and this is problematic), there may be repercussions elsewhere in society as anger at a repressive and oppressive school environment is vented in the more anonymous atmosphere of community and street life. To that extent, attacking symptoms is likely to prove less effective than attempting to get at root causes. As a lever to get at the roots of the problem, insofar as schools can do so independently of the social conditions within which they exist, a cultural approach would appear to be the most promising.

Indeed, it is the school's culture that is the target of the organizational change effort discussed previously in this paper: that is, restructuring the school is done precisely to create a culture that is conducive to teaching and learning; such a culture includes order and discipline and a seriousness of purpose about the work of students and teachers alike (see Purkey and Smith, 1985). Organizational changes, therefore, are sought that will facilitate, if not directly cause, a new, more productive culture to slowly replace that which currently exists.

Operationally, *school culture* refers to the values or guiding beliefs and to the norms or daily behavior and practices of the people within the school; current research has revealed the following about this vague but powerful construct called "school culture" (adapted from Patterson, Purkey, and Parker, 1986, pp. 97-98):[1]

1. School culture does affect the behavior and achievement of elementary and secondary school students (though the effect of classroom and student variables remains greater).

2. School culture is created by and thus can be manipulated by people within the school.

3. School cultures are relatively unique; whatever their commonalities (e.g., sense of leadership, clear and shared goals), no two schools will be exactly alike—nor should they be.

4. The elements of school cultures interact with each other to produce a whole that is greater than the sum of its parts; although individual aspects of the school culture can affect a child for better or worse, it is the child's encounter with the entire school culture that seems most influential.

5. Particularly, but not exclusively, at the secondary level, different groups of students experience the school's culture dif-

ferently; similarly, student peer cultures and/or community cultures may not be in harmony with the school culture.

6. To the extent that it provides a focus and clear purpose for the school, culture becomes the cohesion that bonds the school together as it goes about its mission.

7. Though the positive aspects of culture are emphasized here, culture can be counterproductive and an obstacle to educational success; culture can also be oppressive and/or discriminatory for various subgroups within the school.

8. Lasting, fundamental change (e.g., in student attitudes or teacher behaviors) requires understanding and, often, altering the school's culture; cultural change is generally a slow process.

The above notwithstanding, school culture remains difficult to define (Anderson, 1982). To that can be added the confusion generated by the use of multiple terms for what seems to be essentially the same phenomenon (e.g., Rutter et al., 1979, use the term *ethos*; Goodlad, 1984, speaks of *school climate*; Hawley et al., 1984, refer to the *learning environment*), and the difficulty of measuring and evaluating culture (Patterson, Purkey, and Parker, 1986). Nevertheless, research persists in identifying culture as a significant variable separating effective, and therefore orderly, schools from ineffective, often disorderly schools. This should not be surprising, because when culture is broken down into its constituent parts, it is evident that the concept incorporates many of the factors usually associated with an orderly school environment. In other words, school discipline, like student achievement, is a result of a web of factors that have a cumulative impact on staff and student behavior. Translating this into concrete practice is the problem, of course, but altering organizational culture is not an impossibly complex task (see Deal and Kennedy, 1982, 1983; Patterson, Purkey, and Parker, 1986).

School discipline understood as a problem of organizational structure and culture is a more useful and pragmatic approach than searching for a one-best technology that probably does not exist. A cultural perspective also reminds us that it is students' experience with the whole school, as well as the congruence between the values and norms of the school and those of the students' homes, neighborhoods, and workplaces, that determines whether groups of students will comply with school regulations and expectations or resist them. (Note, however, that *individual* students, although certainly subject to the same forces, make individual choices in any given situation; manipulating school culture is designed to encourage certain choices over others.)

CULTURE AND COMMUNITY

In accordance with the cultural change approach advocated here, Cohen (1983) suggests, in a review of the school and teacher effectiveness literature, that schools must be communities with a moral order that relies on "the internalization of goals, the legitimate use of authority, and the manipulation of symbols, as means of controlling and directing the behavior" of their members (p. 31). Lightfoot (1983) argues that good schools, however imperfect they may be, have gained control as part of the "development of a visible and explicit ideology" that has provided cohesion within the school community and engendered feelings of identification, affiliation,and loyalty. Finally, Lipsitz (1984) describes successful middle schools as developmentally healthy communities having distinct cultures that include, among other things, the *means* by which order is generated, reciprocal human relations, leadership, and clarity of purpose.

Discipline is vital to the success of these schools, but order is achieved within the context of rather unique cultures that establish communities of purpose. And, just as organizational culture can be manipulated, so too can community be established within schools via such things as cooperative work activities, relationships between students and faculty that extend beyond the classroom, democratic governance, the use of ceremony and ritual to express shared purposes and commitments, the recognition and acceptance of diverse talents, skills and personal attributes of staff and students alike, and so forth.[2] Contrast this approach, in its intent and its philosophical base, with the opposite approach, which would impose order by the essentially punitive use of increased control, surveillance, and monitoring mechanisms.

CULTURE AND CURRICULUM

Finally, adopting a structural-cultural change approach to improving student discipline reminds us that curriculum and instruction are school-level variables. Although schools have often been criticized for unchallenging curricula and instructional methods that promote emotional passivity and intellectual sterility (e.g., Boyer, 1983; Everhart, 1983; Goodlad, 1984; McNeil, 1983), it is equally true that different forms of curricula and instruction can engage students in authentic learning activities that are intrinsically satisfying. Abstractly, this suggests integrating knowledge across subject areas, linking knowing and doing, connecting schoolwork to the ongoing life of the community, emphasizing student participation in the creation of knowledge, providing opportunities for cooperative work, employing inquiry and problem solving, encouraging academic work that requires synthesis or creativity, and holding students to high standards of quality (see Newmann, 1981; Sizer, 1984). Concretely, it might resemble the Foxfire program in Rabun Gap, Georgia (Wigginton, 1985), Greendown Community School in West Swindon, England (Matthews, 1987), or the Key School in Indianapolis (Olson, 1988). In each, the curriculum seems to meet several, if not most, of the criteria listed above. Though the Key School is far too new to enable educators to draw firm conclusions from its experience, both Foxfire and Greendown demonstrate rather convincingly the power of a rich, integrated curriculum to create a culture in which the norm is the orderly engagement of students in their academic work. Again, in both schools discipline seems to be a relatively natural outgrowth of the culture and a curriculum which sustains that culture.

Put another way, just as stimulating curriculum and instruction in a single classroom contribute to its orderly atmosphere (which is not necessarily quiet), so too can intrinsically satisfying and engaging curriculum and instruction across all classrooms result in a purposeful and orderly school. Without denying the importance of clear rules, consistently enforced and fairly applied, order and discipline that stem from the nature of the academic work in schools is certainly preferable.

Granted, there is little in the way of quantifiable data demonstrating conclusively, at the school level, the effectiveness of this strategy for improving student discipline (for one exception, however, see Lipsitz, 1984). It is clear, also, that significant changes in organizational culture may be necessary to alter the prevailing forms of curriculum and instruction, and that such fundamental change is exceedingly difficult. Nevertheless, models do exist, even if primarily at the classroom level, and there is no compelling reason to think they cannot be replicated throughout schools given the necessary conditions for implementing any major cultural change.[3] In any event, if successful, improving discipline by altering the dominant forms of curriculum and instruction within schools is, in the long run, likely to be an enduring strategy because it addresses the more significant sources of student opposition to schooling than does the historically bankrupt effort to end misbehavior by relying on institutional control via closer monitoring and stricter punishment.

CONCLUSION

In brief, then, it is the contention of this paper that in the absence of a one-best method for imposing discipline on presumably passive students and staff, both groups would be better served if schools focused on altering their organizational structure to promote the emergence of a culture that creates a healthy, engaging environment in which to work and learn.

Finally, two crucial points must be made. First, although schools are treated here as isolated institutions, in reality the external environment intrudes on them in myriad ways. This can be critically important for the issue of discipline—in fact, for all questions of student performance in schools. For example, to the extent that students perceive a bleak future outside of school, or encounter peer or other reference groups whose beliefs and values run counter to the official message of the school, students will be less willing, especially at the secondary level, to comply with school rules. This may be particularly true for those economic groups whose experience has convinced them that the historical contract alleged between getting an education and getting a good and satisfying job has been broken. That is why projects such as the Boston Compact may, potentially, be a better *single* disciplinary strategy than any one school-level proposal (see Farrar and Cipollone, 1985). (See Willis, 1977, and Ogbu, 1978, for an extended discussion of the manner in which school can conflict with the cultural values and norms of students' nonschool lives and the implications of this conflict for student behavior.)

Second, to the extent that student misbehavior is associated with poor performance in school (see, for example, Gottfredson in this volume), programs that can improve students' academic skill development in the elementary grades are also likely to significantly reduce schools' discipline problems. Therefore, at the other end, so to speak, school discipline might also be attacked by early childhood education programs such as the Perry Preschool Project in Ypsilanti, Michigan (see, for example, Berrueta-Clement et al., 1984).

Although neither a "head start" nor a good job is sufficient alone or in combination, these sorts of nonschool strategies, together with the organizational, cultural change approach discussed previously, must be a part of any long-range strategy for improving school discipline if discipline is to be the means to a better education for all and not simply the "end" of increased control.

4

Improving School Discipline Through Student-Teacher Involvement

Willis J. Furtwengler

Reaching Success Through Involvement (RSI) is a school organizational development process which appears to have significant promise for improving school discipline. It has been tested successfully in a variety of school settings in sixty-one schools. Discipline improved in each school and significantly in schools that exhibited considerable discipline problems. This chapter describes the RSI's development, the basic framework on which RSI is based, and the activities of the RSI process. It then discusses the major results from past implementations and presents some examples of how discipline improved in schools that implemented RSI. Lastly, tentative research findings from the implementations are described.

The RSI change process evolved from the author's repeated attempts to help schools improve school discipline effectiveness. Discipline effectiveness is the extent to which the students' behaviors are: (1) viewed by the faculty and community as appropriate social behaviors, and (2) self-governed. Another way of stating the definition is that discipline effectiveness is the appropriateness of student behaviors and the willingness and abilities of students to govern their own actions in a school.

Research from the areas of organizational development (Schmuck and Runkel, 1984), effective schools (Purkey and Smith, 1983; Lezotte and Bancroft, 1985), and the cultural and symbolic management of organizational change (Deal, 1987; Schein, 1986; Fullan, 1982) has supported the development of the RSI framework for implementing change to improve discipline in schools. The framework consists of these four processes: (1) *the involvement process*, which is directing the active attention of the formal and informal leaders (teachers, students, administrators, and a few from the local community) toward the school's achievements and activities; (2) *the problem-solving process*, which is the active involvement of the above personnel in identifying and proposing solutions to school problems; (3) the *identification process*, which is the changing of personal boundaries, roles, and areas of responsibility to assume new roles and shared responsibilities for implementing solutions to school problems; and (4) the *monitoring process*, which is the systematic collecting of data regarding the effectiveness of actions designed to improve or maintain the effectiveness of the school. The monitoring process also includes determining the effectiveness of each of the four processes used in the framework for creating and maintaining an effective school.

RSI is defined as a systematically planned and sustained effort for school (unit) self-study and improvement that focuses explicitly on changing the culture, climate, and productivity of the unit. Culture is defined in this context as "the way we do things around here," and climate is defined as the way people *feel* about the "way we do things around here." RSI was designed to alter the culture and climate of schools as a means of increasing discipline effectiveness (Furtwengler and Konnert, 1982). Implementation of RSI includes four sets of activities for achieving four central purposes: assessing the organization's productivity and health (climate and culture); planning for improvement of the organization; implementing plans through groups of individuals who, according to the bureaucratic structure, have differing roles and responsibilities; and assessing the organization's productivity and health a second time to plan again for improvement.

The RSI framework has been implemented in sixty-one schools with encouraging results. The schools were located in a variety of geographic locations within the eastern, southern, and midwestern states. Approximately one-third of the schools were secondary schools, another third were schools for the middle grades, and a third were elementary schools. In a specific study of fourteen of these schools, thirteen improved some aspects of their learning and/or social milieu, including discipline effectiveness (Furtwengler, 1986). Moreover, the schools which showed the greatest improvement had been classified as "less effective."

The use of this framework appears to increase the school members' feelings of being empowered (Furtwengler, 1985). This empowerment, or perception of control, is directly related to the extent to which school participants believe they have "a stake" in the school and feel responsible for its well-being and success. As members implement the processes in the framework and participate in the four sets of activities, their motivation to improve the school and its discipline effectiveness appears to increase, as does their use of group problem-solving skills.

FIVE STAGES OF RSI DEVELOPMENT

Development of the RSI process evolved through five stages of use and refinement. The process was altered at each of the five stages to increase its ability to improve discipline effectiveness.

Stage I: One-Day Teacher In-service

The first of five stages consisted of one-day in-service training for a school's faculty. Stage I activities were conducted beginning in the fall of 1974 through the spring of 1975 and involved workshop activities in twenty-six schools. During this first stage, it was believed that one-day in-service training sessions would help improve discipline effectiveness in schools. These one-day affairs, conducted by the author, were usually not related to other in-service training topics conducted at the school. For example, a workshop on improving student behavior was not related to a later workshop entitled "Student Learning Styles." The specific focus for each of the one-day sessions was defined by the school administrator or faculty representatives or both.

Results of the efforts during the first stage of development were disappointing. No significant improvement in discipline effectiveness occurred as a direct consequence of these one-day in-service sessions. The ideas presented were determined to be relevant by the faculty when its members had input into the selection of the topics, but teachers had difficulty changing their school and classroom behaviors. Teacher in-service sessions were "good," but were not enough to help them improve discipline in their classrooms and schools. When asked why they were not able to implement the new ideas, the teachers replied, "Because that is not the way we are accustomed to doing things around here."

Stage II: Three-Day Teacher Workshops on Discipline Improvement

In the second stage of development, the one-day in-service sessions were replaced with two- or three-day workshops partially designed by teachers and usually conducted prior to the beginning of the school year. Stage II was initiated in the fall of 1975 and extended through the fall of 1976; it involved eighteen schools. The three-day sessions were planned individually by teacher representatives at each school. During these sessions, the faculty members defined the school's discipline problems and directed their attention to learning from the consultant and to learning from each other in small groups. At some sessions, they spent the first day examining the problems and climate in their school. A second day typically included time for reaching agreement on (1) the level of seriousness of specific student actions, (2) the use of penalties and corrective measures for specific inappropriate student actions, and (3) the use of methods to prevent inappropriate student behaviors. The third day included such activities as simulations dealing with ten cases of inappropriate behavior. Teachers also made decisions on how they would all approach teaching students appropriate social behaviors for that year.

Results from the three-day workshop stage were encouraging. In most instances, discipline during the first two months of the school year was improved in comparison with the first two months of the previous year. When the entire year was considered, however, the three-day workshop failed to improve discipline effectiveness in the schools.

Teachers reported that it was difficult to remember what they were to do and what they had agreed to implement during the year. They indicated that it was not natural to do things in the new ways designed prior to the opening of school because it "was not the way we were used to doing things around here." During the second stage, the invisible wall of "the way we do things around here" emerged as a major obstacle to improving discipline effectiveness. The invisible wall appeared to be formed by each person's subconscious agreements to take certain actions in the context of situations. Teachers tended to do what they always had done in the school and classrooms. Clearly, something else was needed if discipline effectiveness was to be improved.

Stage III: Problem Solving as In-service Training

Stage III included a first attempt to improve discipline effectiveness through a one-year, problem-solving approach to in-service training.

Stage III was begun in the fall of 1977 and extended through the spring of 1978. This stage involved work with four schools. The one-year consultation design included the formation of a planning council, including representatives of teachers and administrators, which served as a problem-solving group to accomplish two things. First, it helped design in-service events during the year to increase discipline effectiveness. These in-service sessions were related and built on each other; adjustments were made as the year progressed. For example, at one in-service meeting, the faculty in small groups developed a list of alternatives to sending students from the room for inappropriate student behavior. At a subsequent meeting, the faculty identified methods for helping students learn to take responsibility for the classroom and their school. In most instances, the two- or three-day workshop conducted before school began was a part of the year's plan for in-service.

A second purpose of the faculty planning council was to monitor data on student infractions and teacher problems. This activity included the assumption that the council would search for solutions that it would recommend to the faculty. The author's role as consultant to this process was to be responsive to their requests for various in-service assistance and to make suggestions regarding ways to improve the process and discipline effectiveness.

During this stage, the concept of developmental consultation services to the school was initiated. Developmental consultation is designed to help the school or organization create and maintain its effectiveness over an extended time period. For example, teachers involved in stage III suggested that a planning council be formed and that, throughout the year, it should find ways to reinforce the shared values which the faculty had established at the beginning of the year. In response to this suggestion, two schools held celebration activities prior to or following in-service sessions during the year.

Results from the ongoing, problem-solving approach and related in-service training programs were extremely encouraging from one point of view. The staff in each school became a closer working team and, as a result, their overall supervision of the school improved:that is, teachers were better able to monitor students' actions and to prevent some inappropriate behaviors from occurring. The structure and order of the school also improved. The operation of the school was smoother and the teachers were more consistent in their approaches to handling inappropriate student behavior. The frequency of inappropriate student behaviors actually decreased for the year despite reports of increased student apathy in classrooms. This third stage of development provided evidence that the invisible wall of "the way we do things around here" among the teachers could be altered.

Two schools identified specific aims to decrease the number of students tardy to classes. In both schools, progress was made in decreasing the number of students late to classes, but both schools had increases in other forms of inappropriate student behaviors. As one teacher said: "This is crazy. We decreased the number of students who are late to class, but we have increased the number of fights in the school. It is like a tube of toothpaste. When you attempt to patch a break on the tube it squeezes out somewhere else. Should we be attempting to improve discipline on all fronts at the same time?"

During this stage of the RSI development, teachers reported that they believed they had more control over events in their lives and their school. Hence, they felt as though they had more ownership of the school. They also reported that they felt more responsible for the school than they had during previous years. But now they were burdened with feelings of carrying too much responsibility for the students' behaviors. They had their act together as teachers, but the school had become a "we" (the faculty) and "they" (the students) institution. One teacher was quoted as saying: "Students dare us to try to teach them. Somehow it is all twisted around. We now are the persons who appear to be solely responsible for both their discipline and what they learn about their subjects. Surely, something is wrong." Another teacher reflected the sentiments of the majority when she said: "Most of us (teachers) are now working better as a team, but a small core of teachers continues to do things the way we used to do them. They could help us so much if they only would."

What was apparent from these discussions with teachers was (1) their frustration over having to devote so much of their energy to controlling student behavior, (2) their skepticism toward targeting specific inappropriate student behaviors apart from dealing with misbehavior on a broad front, and (3) their concern about those teachers who were not contributing to the efforts of the majority of faculty members.

Students reported "prisonlike conditions" in their views of their school. They had lost opportunities to "have fun" or to make decisions because their actions were so closely monitored. Students reported that they liked the fact that the system of rules and regulations worked. They said that more fairness, firmness, and consistency was evident in the discipline process. Students also reported loss of control in the school and feelings of less ownership of their school.

They viewed themselves as not being responsible for contributing to their school. When asked what had changed about student misbehavior at the school, they reported that the obvious offenders were becoming less obvious. Students, they said, were more secretive about their misbehaviors, and they worked harder and more cooperatively with other students at avoiding being caught by the teachers. Asked why they did not study more or why they did not contribute more to the "good" of the school, the students reported that "that was not the way they did things at the school." One student said: "Are you kidding? This school has always been known for students who screw around. That is one reason why it will not change."

It was obvious to the author at this stage of RSI development that three problems kept discipline effectiveness from being increased. First, students, like teachers, had an invisible wall ("the way students do things around here") which kept them from altering the way they acted at the school. Students appeared bound by their own set of subconscious agreements concerning "the way we do things around here."

A second problem was teachers who opted not to become involved in the effort. They were notorious for saying, "We do not have a problem with discipline effectiveness" or "We do not want to alter what we do in any way" or that it is "the students these days." These teachers did not perceive a problem. One possible reason for this situation was the lack of information concerning the status of discipline effectiveness and the status of the invisible wall among teachers. The other possible reason for the situation was that the information which was provided to faculty members was not convincing to teachers who, for example, were teaching "the good kids."

A third problem associated with this stage was the assumption that inappropriate behaviors such as tardies are unrelated to other student behaviors. There was an assumption among the faculties that students would not alter their other behaviors while the school was making an effort to reduce the numbers of students who were late for classes. Teachers were surprised to learn that solving the problem of class tardiness was associated with the rise of other inappropriate student behaviors. It is doubtful that the attention and energy directed toward correcting one problem created the others, but it is likely that the narrow focus on specific inappropriate acts may have resulted in a lack of normal attention to other areas of student behavior. It appeared that a broad problem-solving effort to increase discipline effectiveness might have been more effective than a single narrow-focused approach.

Stage IV of RSI process development included two significant additions to the process. The first was to involve students in the process, and the second was to significantly improve the measures of discipline effectiveness. These were designed to solve the three problems encountered during stage III.

Stage IV, Part A: Student Involvement

The fourth stage in RSI's development yielded a high return on faculty and student investment. During this stage, the problem-solving in-service approach guided by the faculty planning council included treating students as a major school resource to be included in the RSI process. Methods were discovered for tapping that resource to improve discipline effectiveness. In effect, the students' invisible wall of "the way we do things around here" was altered. Stage IV was initiated in the fall of 1978 and continues to the present. Sixty-one schools have initiated the RSI process since 1978.

Planning councils, after convincing the majority of their respective teacher groups that students might be a resource, asked teachers to help select the formal and informal student leaders in their schools. At the elementary levels, student participation began with grade four. The planning councils scheduled two- and three-day leadership workshops which were held prior to the opening of school. These workshops, called "school retreats," included formal and informal student leaders, a small group of community leaders, and a core of formal and informal faculty leaders (Furtwengler and Farley, 1987). At these training and problem-solving sessions, students and teachers joined forces to form action teams. Each action team identified problems related to improving discipline effectiveness in their school. For example, separate action teams worked on the problem of tardiness to school and classes, on increasing student involvement, and on chemical abuse among students. Still other teams became committed to increasing school spirit and pride.

The action teams worked all year at their school to implement their plans and to involve other students in completing their action plans. Teams had such labels as the "school pride bunch," the "let's get involved group," and the "keepers of building and grounds." Students indicated that they believed they had more choices and control over what happened in their lives, that they believed the school was their school, and that they felt a new sense of responsibility for their school. Students took charge of their own actions and demonstrated their abilities to exercise self-governing behaviors.

The planning council also coordinated the topics for faculty in-service and problem-solving activities with the aims of the action teams.

Results from stage IVA showed dramatic improvement in schools that had low initial levels of discipline effectiveness (Furtwengler, 1985; 1986). Teachers reported that they felt a greater sense of shared responsibility with students despite their loss of control regarding some of the decisions they were accustomed to making. One teacher reported, "It is no longer a "we-against-them" (students) situation. We now have some allies who are working with us. Every time I see one of the students from the retreat, I know that we share some similar aims for the school. Several of our worse characters have become powerful positive forces in our school." Students were much more involved in preventing inappropriate student behavior. The implementation experience during stage IVA made it evident that changing the invisible wall of "the way we do things around here" among both students and teachers can be accomplished through collaborative problem-solving activities involving teachers, students, and members of the community. A big event, such as a retreat, is needed to make a symbolic organizational statement that "the way we do things around here is about to change."

The second problem which emerged from implementing the RSI process as developed through stage III was the time it took for some teachers to develop a broad sense of ownership and responsibility for the school. This deficiency led to stage IVB of development of the RSI process for creating and maintaining discipline effectiveness.

Stage IV, Part B: The RSI School Report Card

Stage IVB of RSI's development included the design and testing of an extensive process for building an RSI School Report Card. Part of this report card gave the school a much better picture of its discipline effectiveness.

Schools were encouraged to use their own personnel to develop methods for collecting information on discipline effectiveness. The key need was for information that would be viewed by all teachers as credible data and reliable sources for making valid judgments regarding the discipline effectiveness of the school. Typically, data regarding discipline effectiveness were collected through (1) interviews with school personnel, including students and, usually, parents; (2) compilation of written inventories developed for schools—such as the Climate Effectiveness Inventory, School Culture Inventory, Public Image Inventory, Student Opinion Inventory, Inservice Choices Inventory,

Leadership Inventory, Burnout Assessment Inventory, Learner Needs, Learner Methods, Learner Self-Image, and Learner Behavior (Furtwengler, 1978-1987); (3) observations of personnel and activities in the school; and (4) reviews of records kept by the school regarding discipline.

In addition to data on discipline effectiveness, the RSI Report Card included measures of the school's culture ("the way we do things around here at the school"), an assessment of the way teachers and students felt about their culture, and perceptions of the school's image held by parents, teachers, and students. Each school's planning council determined those inventories to be used in the data collection process. The council also helped to determine how the information would be collected. In a sense, the council determined the paint to be used in painting a portrait of the school.

Determining a school's ratings on the report card was done by a team of RSI facilitators in consultation with the school's planning council. Data gathered and analyzed were compared with (1) similar data from other schools, (2) the school's previous record, and (3) the school or district's standards or aims for that particular school. These comparisons were made through a consensus decision-making process involving RSI facilitators. These preliminary findings were then reviewed with the school's planning council. A four-point rating system with a brief narrative was developed to summarize the school's level of discipline effectiveness. The rating standards used reflected four conditions: excellent; effective but in need of improvement; in need of improvement and being worked on; and in need of immediate improvement and nothing being done to correct the situation.

Results from implementations of the RSI process during stage IVB showed that the motivation of most teachers to act on the problems of the school was increased. Teachers, after reviewing the report card data, concluded for themselves that improvement was needed in many areas within the broad scope of discipline effectiveness. More teachers volunteered to help serve on action teams once they were aware of measured needs: for example, to improve structure and order, or to increase the teachers' and students' sense of belonging to the school.

The RSI process as designed through stage IVA and stage IVB has been tested in a variety of school settings. Initial development involved inner-city secondary schools that had relatively high incidences of inappropriate student behavior. Since 1981, development of the process has occurred in a wide variety of school settings, including rural, inner-city, and urban schools and elementary, middle, and high schools. The tentative findings suggest that the RSI process is effective in increasing the level of discipline effectiveness of almost any school: that is, it can reduce the number and seriousness of inappropriate student behaviors and can move the students toward assuming responsibility for their own behavior. A later section of this chapter presents evidence for this conclusion.

STEPS IN THE RSI PROCESS

As previously stated, implementation of RSI includes four sets of activities for achieving four central purposes: assessing the organization's productivity and health, planning for improvements, implementing plans through groups of individuals having differing roles and responsibilities, and reassessing the organization's productivity and health to plan for continued improvement. These four central processes are subdivided into a set of twelve steps. Each step requires a functional activity and specifies who participates in the activity. Implementation of each step is described in the following exposition of the sequence in which the steps usually occurred in the schools (Furtwengler, 1985).

Steps 1 through 5 were completed during the first school year of implementation.

1. The building administrators recognized and accepted their responsibility for their schools' discipline effectiveness.

2. Each principal appointed a planning council consisting of ten to fifteen teachers to guide the implementation of the RSI process. The council determined changes that the school should make to increase discipline effectiveness. The RSI facilitators, with the help of the council, collected and analyzed information about the status of the school (the RSI School Report Card), including the level of discipline effectiveness in the school. The council prepared a report on its findings.

3. The planning council presented its report to the rest of the faculty, along with its recommendations and plans for action related to improving discipline effectiveness. Usually the council recommended some in-service training sessions to be held prior to the establishment of a student leadership group.

4. In secondary and middle grade schools, the council used recommendations received from teachers, students, admin-

istrators, and parents to establish a student leadership group of fifty to one hundred youngsters. Some elementary schools also followed this procedure.

5. The entire planning council and several members of the student leadership group planned a two- or three-day retreat focusing on leadership training and school problem-solving activities. Some schools also began the involvement of formal and informal community leaders in the process at this step.

Steps 6 and 7 occurred during August or September of the second year.

6. The planning council and the entire leadership group of students took part in a retreat. The retreat ceremony helped some students and teachers adjust to role changes, and it provided for students the rite of passage to increased responsibility (Furtwengler and Farley, 1987).

7. During the retreat, teachers and student leaders joined forces to form a school leadership team. This leadership team was divided, according to members' interest, into several task forces charged with solving specific school discipline problems. These task forces typically found ways of involving large segments of the student body in their improvement efforts. Planning councils at elementary schools held faculty retreats and/or faculty-student retreats that included students from the fourth grade and up.

Steps 8 through 12 were completed during the school year following the retreat.

8. An executive committee of the school leadership team held regular meetings to establish agendas for four half-day meetings of the action teams. These half-day meetings were held throughout the year to assess the progress of the action teams and to rededicate the action team members to the mission of improving discipline effectiveness.

9. Members of the planning council planned in-service training to meet the needs of the faculty. These activities typically covered such topics as how to help individuals and groups assume more responsibility for their behavior; how to alter the culture within the school and classrooms; and how to increase cooperative student learning.

10. As the school year progressed, changes in discipline effectiveness of the school were documented. The action teams presented these findings to the school leadership team, to the entire faculty, and to the student body. Special celebrations were established for the progress.

11. Prior to the end of the school year, a second RSI School Report Card was developed to show the extent to which discipline effectiveness had changed in the schools. The planning council prepared and presented a report and recommendations to the entire faculty. Step 11 essentially repeated steps 2 and 3.

12. The planning council established a procedure for electing or appointing new members to the council each year. The new planning council completed plans for the second annual retreat to be held in August or September. This step repeated the functions of steps 4 and 5.

13. Steps 6 through 12 were repeated annually to provide continuity to the RSI process.

The timing of each step in the RSI process varied according to the school's initial level of discipline effectiveness. Schools with high levels of discipline effectiveness quickly focused on increasing students' involvement in the RSI process. These schools tended to quickly implement the steps that were related to student involvement.

Staff members in schools with moderate levels of discipline effectiveness, by contrast, were somewhat anxious about student involvement. They wanted first to develop procedures that would ensure fairness, firmness, and consistency in their dealings with students. It took more time for school personnel to view students as an untapped resource for increasing discipline effectiveness.

In schools with low levels of discipline effectiveness, the teachers were interested first and foremost in survival. It typically took six months for faculty in these schools to feel secure enough to entertain the premise that students can make a positive contribution to the school as an organization. The planning council in such schools focused on helping the faculty, through in-service, reach agreements on how to establish a dependable order and structure and see that their system of rules and procedures was working.

In general, the timing of RSI implementation will vary according to the existing level of discipline effectiveness. The more severe the discipline problems, the more likely faculty will not want to involve students as members of the organization. The more secure teachers become through functioning as members of the planning council and on faculty committees, the more open they will be about involving students in the efforts to improve discipline effectiveness.

Two aspects of these twelve steps are believed to be critical to the RSI process of improving discipline effectiveness. First, the change agents must assemble and integrate information from a variety of sources to develop a picture of the school's level of discipline effectiveness. Second, students as well as faculty must be involved in the process if effective change of the invisible wall among students is to occur. Moreover, informal student leaders as well as formal leaders should take part in the schoolwide effort.

RESULTS AND FINDINGS FROM RSI IMPLEMENTATION

Results from the RSI implementations to improve school discipline varied depending on the status of discipline effectiveness at the school when the program was initiated. Schools with low levels of discipline effectiveness benefited the most from implementations of the RSI process. Schools with relatively high levels of discipline effectiveness improved slightly. Schools with moderate levels of discipline effectiveness showed more increases in discipline effectiveness after or during RSI implementations than did schools with high levels of discipline effectiveness.

Schools with low levels of discipline effectiveness usually displayed these characteristics: (1) numerous and serious discipline problems, (2) low levels of student and teacher involvement in school activities, (3) little structure and order, (4) few social interactions and little acceptance of people as individuals, (5) strong support for *dependent* thinking and little support for collaborative problem-solving in learning activities, and (6) little or no commitment to a school purpose and/or mission. In addition, teachers and students in schools with low levels of discipline effectiveness appeared to have feelings of quiet desperation, fears of being harmed, and general feelings of hopelessness. Schools with moderate and high levels of discipline effectiveness displayed characteristics which were the opposite of those in schools with low levels of discipline effectiveness. As one might expect, the schools with moderate levels of discipline effectiveness displayed characteristics which were lower than those of schools with high levels of effectiveness.

Schools with low levels of discipline effectiveness showed significant improvement in all measures of discipline effectiveness. For example, a suburban high school enrolling approximately 1,000 students from middle- to upper-income families, 65 percent of them minority, suspended 170 students during the 1978-79 school year. Suspensions dropped to 150 in 1979-80 during the first year of the RSI program and to 126 during the 1980-81 school year. The total days of suspension, which stood at 2,068 in 1978-79, dropped to 1,025 in 1979-80 and then to 542 in 1980-81. Meanwhile, the average daily attendance, which stood at 86 percent in 1978-79, rose to 91 percent in 1979-80 and to 94 percent in 1980-81.

A second example of the results obtained from an RSI implementation was in a school with an enrollment of 1,100 students, about 55 percent of them white and 45 percent of them black, who came from families with moderate incomes. In this school, there were 2,258 incidents of inappropriate behavior referred to the office for disciplinary reasons in 1980-8l, but only 543 such referrals to the office for disciplinary reasons in 1981-82, the first year of the RSI implementation. During the same interval, the number of classes cut fell from 9,248 to 2,766, the number of three-day suspensions dropped from 337 to 61, and the number of ten-day suspensions fell from 124 to 36. Meanwhile, average daily attendance rose from 81 percent to 86 percent.

In both of these schools, student and teacher involvement in school activities increased, as did the structure and order. The number of fights among students decreased, indicating an increase in the level of social acceptance. The number of formal collaborative problem-solving activities increased among students as they met to work on school problems. The students' level of commitment to the mission of the school increased and was demonstrated through their actions to improve the school. Faculty fears of being harmed and their general feelings of hopelessness were replaced with beliefs that they had some allies in the student body. As one teacher commented: "The we (faculty) versus they (students) divisions are beginning to disappear."

Information from attempts by schools to implement the RSI process suggests that some schools need an outside consultant to help them "stay on task" over the period of a couple of years. Many of the political, structural, and human resource demands on local administrators almost prohibit them from working toward long-range aims. A consultant, while providing assistance, is a form of accountability self-induced by the school. During the past decade of implementations, at least eight professional educators have been trained to facilitate RSI implementations. Their demonstrated ability suggests that educators can be trained to assist schools that need help in implementing the RSI process.

Data from the implementation of RSI suggest some important findings. Past results seem to indicate that the behavior of both teachers and students is strongly influenced by the organizational culture of their school: that is, they tend to continue doing what they do because "that is the way we do things around here." It also appears that RSI implementations lead to changes in the culture of schools. It seems that students and teachers, through the process of involvement in solving school problems, collaboratively develop a new set of shared priorities or a new shared sense of reality. Agreements between students and teachers that both share responsibilities for the status of discipline effectiveness can be established. (When students' actions help to reduce inappropriate student behaviors, it is assumed that students have altered their agreements concerning "the way we do things around here.") When agreements to share responsibility for discipline effectiveness exist among students and teachers, the level of discipline effectiveness improves. Positive changes in the culture of the school lead to increases in discipline effectiveness.

Two other findings from RSI implementations appear useful to efforts to improve school discipline. First, it appears that when students have opportunities for making choices about strategies to improve their school, their perceptions of control increase, which in turn increases their feelings of school ownership and their feelings of being personally responsible for helping to achieve the aims of the school. Students and teachers developed shared feelings of responsibility for increasing discipline effectiveness when they, individually and collectively, identified school problems related to discipline and participated jointly in planning to solve those problems. Their feelings of being responsible for the discipline effectiveness were wedded to their perceptions of being able to alter "the way we do things around here" (control of their environment). The involvement of formal and informal student leaders in school problem-solving activities led to their own redefinition of their roles and responsibilities relative to discipline effectiveness at the school. With that redefinition, the sense of school ownership grew among the students. There also was an increase in their feelings of being responsible for what happened or failed to happen relative to the actions of students and teachers. Lastly, students displayed a heightened interest in monitoring discipline improvement efforts; they wanted to know what was working.

The second potentially useful finding for improving school discipline was the further identification of the variables of school culture initiated by Purkey and Smith (1983). The heart of RSI implementations to increase discipline effectiveness was altering "the way we do things around here," or organizational culture. Administrators and planning councils were anxious to know which areas of "the way we do things around here" needed to be altered to improve discipline effectiveness. The variables of school culture and assessment of their status (Furtwengler, 1987b) showed school planning councils and action teams which categories of agreements at a school needed to be altered through the RSI implementations. Several of these variables were altered through RSI implementations to improve discipline effectiveness (Upton, 1986).

For example, one school interested in improving discipline effectiveness discovered during its status review that the cultural variable of structure and order was below that of schools with high levels of discipline effectiveness. One action team was formed at the retreat to improve the overall attractiveness of the school building. This action team instituted an awareness campaign to reduce the daily dropping of paper in the halls of the school. Three weeks later, only one-third as much paper was thrown on the floor. It was a marked improvement in the school. The action team expressed appreciation to the school and instituted the "golden hall award" to be given out monthly to the school wing with the cleanest hall. The agreements among students regarding "the way we do things around here" were altered. These agreements were identified as improving the structure and order factor of school culture.

Three additional findings from the RSI implementations are important to those interested in implementing RSI. It appears that the more credible the information collected concerning the school's discipline effectiveness, the more powerful the data become in helping teachers and students conclude that there are problems which need their attention. When three or four different sources of data suggested that the same problem existed, both "new" teachers and the "old guard" were convinced that there was a problem. Some teachers still agreed to blame others for the problems, but most teachers contributed to solving the problem.

Evidence to date also suggests that schools that stressed "school as a place of business—the business of teaching and learning" were better able to utilize the involvement of students in helping to increase discipline effectiveness. Students in schools which had a clearly defined purpose, slogan, or mission that was communicated to them frequently asked and answered the following question: "What can I do to help make the school a better place for learning?" Students in schools without a clear sense of purpose tended to ask and answer the question: "What can the school do for me without giving of myself to improve the school?" Student involvement in the RSI process occurs in the context of an effort to achieve the aims of the school.

Data from the topics identified by retreat participants show that seven broad categories of discipline effectiveness problems emerged repeatedly during RSI implementations. The retreat groups identified discipline problems associated with student apathy, human relations, school spirit and pride, buildings and grounds, school image, chemical abuse, and student involvement. Changes in the culture of the school were targeted in all of these areas in most schools and in unique areas in a few schools, such as school rules and after-school transportation.

CHANGES IN ASPECTS OF SCHOOL CULTURE

Teachers and administrators can focus their attention on these variables of school culture as they collect data in the RSI implementation process. Information regarding these variables helps planning councils and administrators examine the culture of their schools relative to increasing discipline effectiveness (Upton, 1986). The categories and their definitions are listed below and can also be found on the School Culture Inventory (Furtwengler, 1987b).

STRUCTURE AND ORDER is the smoothness with which school policies, procedures, and management roles are implemented in schools. This category of culture is composed of five subcategories. *Environmental Support* is viewed as an orderly school environment, including student behavior, that supports the goals and purposes of the school. *Consistency* refers to the regularity with which school policies, standards, and operational procedures are followed. *School Operations* is the smoothness of the flow of daily activities in the school. *Role Clarity* is described as the extent to which the various roles and responsibilities are clear within the school. And *Discipline* is viewed as the social order within the school and respect for the external system of governance.

Most schools with serious discipline problems need to increase their level of structure and order. On the other side of the ledger, at least one school which implemented RSI had too much structure and order: that is, everything which occurred in the school was predictable and unchanging. Teachers did not have faculty meetings because they already knew the rules and answers for handling most of their problems. The boredom which had set in at the school resulted in high levels of student and faculty apathy.

SOCIAL ACCEPTANCE is the presence among most individuals of a sense of belonging to the organization. It is the extent to which teachers and students believe that they are accepted by others as a part of the school. In one school, it was found that teachers disliked each other. They seldom conversed informally, and they never met socially. Administrators seldom involved them in the decision-making processes.

MISSION AND VISION is defined as the reasons for being and doing and the long-term goals of what the school is to become. Faculty and student agreement regarding the purposes for the school is important. But too much emphasis on defining these and attempting to reach agreement on them can lead to a failure to live life as it is and enjoy the "here and now." The school's culture can be strengthened through participation in celebrations and "here and now" events that reflect those shared values for which the school stands.

ACADEMIC EMPHASIS is the general and continuous support for the teaching/learning activities in the school. It is the extent to which there is a high level of support among school personnel for identifying and solving problems related to curriculum and instruction. In one school, the supplies and materials for the instructional process were selected and ordered by the business manager. Not only did the supplies come late in November when they were needed in September, but they were not the supplies and materials which the teachers could use effectively. Academic emphasis was low. An action team was formed to improve the support for the teaching and learning process at the school.

DEDICATION is the teachers' consensus on, and shared commitment to, school purposes, goals, and improvement. It is the extent to which teachers (1) share the same broad aims, (2) express strong commitment to the aims of the school, (3) hold high expectations for students' academic performance, and (4) display a commitment to constantly look for ways to improve. One elementary school had a very high level of discipline effectiveness. Its faculty had a strong shared commitment to the slogan "living, loving, and learning together." Teachers were constantly searching for new teaching strategies and had high expectations that students would be successful.

PROFESSIONAL SELF-WORTH is the presence among teachers of a sense of competence and their value to the organization. It is the extent to which teachers believe they are respected by their colleagues, treated as equals among their colleagues, consulted before decisions are made or actions taken, and able to influence what occurs in the school. One school principal made it a practice to confer with his teachers before making any decision which would affect the school. He was viewed by some of his colleagues as being indecisive. However, the teachers in his school held him in high regard, considered themselves to be strong instructional leaders, and had a strong sense of professional worth.

PROBLEM SOLVING is the systematic identification and resolution of problems in the school. It is the extent to which problems are consistently confronted and resolved and to which staff and students are involved in these processes. One of the significant differences among schools that affected their discipline effectiveness was their respective problem-finding abilities and desires and their willingness to engage in problem-solving practices. Data on school culture were collected in fifteen schools which did not implement the RSI process as well as in those schools with RSI implementations. Schools that were willing to confront their problems of poor discipline and that implemented a collaborative problem-solving process increased their discipline effectiveness. Many schools that were willing to confront problems had principals who were new to that school.

CULTURAL AND SYMBOLIC MANAGEMENT is the communication of the school's mission and vision that emphasizes teaching and learning and an ongoing process to monitor progress and implement changes as needed to achieve school goals. The principal of one outstanding suburban junior high school used much of her time looking for opportunities to communicate the mission of the school to the faculty, students, and parents. She frequently created school events which emphasized the aims of the school. These events usually involved students, teachers, and parents. She welcomed visitors, and held daily student and teacher recognition ceremonies. Problems were always addressed promptly. She viewed problems as opportunities to strengthen the culture.

These several variables of school culture are closely related to each other. Hence, positive change in one variable usually is related to positive changes in the other school culture variables.

ADDITIONAL RESEARCH NEEDS

Additional research is being conducted to determine the factors which influenced the continued improvement of discipline in some schools over a number of years. Another question which needs to be answered is, what were the factors in the schools' culture which influenced the schools' tendency to repeat the use of the RSI process? Some data regarding the continuation of the RSI process and the continued increase of discipline effectiveness suggests that an important variable in the implementation process may be the involvement of one or more members from the central office staff. It appears that central office support for the continued improvement of discipline is enhanced when district office personnel are participants in the RSI process. Central office personnel develop a clear understanding of the shared agreements, priorities, and values of the school through their participation in the process.

More research will be conducted to answer a number of questions. RSI is being implemented in a variety of educational settings which were selected to determine the adaptability of the framework. These settings include schools in cities with strong union leadership, rural schools, large schools with more than two hundred teachers, and small schools with as few as three teachers. The process has been adapted for use at the district level in one school system and with a division of instruction in one state department of education.

SUMMARY

The RSI approach appears to be one effective method for improving discipline effectiveness. Its development evolved through five stages of working in various schools over the past decade. The twelve steps of the RSI process provide a guide for implementing the four fundamental components of RSI's framework. The basic framework components, in review, are as follows:

1. The involvement of informal and formal leaders in efforts to increase discipline effectiveness

2. A systematic student-teacher-administrator (and sometimes parents) consensus approach to identifying and solving school problems related to discipline

3. Providing opportunities for students and teachers to act on their agreements to assume new or redefined roles and responsibilities

4. Collecting information on the extent to which the teachers' and students' solutions and the decision-making processes of cooperative problem-solving are working

RSI implementations in schools increased discipline effectiveness. The improvement was greatest in schools with frequent and serious incidents of inappropriate student behavior. Data from the development of the RSI process indicate that a school's culture can be a serious impediment to increasing discipline effectiveness. Using the RSI process of student-teacher involvement appears to alter the school's culture or "the way we do things around here," and thereby to increase discipline effectiveness in schools.

5

Samuel Gompers Vocational-Technical High School: A Case Study of Collaborative School Improvement

Victor Herbert

In 1979, Samuel Gompers Vocational-Technical High School in the South Bronx section of New York City was widely viewed as a "war zone." Alcohol, drugs, and fights in the halls were all commonplace. Assaults on teachers and fires in the classrooms were not uncommon. Located amidst the urban devastation that attracted President Jimmy Carter to the area around that time, the school had an official enrollment of 1,100, down from 1,500, but actual attendance averaged fewer than 800 students, with most in the hallways, not in the classrooms. Gompers had become "the guidance counselor's solution," the dumping ground for kids who couldn't make it anywhere else. Only 45 percent were reading at or above grade level; and only one hundred made it into the senior class.

One teacher named "the violence being done to the students" as cause for their violent behavior. Physical conditions at the school had decayed. The number of teachers was down to fifty, and reports were that during that year over 40 classes each day simply had no teachers, leaving hundreds of students biding their time in the auditorium. Courses required for graduation were not being offered; and many students were misprogramed into those classes that were. The all-male student body—nearly all black and Hispanic youth—was out of control.

By 1984, Samuel Gompers was a very different high school. Enrollment exceeded 1,800 students, and the competition for entrance was stiff—there were 5,000 applicants for 500 declared seats. The senior graduating class doubled, and over 60 percent went on to attend higher education. Attendance averaged 80 percent, and 67 percent of the students were reading at or above grade level. The dropout rate was down to 6.2 percent. The number of student suspensions fell to 22, down from 208 in 1981. The faculty of 110 teachers and paraprofessionals offered a full academic curriculum in addition to trade specializations in computer technology and electronics, including biomedical technology and pre-engineering. Finally, nearly one-quarter of the student body was female.

The halls of the fifty-year-old art deco building were clean and clear. Basketball and softball teams for both boys and girls competed citywide, and for the first time ever, the boys took the New York State basketball championship for small schools. Statewide, the school had a strong reputation for its student jobs program offering part-time winter and full-time summer jobs, and a reputation internationally for its success in moving toward sex equity. Three representatives from the Irish Department of Education visited the school to study how Gompers had succeeded in enrolling so many girls in such a short period of time.

The Gompers Chorus performed for residents of nursing homes, and the Gompers chapter of the Future Business Leaders of America helped community members fill out their tax forms. Clearly, the school was alive and well, living in the South Bronx.

Early on, the task at Gompers required taking back the halls, the bathrooms, and the schoolyards, in essence establishing an environment conducive to teaching and learning. A student apprehended in the act of "cutting out" asserted that he would attend class only when he could use the toilets safely. Classroom changes had to wait. Three incidents typify that first year:

- Taking control of the school—or—"When the bell goes off, the cuckoo comes out":

  The setting off of the fire alarm system had become so common at Gompers that some people no longer even noticed its ringing, and everyone ignored it as a warning system. Teachers were asked to stand in their classroom doorways and indicate whether the alarm nearest them was the one ringing. At the sound of the bell, the principal would race from the office on the first floor and cover the full four floors of the school at a run until he found the active alarm, and if lucky, the culprit.

The first five times, he captured three of the guilty students. They stood where they were assured that nothing would happen, that no one would respond. As the news of the new response spread, it became more difficult to catch the guilty parties, so he marked each alarm box with indelible grease paint. Then he went to the main entrance of the school and greeted each student with a warm handshake. It was a game the innocent students loved, and, in the process, it helped to establish a rapport with the student body.

- Setting the code of conduct—or—"Stopping the cold weather crime":

    Establishing the difference in students' minds between minor and serious crimes—the difference between smoking in school and carrying a gun; between writing on the walls (which drove the principal up the wall) and selling drugs—was another critical element of reclaiming the school. The cold weather crimes were one example. On the first cold day of winter, the boys would wear their expensive "bomber" jackets, and within that day, twenty or more of them would be stolen. The principal would again greet each student at the front door and advise the younger students to return home for a change of jacket, thereby removing a thief's opportunity.

- Establishing authority over the students—or—"The Pied Piper in Reverse":

    Leaving the school building during the day was fairly common for students, and the principal had to move to herd them back in. He went out to the school yard one day during classtime to bring in a group of Gompers students who had left for a game of football. "You've got the wrong idea," they told him. "The school is yours; the schoolyard is ours." "I'm changing that," he replied. "Now it's all mine." But instead of following, the students set out for the local park. Halfway down the first block they broke into an enthusiastically impromptu version of the summer's big song, "Come on, White Boy, Play that Funky Music." The neighborhood patrol car coincidentally passed by, and the policeman— someone feared by the students—stepped out to offer assistance by reining in the quarterback, who broke into tears. The principal put his arm around the frightened boy and walked him back to school. Naturally, the crowd followed for the first of many cafeteria conferences.

Other actions taken that first year were designed to define the school as "sanctuary," as a unit apart from the stresses and demands of the outside community. Outlawing gang colors from the school—in particular those of the Zulu Nation, the Ball Busters, and even the Guardian Angels—was one move. Soon the Gompers school jacket and the Gompers colors began to take their place. Although these incidents hinted at a turnaround, it was clear that substantial changes could not have occurred if the students and staff did not want it to happen. Early reluctance to participate was understandable as students and staff reflected past events: drug sales, criminal assault, and constant neighborhood tension.

The task was to build the confidence of students, teachers, and administrators. Then they took over. Somehow, students, staff, and community had to believe that Gompers was recovered from past ailments. Once converted, they became the preachers of the "Good News." During this period, three major areas became the focus for improvement: the curriculum, the student body, and the teaching staff.

The directive to alter the curriculum was part of a dream to make Gompers the Technical Center of the Bronx. Nevertheless, it raised controversy among some faculty affected by the changes. The move to an innovative, modern curriculum in technical electronics and computer technology meant better prospects for student recruitment and opened up promising new avenues of employment for students both during their school years and after graduation. Some teachers feared that they would be left behind. Fortunately, private industry offered staff development opportunities, and a dozen eagerly participated in on-site and industrial center training sessions. The "nay" sayers were soon silent.

In 1981, Samuel Gompers became a coed school, and the first 30 girls entered the program. Three years later, there were 350 girls, or nearly one-quarter of the student body. The difference resulted from active recruitment and retention strategies related to the return of school discipline and good order. Many warned that the girls would bring even more trouble. Actually, once the initial curiosity passed, the androgynous experience more accurately reflected the student day beyond the school and brought a calming of tensions. There were still occasional cafeteria and classroom fights—the cause, a much more reasonable one than earlier causes—was one Gompers could live with: love.

Given the nature of the curriculum, aggressive efforts were needed not only in recruitment, but also to provide support services for those girls entering the more nontraditional trade areas. Recruitment of girls and new students in general became an area of top priority that continues to receive a great deal of attention today. Each fall, volunteer groups of students visit neighborhood schools to explain what Gompers has to offer.

Building the esteem of the Gompers faculty was the next major item on the agenda for change. Communication and participation were encouraged at all levels through the establishment of formal committees. Established during that time was a Committee of Administration; the School Improvement Committee, consisting of nine volunteer teachers with a rotating chair who examine the key issues for improvement; and a Consultative Council of students that today handles concerns such as improving the condition of the hallways and keeping up attendance levels. Traditional faculty meetings were held once a month, and each department also met once a month with its assistant principal. In all, the effort to broaden participation and therefore increase ownership was encouraged. Obviously, student discipline was a major concern at each conference. Department heads at Gompers were encouraged to continue that same style with their staff, combining respect, open communication, and support.

Recruiting good new teachers, helping to support weaker teachers, and encouraging ineffectual or incompetent teachers to transfer or leave the system were other elements in the rebuilding of the school. Perhaps 25 percent of the teachers on the faculty at Gompers in the early days were not effective. That high rate was in part a function of the condition of the school at that time. When disciplinary problems plague a school, attention is devoted to solving them before attention can be paid to the teaching that goes on inside the classroom. Clearly, complete harmony requires both. Emphasizing improved instruction in a chaotic school seemed a reversal of priorities.

Incompetency of a certain percentage of individuals is a facet of every profession. The staff knew who was carrying or shirking the load. Local teacher union officials agreed not to block the efforts to remove clearly incompetent or unethical teachers in exchange for agreements to work together to offer support for another faculty member. It was a very important temporary pact.

A school is a community without secrets. What one member knows, eventually all come to know. In the past, a union decision to protect individuals indiscriminately without regard for the greater community often resulted in chaos. Subtly or overtly signaling to students that attendance was not required solved teachers' problems but contributed to school disorder. With time to kill, the students wandered through the halls engaging in mischief at best, violence at worst. Strict compliance with the letter of the contract rather than the spirit allowed some teachers to shirk responsibility, and colleagues knew who they were. Students, their education, and the future of the school had to take precedence. That it did speaks for the eagerness of the majority to return Gompers to its proper educational stature.

New teacher recruitment was the next critical effort. Teachers were sought out not only because of their professional knowledge but also for their empathy for Gompers students. There were some limitations here, since pedagogical personnel are assigned centrally. Nonetheless, since Gompers of the past was not viewed as a plum assignment, it was not too difficult to have volunteers assigned.

Again, support of the United Federation of Teachers local chapter at Gompers provided freedom for collaborative movement, mutually beneficial to administration and other staff. An Executive Committee met formally once a month, and together worked toward acceptable solutions to common problems. Anticipation of problems also led to many informal negotiations with the union representatives. In the early days of change, the formal union posture was neither supportive nor adversarial; although the union did not step forward to take a proactive stance, neither did it block the way for change. The concerns of the union then centered on teacher safety, parking, and classroom scheduling. Eventually, a give and take on both sides promised relief from the unbearable teaching and learning conditions.

The Gompers story telescoped here began with a school in total disorder and evolved over five years into a nationally recognized "school of excellence." The neighborhood, although also improved, remained among the poorest congressional districts in the country. The students came from the same deprived conditions, broken homes, drug-pervasive streets, and other all-too-common life-styles of the urban poor. Nevertheless, the school was different: out of chaos came order; out of crime and violence came safety and discipline. The tale was a collaborative one involving students, staff, parents and guardians, the community and the private sector. Unfortunately, there was little research into the evolution of this change nor were research findings applied in a conscious way to the change process. Although there may be many reasons to explain this failure to interact more deliberately, a feeling of isolation from the mainstream led to independent action rarely planned beyond immediate outcomes, particularly in the early days. Later, participants brought more to the table from personal reading and course work.

The Gompers transition from chaos to order often draws the question "how?" Certainly, there is no simple answer. Gompers needed everything—determined staff could do nothing wrong except to do nothing. An important ingredient was patience. Priorities for safety and security had to be set with full awareness that other problems would have to wait. There were risks involved. An evaluator from the certification department recommended the dismissal of the principal because he spent "too much time in the halls." Unfortunately, early on, that was where most of the students were. There were setbacks, failures, and frustrations. Nevertheless, the satisfactions far outweighed the disappointments. Christa MacAuliffe said it best: "I teach because I touch the future." Gompers provided a future for many who had none by becoming an educational sanctuary in a most unexpected location.

PART II
Classroom Strategies

INTRODUCTION:
Classroom Strategies Section

This second section of the book is devoted to an analysis of classroom strategies to reduce student discipline problems. These three chapters deal with very different strategies. In the first, Walter Doyle approaches the problem from the standpoint of principles and techniques of classroom management. In the second, Edmund Emmer and Amy Aussiker analyze studies on the effects of three common discipline training programs for teachers. In the third, Edward Wynne discusses various ways of improving both student discipline and character by the actions of teachers, parents, and school administrators. Each of these chapters draws implications to assist teachers in the classroom.

Doyle's paper reviews various concepts and research findings on classroom management techniques, beginning with strategies for monitoring and guiding classroom activities. He argues that order is not so much determined by the teacher's reactions to misbehavior as it is conditioned by the way teachers organize the system of classroom activities and academic work, even from the first few days of school. Doyle also discusses the importance of classroom rules, issues in developing rules, types of misbehavior, and punishments ranging from reprimands to suspension. The paper ends by suggesting ways to use knowledge for more effective practice. The conditions for using different forms of punishment and their effects on students also are explored.

The chapter by Emmer and Aussiker examines research, much of it unpublished, on three widely used discipline programs: Assertive Discipline, Teacher Effectiveness Training, and Reality Therapy. They look for effects on the attitudes, perceptions, and behavior of teachers and students, and find only limited support for training teachers in these programs. Some differences in effects among the programs are noted. Emmer and Aussiker conclude that training in discipline programs should be viewed as supplemental to a more comprehensive approach to discipline and classroom management.

Wynne approaches the question of classroom strategies from yet another angle. He takes a "pro-tradition" perspective on policies affecting student discipline and character development. He argues that differences in the definition of discipline, and the underlying value judgments these represent, are an important source of the discipline problems confronting schools. Acknowledging that the research support for some recommended discipline practices is unclear, Wynne nevertheless provides an important analysis of a wide variety of strategies. He discusses assigning students to classrooms, courses for developing character, role modeling by educators, systems of rewards and sanctions for student behavior, and parent roles in discipline. Clear statements of school rules and firm consequences for misbehavior, advocated by many and well grounded in the research literature (Gottfredson and Gottfredson, 1985; Metz, 1978; National Institute of Education, 1978), also form part of Wynne's picture of the orderly school. Various ideas to help school administrators are offered.

The discussion of role modeling by educators goes to the heart of social learning theory. Observing and imitating others is a powerful means of learning. When teachers are dedicated, dynamic and interesting, present material clearly, and motivate students to pay attention, the behaviors they model are more likely to be copied. Praise, grades, and other means of pleasing the teacher motivate students to continue these new behaviors (Bandura, 1977).

The definition of misbehavior is confronted directly in these chapters. Doyle sees it as any student act which competes with the ongoing program of activity. Thus talking out of turn is not misbehavior when it moves the lesson forward. Wynne would define misbehavior as actions against the rules of conduct of mainstream adult society; such misbehavior might not be overtly disruptive of the learning process for others. He contends that deviant behavior, allegedly non-disruptive, is tolerated too often, and this leads to confusion and tension among pupils and faculty. (See also the chapter by Toby and Scrupski for a discussion of the nature and development of misbehavior.)

Definitional issues are difficult to resolve. The authors of these and other chapters would probably classify certain student behaviors differently, and the interpretation of what is misbehavior or responsible behavior will ultimately be made by each teacher and administrator. It is then a matter of determining the consequences of that interpretation for the individual student, the class of students, and the school.

These three chapters show that classroom discipline cannot be achieved by reliance on any single technique. Instead, a range of actions and strategies are necessary from first contact with students, and these must be adapted to the specific classroom situation and type of misbehavior. Management strategies can help prevent classroom misbehavior from developing in the first place, as well as treat misbehavior when it occurs.

Intervention strategies centered on rewards and punishments are discussed prominently in these papers. Assertive Discipline uses both, whereas Teacher Effectiveness Training discourages both as barriers to open communication. Wynne recounts certain principles regarding sanctions: sanctions need to be graduated, capable of being applied quickly, and significant to students. Doyle considers the motivations for misbehavior, and states that punishment should be tailored to those motivations. For example, suspending chronic truants may simply be giving them what they most desire. He notes that successful interventions occur early, are initially brief and "soft," and minimize the possibility of further reactions from students. But Doyle recognizes that serious and chronic misbehavior may require more, and he weighs factors to consider in deciding on other punishments and suspension.

The possibility of contagion in the classroom and gaining peer status from misbehaving is very real. A national longitudinal study of the development of delinquent behavior shows that association with mildly delinquent peers precedes the onset of delinquent acts (Elliott, Huizinga, and Menard, 1988). The school and classroom in many places provide sustained opportunities for such associations. Sending serious troublemakers to time-out rooms and alternative schools, and in other ways isolating them from other students, are means of reducing the influence of such associations, but there are no easy solutions to this problem.

Enthusiasm for any particular approach or strategy needs to be tempered by systematic research and dispassionate analysis of its implementation and effects. As an example, Assertive Discipline is widely used by teachers. In view of this popularity, it is somewhat surprising that Emmer and Aussiker found only two studies dealing with changes in teacher behavior. Moreover, the ten studies of student behavior change generally did not support Assertive Discipline training. Emmer and Aussiker outline the kinds of information that would be needed to detect effects of in-service training programs, and suggest that more use of social science models and theories could help guide and interpret studies. In addition, the possibility that some aspects of student discipline-related training programs are more beneficial than others has gone largely unexplored.

One approach to improving student discipline assessed by Wynne is the development of pro-morality courses and didactic teaching materials. These are appealing because they seem to address the issue head-on. However, as he notes, the didactic approach must be analyzed carefully, and its benefits may depend on the context in which materials are presented.

Another promising curricular example, law-related education, has been developed by several legal organizations and has been used widely in recent years. It teaches students about their rights and responsibilities under the law, and how the law and the courts operate. Evaluations show that many students become better informed about these subjects, and report that they commit fewer infractions of school rules than do control groups. The amount of change is contingent on the competence and dedication of the teachers, their experience with law-related education, and the number and types of outside speakers (Johnson and Hunter, 1985). The classroom context here seems to make an important difference. The benefits of outside speakers presage the fuller treatment of school-community relationships in the next section of this book as the broader context which may influence the functioning of both schools and classrooms.

6

Classroom Management Techniques

Walter Doyle

The purpose of this chapter is to review concepts and research findings on classroom management techniques with special attention to how these techniques are related to student discipline strategies. The discussion opens with a survey of the descriptive and experimental research recently accumulated on classroom management processes, with special attention to strategies for monitoring and guiding classroom activity systems. The second section focuses on classroom rules and procedures and on common forms of classroom discipline, particularly reprimands and other techniques teachers use to sustain order. The bulk of these first two sections is drawn from an extensive and detailed analysis of research (see Doyle, 1986). In the third section, a sampling of the literature on punishment and suspension is examined in order to assess their effectiveness as discipline strategies for serious classroom disruptions. In this section the applicability of behavior modification procedures to classroom settings is also discussed briefly. In the concluding section, the general state of research on classroom management and discipline is assessed and implications for research and practice are identified.

Because of space limitations, an exhaustive review and analysis of the relevant literature is not feasible in this chapter. The focus, therefore, is on studies that were judged to be representative of the main lines of inquiry in classroom management and to reflect the general findings in the field. Where possible, previous reviews are cited if they were judged to be sufficiently comprehensive to be reliable and to reveal broad trends in the development of knowledge. Given the state of research in this area, a quantitative synthesis of the effects of classroom management practices is not possible. Special attention is given, therefore, to conceptual coherence and consistency across studies. Finally, the emphasis throughout is on management in ordinary classrooms. No attention is given, therefore, to special management systems such as mastery learning or cooperative learning.

CLASSROOM ACTIVITIES: THE CORE OF MANAGEMENT

Classrooms are crowded and busy places in which groups of students who vary in interests and abilities must be organized and directed in ways that maximize work involvement and minimize disruptions. Moreover, these groups assemble regularly for long periods of time to accomplish a wide variety of goals. Many events occur simultaneously, teachers must react often and immediately to circumstances, and the course of events is frequently unpredictable. Teaching in such settings requires a highly developed ability to manage events.

Traditionally "misbehavior" has been the dominant theme in discussions of classroom management. This emphasis is understandable since the need for management and discipline is most apparent when students are misbehaving. Yet, order in classrooms is not a consequence of reactions to misbehavior but a condition established and sustained by the way a teacher organizes and guides a complex system of classroom activities and academic work. Moreover, the effectiveness of interventions to restore order when misbehavior occurs depends upon the existence of structures of orderliness in the first place. To understand management, therefore, it is necessary to examine what teachers do to structure and monitor classroom events before misbehavior occurs.

Classroom Activities

From an organizational perspective, the central unit of classroom order is the *activity*. An activity can be defined as a segment of time in which participants are arranged in a specific fashion and communication follows an identifiable pattern (see Gump, 1969). A segment of classroom time, such as a spelling test, writing lesson, or study period, can be described in terms of (1) its temporal boundaries or duration; (2) the physical milieu, that is, the shape of the site in which it occurs, the number and types of participants, the arrangement of participants in the available space, and the props or objects available to participants; (3) the behavior format or program of action for participants; and (4) the focal content or concern of the segment.

The concept of 'program of action' is key to modern understandings of classroom management and order. Each activity defines a distinctive action structure that provides direction for events and "pulls" participants along a particular path at a given pace (see Gump, 1982). In seatwork, for example, students are usually expected to work privately and independently at their desks, attend to a single information source such as a textbook or worksheet, and finish within a specified time. In whole-class discussion, on the other hand, students are expected to speak publicly and monitor information from multiple sources. To say a classroom is orderly, then, means that students are *cooperating in the program of action defined by the activity a teacher is attempting to use*. Misbehavior, in turn, is any action by students that threatens to disrupt the activity flow or pull the class toward an alternative program of action. If order is not defined in a particular setting, that is, if an activity system is not established and running in a classroom, no amount of discipline will create order.

Major findings from research on classroom activities, most of which has been conducted in elementary classes, can be summarized as follows (for details, see Doyle, 1986).

1. Types of activities are systematically related to the behavior of students and thus place different classroom management demands on teachers. In a study of third-grade classes, Gump (1969) found, for instance, that involvement was highest for students in teacher-led small groups and lowest for pupil presentations. Between these extremes, engagement was higher in whole-class recitation, tests, and teacher presentations than in supervised study and independent seatwork.

2. The physical characteristics of a classroom, including the density of students, the arrangement of desks, and the design of the building (open space vs. self-contained), also affect the probability of inappropriate and disruptive behavior as well as the difficulties a teacher encounters in preventing or stopping such behavior (Gump, 1982; Weinstein, 1979). In general, the more loosely structured the setting and the

weaker the program of action, the higher the probability that inappropriate behavior will occur. Similarly, the greater the amount of student choice and mobility and the greater the complexity of the social scene, the greater the need for overt managing and controlling actions by the teacher (Kounin and Gump, 1974).

3. The type of work students are assigned affects classroom order (see Carter and Doyle, 1986). When academic work is routinized and familiar to students (such as during spelling tests or recurring worksheet exercises), the flow of classroom activity is typically smooth and well ordered. When work is problem-centered, that is, when students are required to interpret situations and make decisions to accomplish tasks (such as during word problems or essays), activity flow is frequently slow and bumpy. Managing higher-order tasks requires exceptional management skill.

Establishing Classroom Activities

Recent classroom studies have shown that the level of order created during the first few days of school reliably predicts the degree of student engagement and disruption for the rest of the year (see Emmer, Evertson, and Anderson, 1980). Most studies indicate that successful classroom managers rely on three basic strategies to establish order at the beginning of the year: simplicity, familiarity, and routinization (for a summary, see Doyle, 1986). Early activities, in other words, have simple organizational structures which are typically quite familiar to students (e.g., whole-class presentations and seatwork rather than multiple small groups). The first assignments, in turn, are easy for the students to accomplish in relatively short periods of time, have clear specifications, and are run at a brisk pace. Moreover, they are often based on work the students can be expected to have done the previous year. A significant chunk of the management task, then, is solved by selecting appropriate activities and assignments for the opening of school.

Proper selection is supplemented by routinizing the activity system for the class (see Yinger, 1980). Teachers repeat the same activity forms for the first weeks to familiarize students with standard procedures and provide opportunities to rehearse them. This routinizing of activities helps sustain classroom order by making events less susceptible to breakdowns because participants know the normal sequence of action.

Monitoring and Guiding Classroom Events

Monitoring plays a key role in establishing and maintaining classroom activities. Teachers must be aware of what is going on in a classroom and be able to attend to two or more events at the same time (see Kounin, 1970). The content of monitoring—what teachers watch when scanning a room—includes at least three dimensions. First, teachers watch *groups*, that is, they attend to what is happening in the entire room and how well the total activity system is going. Localized attention to individual students must be scheduled within the broader framework of the group activity. Second, teachers watch *conduct or behavior*, with particular attention to discrepancies from the intended program of action. This enables teachers to recognize misbehavior early, stop it before it spreads, and select the appropriate target for intervention. Third, teachers monitor the *pace, rhythm, and duration* of classroom events. Several studies have shown that pace, momentum, and rhythm are key factors in maintaining an activity in a classroom (Arlin, 1982; Erickson and Mohatt, 1982; Gump, 1969). Excessive delays in the flow of classroom events or abrupt shifts in direction are often associated with inappropriate or disruptive student behavior.

Obviously, situational factors influence the monitoring and guiding processes in classroom management. The more complex the arrangement of students in a class and the greater the demands on the teacher as an actor in the activity system, the more difficult monitoring and cueing become and, thus, the greater the probability of a breakdown in order.

In summary, teaching in classrooms demands an ability to predict the direction of events and make decisions rapidly. For this reason, management is fundamentally a cognitive activity based on a teacher's knowledge of the likely trajectory of events in classrooms and the way specific actions affect situations (see Carter, 1986). Specific management skills are, for all practical purposes, useless without this basic understanding of classrooms.

RULES AND REPRIMANDS: THE CORE OF CLASSROOM DISCIPLINE

Because classrooms are populated by groups of students assembled under crowded conditions for relatively long periods of time to accomplish specified purposes, life in these settings is governed by a variety of explicit and implicit rules and procedures (see Blumenfeld et al., 1979, on elementary schools, and Hargreaves, Hester, and Mellor, 1975, on secondary schools). The rule-making process is especially salient in the present chapter because most incidents of misbehavior and discipline involve the violation of classroom or school rules.

The Importance of Rules

Classroom rules are usually intended to regulate forms of individual conduct that are likely to disrupt activities, cause injury, or damage school property. Thus, there are rules concerning tardiness, talking during lessons, gum chewing, fighting, bringing materials to class, and the like. In addition, there are a large number of implicit rules (e.g., patterns of turn taking in discussions or conventions for social distance between pupils) that affect social interaction and interpersonal relationships in classrooms (see Erickson and Shultz, 1981). Finally, there is typically a set of classroom procedures, that is, approved ways of taking care of various responsibilities and privileges, such as handing in completed work, sharpening pencils, getting a drink of water, going to the restroom, or forming groups for reading or math.

Studies at the Research and Development Center for Teacher Education (Emmer, Evertson, and Anderson, 1980; Emmer et al., 1982; Emmer et al., 1981) have indicated that effective classroom managers in elementary and junior high school classes are especially skilled in establishing rules and procedures at the beginning of the year. In elementary classes, the investigators found that nearly all teachers introduced rules and procedures on the first day of school. In classes of effective managers (selected on indicators of management processes and student achievement), however, rules and procedures were concrete and explicit and covered matters directly related to work accomplishment. In addition, effective managers deliberately taught their operating systems to the students. They clearly explained rules and procedures to students, established signals to indicate when actions were to be carried out or stopped, and spent time rehearsing procedures. In addition, effective managers anticipated possible interruptions or problems and had procedures readily available to handle these situations. Finally, effective managers monitored classes closely, stopped inappropriate behavior promptly, and continued to remind students of the rules and procedures during the first weeks of school. In contrast, less effective managers either failed to anticipate the need for rules and procedures covering important aspects of class operation or tended to have vague and unenforceable rules (e.g., "Be in the right place at the right time"). Moreover, they neither explained their rules and procedures clearly to students nor monitored and enforced compliance. They seemed, rather, to be preoccupied with clerical tasks and disoriented by problems and interruptions.

In junior high school classes, the researchers found that all teachers presented rules and procedures at the beginning of the year, and there were few differences across teachers in the time spent on these matters. Differences were found, however, in the clarity and thoroughness of presentation and in the monitoring and enforcement of compliance. Successful managers, in contrast to their less effective colleagues, anticipated problems, communicated rules and expectations clearly, watched students closely, intervened promptly, and invoked consequences for behavior. These results were consistent with those for elementary classes, but less time was spent teaching and rehearsing rules and procedures at the junior high level.

Rule Making and Enactment Processes

Creating a rule system in a classroom is a difficult task to accomplish for at least three reasons. First, classroom rules are situational: different rules apply to different phases of lessons (see Bremme and Erickson, 1977; Hargreaves et al., 1975). Quiet talk among peers, for example, is allowed during entry and seatwork but not during teacher presentations or recitations. Similarly, orderliness in group activities that involve speaking, listening, and turn taking differs substantially from that required for seatwork. Second, order is "jointly constituted" by the participants in activities (see Erickson and Shultz, 1981; Sieber, 1979): that is, order is achieved *with* students and depends upon their willingness to follow along with the unfolding of an event. Whether or not students play an official role in defining or choosing classroom rules, they shape, through cooperation and resistance, the rules that are actually established in a particular class. Finally, teachers must balance activity management with rule enforcement. Time taken to deal publicly with rule violations distracts attention away from the main activity system. And, if rule violations are frequent, misbehavior rather than academic work can become the operating curriculum in a class. For this reason, experienced teachers tend to push ahead with activities and endeavor to make reprimands brief and private (see Carter, 1986). (This point will be discussed more fully in the following section on misbehavior and interventions.)

Research suggests that rules and procedures in classrooms must be both announced and enforced and that rule making involves complex processes of interaction and the negotiation of meaning. The implication here is that rule making cannot be easily captured in a list of directives or techniques. To be effective participants in the rule-making process, teachers must understand what they are attempting to orchestrate and how situations shape actions.

Misbehavior and Interventions

The central message of modern research on classroom management is that misbehavior and actions teachers take to stop it are embedded in the activity system of a classroom. This viewpoint has implications for understanding the nature of misbehavior and the character of appropriate disciplinary strategies for classroom use.

Misbehavior.   Despite popular reports of violence and crime in schools, most problems of misbehavior in classrooms are related to attention, crowd control, and getting work accomplished (see Duke, 1978). The key to understanding misbehavior in classrooms is to view what students do in terms of its consequences for the main program of activity for the class. From this perspective, misbehavior is any student act that initiates a competing vector or program for the class. Vectors perceived as misbehavior are likely to be *public*, that is, visible to a significant portion of the class, and *contagious*, that is, capable of spreading rapidly or pulling other members of the class into them. For classes in which the primary vector is weak (i.e., students are easily distracted from academic work) and actions outside the primary vector are frequent, misbehavior is likely to be common (see Felmlee and Eder, 1983; Metz, 1978).

By this definition, not every infraction of a rule is necessarily misbehavior. Talking out of turn is not misbehavior if it advances the lesson at a time when moving forward is essential. Similarly, inattention during the last few minutes of a class session will often be tolerated because the activity is coming to an end. On the other hand, consistent delays in conforming to directives can slow down activity flow and irritate a teacher (Brooks and Wagenhauser, 1980).

Interventions.   McDermott (1976) has documented that students in both high- and low-ability groups respond almost immediately to departures from the primary program of action and begin to signal through posture and glances their awareness of "disorder." Nevertheless, the teacher is the primary custodian of order in a class and must frequently decide when and how to intervene to repair order.

In a study of third and fifth grade classes, Sieber (1976) found that interventions to stop misbehavior occurred at a rate of about sixteen per hour. Despite their frequency, such interventions are inherently risky because they call attention to potentially disruptive behavior, and, as a classroom event, they initiate a program of action that can pull a class further away from the primary vector and weaken its function in holding order in place. There is, in other words, a "ripple" effect for interventions (Kounin and Gump, 1958). Because of these risks, interventions often have a private and fleeting quality that minimizes their effect on the flow of events. Successful interventions occur early in response to misbehavior, are often quite brief, and do not invite further comment from the target student or students. Thus, teachers tend to use a variety of unobtrusive nonverbal signals (e.g., gestures, direct eye contact, and proximity) to regulate misbehavior, and the majority of spoken interventions consist of simple reprimands: "Shh," "Wait," "Stop," or "No" (Humphrey, 1979; Sieber, 1976).

Decisions to intervene are necessarily reactive and problematic. Most studies indicate that teachers decide to intervene on the basis of their knowledge of who is misbehaving, what the misbehavior is, and when it occurs (see Doyle, 1986). Hargreaves and his colleagues (1975) noted that early cues of possible misbehavior (e.g., concealment) are ambiguous, and yet the teacher has little time to form a judgment and act. To reduce uncertainty, teachers classify students in terms of such factors as their persistence and their visibility in the social structure of the group.

SCHOOL DISCIPLINE STRATEGIES

Management effectiveness studies have established that successful managers plan for and invoke consequences for rule violations (see Emmer et al., 1981). In most instances, a simple reprimand or similar intervention is sufficient to correct a violation, especially in a well-managed class. Indeed, teacher interventions to restore order are remarkably soft, primarily because most misbehavior in classrooms is not a serious threat to order or safety and is only weakly motivated. Most students appear to misbehave to create opportunities for "goofing off" (Cusick, Martin, and Palonsky, 1976), to test the boundaries of a teacher's management system (Doyle, 1979), or to negotiate work requirements (Doyle and Carter, 1984). In some instances, however, serious and chronic misbehavior, such as rudeness or aggressiveness toward the teacher, consistent avoidance of work and ignoring of common rules, or fighting, occurs in elementary and secondary classrooms. In the face of these behavior problems, common classroom forms of management—activity systems and reprimands—are often ineffectual and stronger consequences are needed.

Several comprehensive discipline models have been proposed that deal in part with serious behavior problems (see Charles, 1981; Hyman et al., 1979). In another chapter in this book, Emmer examines these models in considerable depth. In this paper, attention is given to two forms of discipline: (1) the traditional practices of punishment and suspension; and (2) behavior modification.

Punishment and Suspension

Historically, punishment (extra work, detention, paddling) and suspension or even expulsion have been the most common techniques for handling serious behavior problems in schools (see Doyle, 1978). It appears that these practices are still used widely in American schools today (Rose, 1984). In this section, I attempt to delineate the issues and research findings related to punishment and suspension as classroom management strategies.

At an immediate level, suspension is 'effective" for removing a threat to order from the classroom. Similarly, punishment can sometimes inhibit or suppress misbehavior (see O'Leary and O'Leary, 1977), although it is often difficult to administer during class time. But are suspension and punishment effective consequences to use in response to serious rule violations in classrooms? Unfortunately, very little systematic empirical research exists to answer this question (see Hapkiewicz, 1975). Rather, most of the literature on these techniques addresses legal or moral issues and, thus, either ignores or assumes efficacy. How, then, can the strategies be assessed in light of present knowledge?

Decisions about punishment and suspension need to be based on at least two considerations: for whom they are effective and what the effects are. Serious misbehavior is usually exhibited by two types of students: (1) those who are, for a variety of reasons, strongly motivated to be disruptive; or (2) those who, because of ability or inclination, do not readily engage in academic work. The latter students are not necessarily strongly motivated to misbehave, but they are not easily "caught" by the typical programs of action in classrooms. Clearly different decisions about the appropriateness of punishment or suspension are likely to be made depending upon which type of student is misbehaving. It is important to add that minority students are often disproportionately represented among students who are targets for punishment or suspension (see, for example, Leonard, 1984; Parents Union for Public Schools, 1982; Stevens, 1983).

The effects of punishment depend in part upon the type and consistency of the punishment used. Mild forms, such as loss of privileges, demerits, or detention, can effectively communicate seriousness and a concern for civility in classrooms (see Brophy, 1983). Emmer (1984) reviewed laboratory studies by Parke and associates (Duer and Parke, 1970; Parke and Duer, 1972; Sawin and Parke, 1979) on the importance of consistency in the administration of punishment. In these studies it was found that inconsistency in punishing young boys for hitting a doll inhibited the behavior in some subjects but increased it to an extremely high level in others. Moreover, once the response to inconsistent punishment was established, it was very difficult to change by improving consistency.

Stronger punishment, especially corporal punishment, is more controversial. Evidence indicates that corporal punishment is widely used in schools and appears to have considerable "practical" appeal for administrators and teachers (Rose, 1984). Indeed, Hyman (1981) has documented instances of school punishment that are quite extreme:hitting students with sticks, arrows, belts, and fists; cutting their hair; confining them to storerooms; withholding food; and throwing them against walls. Yet most commentators, and especially those who draw upon behavioral psychology, argue that (1) the effects of corporal punishment are unpredictable, that is, it can actually be reinforcing because the student gains attention and status among peers; (2) corporal punishment creates resentment and hostility in the target student, thus making it more difficult to establish a working relationship in the future; and (3) severe punishment inhibits unwanted behavior but does not itself foster appropriate behavior (Brophy, 1983; Hapkiewicz, 1975; O'Leary and O'Leary, 1977). Bongiavanni (1979) reviewed evidence that frequent use of corporal punishment is associated with such undesirable consequences as increased school vandalism. He also reported preliminary results of a survey indicating that most school districts which had eliminated corporal punishment did not experience an increase in school behavior problems.

A similar argument can be made for suspension from school as a discipline strategy. Suspension is widely used (see Stevens, 1983), but there is little evidence that suspension is, by itself, educative. Indeed, suspension denies educative opportunities for precisely those students who need them the most. Moreover, suspension can be inherently rewarding, a vacation from a setting the student is likely to find aversive. Under such circumstances, little long-term effectiveness can be expected from suspension. It is frequently argued that suspension or expulsion makes a school more orderly and effective for the rest of the students who suffer from a disruptive environment. Unfortunately, little systematic research exists to support or refute this hypothesis.

Studies of suspension in Cleveland (Stevens, 1983) and Philadelphia (Parents Union for Public Schools, 1982) indicate that there is wide variation across schools in suspension rates. In the Philadelphia study it was found that schools with low suspension rates had high levels of community involvement, emphasized instruction rather than control, and had a student-centered environment. In high-rate schools, suspensions were used as a means of bringing parents into the school and school administrators concentrated primarily on standards and control rather than on instruction.

Several schools and school districts have established alternative or in-school suspension programs. In many instances these programs emphasize punishment rather than academic work or remediation of behavior problems (see Garibaldi, 1979; Short and Noblit, 1985). More elaborate programs, such as the Portland PASS program (see Leonard, 1984), which include parent and community involvement and student training in academic survival skills, appear to be successful in reducing suspension rates and improving student behavior. The message of these programs is clear: for suspension to have a long-term effect on students' conduct, significant resources must be invested in dealing with the problems that led to the need for suspending a student.

Analysis of the effects of punishment and suspension suggests that these strategies are not, by themselves, educative. To be effective, they must be invoked within a clear system of rules and standards so that appropriate behavior is the essential focus.

Behavior Modification

Techniques derived from laboratory studies of contingencies of reinforcement have been researched extensively and advocated widely as discipline strategies. Controlled studies, often in special settings, have indicated that behavior modification techniques are remarkably successful. Nevertheless, there has been considerable controversy surrounding this approach, and questions have been raised about its practicality for classroom teachers.

Several useful studies, reviews, and collections on behavior modification techniques have appeared recently (see Brophy, 1983; Elardo, 1978; Emmer, 1984; McLaughlin, 1976; O'Leary and O'Leary, 1977; Thompson et al., 1974). The weight of the evidence suggests that most of the early recommendations for elaborate and complex systems of token economies, systematic contingency management, and ignoring undesirable behavior while praising desired behavior are impractical for individual classroom teachers who lack the assistance of independent observers and support personnel and who work with large groups of students in noncustodial settings. Moreover, using rewards for desired behavior or for academic performance can have deleterious effects when intrinsic motivation is moderate to high (see Leeper and Greene, 1978). Moreover, there are problems of generalizing the effects of behavior modification interventions across settings and of maintaining their effects over time (see Phillips and Ray, 1980).

Attention has recently turned to systems for teaching students social skills (Cartledge and Milburn, 1978), coping strategies (Spaulding, 1983), and participation skills (Cohen, 1979) in which appropriate behaviors for classroom settings are identified and systematically taught to students. Along similar lines, some investigators have advocated that students be taught self-monitoring and self-control strategies which enable them to guide their own learning in classrooms (see Anderson and Prawat, 1983; Brophy, 1983). The emphasis, in other words, is moving toward helping students learn to cope with classroom processes rather than having teachers implement behavior modification programs in their classrooms. Such an approach would seem to be especially useful for students who do not readily participate in academic activities and are not strongly motivated to be disruptive. There is less evidence that such an approach will be successful with students who are strongly motivated to be disruptive in school.

APPRAISAL AND CONCLUSION

The need for management and discipline is most apparent when order is disrupted. As a result, interventions to stop misbehavior have often been the primary focus of theory and research in classroom management. Evidence accumulated in the last two decades suggests, however, that interventions are best viewed as ways in which order is repaired rather than created. The quantity or quality of intervention will not predict the degree of order in a classroom unless a program

of action has already been established. Moreover, stopping misbehavior involves complex decisions about the probable consequences
of particular actions by particular students at specific moments in
the flow of activity in a class. And, because misbehavior and a teacher's reaction to misbehavior are themselves vectors of action in a
classroom, successful managers are able to insert interventions
skillfully into the activity flow. They keep everyone focused, in other
words, on the primary vector that sustains order in classrooms.

The research summarized in this paper clearly indicates that substantial progress has been made in identifying effective classroom
management practices and delineating the knowledge structures which
underlie the use of these practices in classrooms. Two important limitations of this work need to be pointed out, however. First, much of
the research on classroom management has been conducted in elementary classrooms. Some junior high school and a few senior high
school studies exist, particularly in research on managing academic
work. Nevertheless, more needs to be known about classroom management processes and strategies at the secondary level and about
differences between elementary and secondary classrooms on dimensions relevant to classroom management and order. Second, the vast
majority of management studies have been conducted in relatively
"normal" or "plain vanilla" school settings. I am not aware of classroom studies that have been done in schools with serious problems of
violence and crime or research that has focused on serious school
disruption as a factor in achieving classroom order. Indeed, there are
few studies (e.g., Metz, 1978) that have given attention to connections between classroom and school-level dimensions.

More field-based research on the effects of school discipline strategies such as punishment and suspension is clearly needed. In particular, we need to know more about the following:

1. The effects of punishment and suspension on the students
   who receive them. Which students are most likely to be
   punished or suspended? Do these students modify their attitudes or behavior when they return to the classroom? What
   is the rate of "repeat" offenders?

2. The effects of punishment and suspension on classrooms
   and schools. Does the use of punishment or suspension
   "improve" classroom order and school safety? Under what
   circumstances? How do school discipline programs affect
   teachers, students, and classroom processes?

Before these questions can be answered, however, there is a need to understand more about school discipline processes themselves. How is punishment or suspension carried out? What conditions trigger a need for such actions? Existing evidence suggests that there is considerable variability among schools serving similar populations on rates of punishment and suspension and that individual schools vary across time. Why is this so? How does it happen? To gain this knowledge we need more detailed case studies of incidents in which school discipline practices are applied.

In planning research on school discipline strategies, however, at least three cautions are in order. First, one wonders how researchable many questions of school discipline are. Discipline problems are emotionally charged and surrounded by legal and moral issues. In such a climate, the disinterested manipulation of variables or passive observation of behavior is not likely to happen. Second, discipline strategies such as corporal punishment and suspension are likely to be applied to cases of serious and strongly motivated misbehavior. In such situations, the probability of success is necessarily quite low. Thus, resolving questions concerning the effectiveness of these discipline strategies is extremely difficult. Finally, one of the clear messages of modern classroom management research is that the search for specific, transportable strategies is misdirected. Classroom researchers found that the answer to management problems lies first in understanding the problem. The knowledge of most use, then, is that which empowers teachers to *interpret* a situation appropriately so that whatever action is taken, whether in establishing conditions for order at the beginning of the year or in responding to misbehavior, will address the problem at hand.

In the end what is needed most are more disciplined ways of thinking about school discipline problems, ways that are consistent with emerging knowledge of how classrooms and schools work and that are grounded in a greater understanding of the texture of school order and disruption.

7

School and Classroom Discipline Programs: How Well Do They Work?

Edmund T. Emmer and Amy Aussiker

This chapter reviews research on three approaches to preparing teachers in the area of classroom discipline: Gordon's Teacher Effectiveness Training, Glasser's Reality Therapy, and Canter's Assertive Discipline. These systems have been used widely for in-service teacher education for a decade or more, although their use at the preservice level has been more recent, and each has adherents and practitioners who support its efficacy. But testimony and endorsement are subject to expectation effects and other biases—and school districts, teachers, and teacher educators should have better evidence upon which to base decisions about adoption or teacher training.

In addition to a concern about general efficacy, numerous other questions and issues are of interest to the potential user: What types of educationally desirable outcomes does a particular approach produce? For example, does training affect mainly teacher or student attitudes, perceptions, or behavior, or some combination of these variables? If a program has effects, how large are they? What components of a discipline system are essential in achieving desired results? Are the training programs offered to teachers effective in producing long-term changes in teacher and student behavior? For what types of teachers does an approach seem to be most effective (or ineffective)? This paper will summarize research on the three models of classroom discipline in order to determine what is known about these and other relevant questions, and to identify areas needing further research. Before examining the evidence, however, a brief description of the three systems will be presented.

TEACHER EFFECTIVENESS TRAINING (TET)

Developed by Thomas Gordon (1974), TET emphasizes a variety of communication and human relations skills derived from a psychotherapeutic model (Brophy and Putnam, 1979). The approach distinguishes two types of classroom situations: those in which the teacher "owns" a problem (e.g., cannot teach effectively because of student behavior) and those in which a student owns the problem (e.g., student is upset because of a poor grade or personal problem). In the case of a student-owned problem, the teacher is trained to use various listening skills in order to facilitate student understanding and resolution of the problem. In the case of teacher-owned problems, "I-messages" and problem solving are stressed. I-messages require the teacher to specify the problem that the student is causing the teacher and then to negotiate a solution to the problem, so that, ideally, both the teacher's and the students' needs are met. The goal of this approach is to resolve problems in ways that are neither authoritarian nor submissive, but rather respect each party's rights.

Other aspects of TET include avoiding barriers to communication and structuring the environment to prevent problems. The former aspect specifies a series of common responses, such as reprimands, lecturing, moralizing, or praising, that may interfere with open communication. Such responses should be avoided in situations when the student expresses a problem or the teacher is engaging the student in problem solving. Structuring the environment to prevent problems is also suggested. Teachers are encouraged to analyze the classroom environment to determine whether reducing, rearranging, enriching, or otherwise modifying it might avoid problems.

Teacher training in TET is often conducted by representatives of Effectiveness Training, Inc., founded and directed by Gordon, using a prescribed course outline and related materials (Miller and Burch, 1979). Typical training sessions total thirty hours, conducted in 10 three-hour classes. Participants read the TET text as background for the training, which consists of lectures over key concepts, demonstrations, listening to tapes modeling desired behavior, practice of skills with other participants, and workbook exercises. Teachers may also be asked to tape-record their interaction with students to use as a basis for self-critique and feedback.

Although teacher education conducted by formally trained TET instructors is no doubt the most common in-service route, other avenues are possible. College faculty, with or without training in TET, might order the Gordon text and use it as the basis for all or a portion of a course. In such cases, of course, there is less likelihood that all components of TET will be covered or that the course activities will correspond to the recommended ones.

REALITY THERAPY

Reality Therapy is an approach to education that was developed by William Glasser (1969, 1978). It assumes that behavior is the result of choices, and that inappropriate and disruptive behavior derive from poor choices made by students. Poor choices occur because of failure in one or another form, and because students do not think through the consequences of their actions. Persons who fail develop maladaptive identities through withdrawal or delinquency. The teacher's task is to help students make good choices by making clear the connection between student behavior and its consequences. The teacher also needs to develop a classroom in which students can succeed and which supports good choices, and in which memory tasks are deemphasized and critical thinking is stressed. The grading system also needs restructuring, according to Glasser, in order to decrease failure. Glasser's principles are operationalized through the use of class meetings, clear specification of rules and associated consequences, the use of plans or contracts, and a series of steps to guide the teacher's actions when dealing with problem behavior.

Class meetings are used for several purposes: they help the teacher become involved in the concerns and lives of the students, they are used to solve problems, and they help students learn to think about and take responsibility for their own behavior. Meetings can focus on social problems, on educational matters, or be open-ended. Glasser recommends that they be frequent—as often as daily in elementary school and two or three times per week at the secondary level.

Classroom rules should be clearly stated and developed with students. Violations of rules should be followed by consequences, and the teacher should make the connection clear. Students who continue to misbehave are dealt with using a prescribed series of steps, including getting the student to admit responsibility for the behavior, using whatever consequences have been specified, and requiring the student to develop a plan for change. Students who repeatedly misbehave are removed from the classroom until they develop a satisfactory plan. The use of Reality Therapy by individual teachers will probably be enhanced by schoolwide adoption of the approach, because consequences for repeated misbehavior and temporary removal from the classroom may need to be coordinated with the principal, counselor, or others in the building.

A variety of teacher-training materials, in addition to books by Glasser, are available. These materials include film strips, films, and video cassettes, which illustrate applications of Reality Therapy, elaborate the concepts, or present the basic components of the approach.

Glasser has recently modified his approach (cf. Glasser, 1986), chiefly by recommending the use of learning teams or cooperative learning groups as a means of helping students accomplish content objectives as well as to satisfy major social needs. It is important to note that the present paper does *not* include reviews of research based upon Glasser's recent revision of his model.

ASSERTIVE DISCIPLINE (AD)

This system of classroom discipline has as its basic premise the right of the teacher to define and enforce standards for student behavior that permit instruction to be carried out in a manner consonant with the teacher's capabilities and needs. Teachers who do this are assertive rather than hostile or submissive. Canter (1976) describes such a teacher as "one who clearly communicates her wants and needs to her students, and is prepared to reinforce her words with appropriate actions. She responds in a manner which maximizes her potential to get her needs met, but in no way violates the best interests of the students" (p. 9).

Assertive Discipline begins with a series of actions that are directed at clearly specifying expectations for student behavior. These actions include the teacher developing a discipline plan that meets his or her preferences for student behavior. These expectations are then translated into a set of rules that specify acceptable and unacceptable behavior. At the same time, the teacher develops a set of punishments to use as consequences for rule violations. The most widely used punishment is a penalty system of names and check marks recorded on the chalkboard, with detention, a note home, time out, or a referral to the principal being assigned in progression, as check marks accrue. Teachers are also instructed to identify rewards for compliance with the rule system. After receiving the principal's approval for the system, it is explained to the students and implemented in the classroom. Not all behavior is responded to using the preceding system; teachers are encouraged to first try hints, questions, directions, and demands.

Teacher training in Assertive Discipline is usually done in workshops conducted by Canter or his trainers (Canter and Associates). In addition, books by the Canters (1976, 1981) as well as a number of film strips and videotape cassettes make the approach easily accessible to both pre- and in-service teacher educators. A typical training course is six hours long and consists of lectures, discussions, workbook exercises, and role plays on the topics of basic concepts; roadblocks to effective discipline (e.g., labeling, excusing); establishing rules, consequences, and rewards; and presenting the system to students.

STUDY DESIGN

Data sources for this review were articles, reports, and dissertations describing the results of research or evaluations of the three approaches. References were sought by searching several data bases: ERIC, Dissertation Abstracts, and the School Practices Information File. In addition, letters were sent to directors of research and evaluation in 120 school districts in the United States and Canada requesting information about pertinent evaluation studies that might have been conducted in their districts. Similarly, letters requesting relevant reports were sent to developers of the systems (Canter, Glasser, and Gordon). Most of the studies identified by this process were dissertation projects. Surprisingly, only a few of the school districts reported evaluation research on the models, in spite of their widespread use (e.g., estimates cited in the literature indicate over four hundred thousand teachers trained in the use of Assertive Discipline).

Once obtained, each study was read and summarized (see Tables 7.1, 7.2, and 7.3). Basic information in the tables includes the number of teachers participating in the study and their level (elementary, secondary, student teachers, etc.). A short summary of study procedures is provided, along with a specification of the type of research design. Most studies were one of three types: a single group study with pre-post assessment, a two-group experimental (E) vs. control (C) comparison with randomization, or an E vs. C comparison without randomization.

Results of the studies are presented separately for teacher outcomes and student outcomes. Differences are noted in the table by a
plus (if a difference for the outcome measure was statistically significant at the p ‹.05 level), by NEG (if the significant difference favored
the control group), or by NS (no significant difference). NA indicates
that a significance test was not reported. Effect sizes were calculated
by computing the difference between the experimental and control
group means, or the pre-post difference, divided by the standard deviation of the measure. Effects were considered small if they were
less than 1/2 standard deviation, moderate if they were between 1/2
and 1 standard deviation, and large if greater than 1 standard deviation; these effects are noted as S, M, and L in the tables. In most
cases effect sizes could be determined directly or by calculation from
the reported results; in a few cases, noted NA, data were insufficient
to estimate the effects. The purpose of presenting effects is to convey
an idea of the *amount* of difference a training program might make.
Significance tests, of course, do not do this. A highly significant result could be obtained for a small effect if a study used a large sample, and a small sample size might produce a moderate or large effect
and yet not result in statistical significance. In the tables, effects are
reported except when a nonsignificant difference was found and the
effect size was small; this latter case is noted with "-" in the
effect column.

RESULTS FOR TEACHER EFFECTIVENESS TRAINING

A summary of results for research on Teacher Effectiveness Training
(TET) is given in Table 7.1.

All eight studies that examined the effects of TET training on
teacher behavior, knowledge, or attitudes found significant changes
from pre to post, or between experimental (E) and comparison (C)
groups after training, on at least one teacher variable. Not all results
were consistent, however; for example, two studies (Dillard, 1974;
Walker, 1982) found no effects on the Minnesota Teacher Attitude
Inventory (MTAI), but Chanow (1980) did find a significant increase
from pre to post using this instrument. Studies (Dennehy, 1981;
Blume, 1977; Thompson, 1975) that assessed teacher behavior after
training generally found evidence that teachers increased their ability to use recommended TET skills. Effect sizes ranged from small to
large, with large effects common. Although a variety of research designs was used, no apparent bias toward stronger effects was noted

in the weaker studies. The results support the conclusion that TET training can change teacher attitudes and behavior in a direction more consistent with the assumptions of the TET model: toward a more democratic view of the use of authority and more concern for student perceptions and feelings, and toward behavior that reflects acceptance of students.

The case with regard to effects on *students* is not as convincing. Six of the studies examined possible impact on students (Dennehy, 1981; Laseter, 1981; Nummela, 1978; Huck, 1975: Thompson, 1975; Chanow, 1980); and among the studies the results are mixed. Dennehy (1981) found significant effects on only one of five observed student behaviors, and in only one of the two E groups. Nummela (1978) found a small effect on student attitudes, although not on student locus of control. Thompson's study (1975) assessed the effect of I-messages (compared to reprimands) on disruptive behavior in two classes. In one class, no effect of I-statements on disruptive behavior could be detected. In the other class, I-messages seemed to decrease disruption initially, but a functional relationship between such teacher statements and reduced student disruptions was not demonstrated, because of a failure to reverse effects during the reversal phase of the experiment. The strongest results for effects on students appear in Chanow (1980), and Laseter (1981). Chanow found that students of teachers trained in TET significantly increased their evaluations of their teachers (e.g., on general impression, interest, competence) more than did students of teachers in a comparison group. However, teachers in the TET group were volunteers, so a self-selection bias is a serious limitation. Laseter's results have the same limitation. In his study, some teachers (but not a randomly assigned group) received TET training and others did not. Lasseter found significant differences in achievement gains of students, related to the number of classes taken from TET-trained teachers. Students having more classes with TET teachers gained more on California Achievement Test (CAT) reading and math achievement than students having fewer classes whose teachers had received TET training. As with the Chanow study, teacher self-selection into training contributes an unknown amount to the effect; also, the absence of separate results for math- and reading-relevant classes and the failure to observe teacher behavior further limits our ability to interpret the results. Finally, most of the effect sizes for student variables were small.

Thus, TET training was shown in most studies to have discernible effects on teachers. Effects on students were less convincing, in part because fewer studies examined student outcomes, in part because student results were less consistent and showed relatively small effects. For most studies of TET, the absence of random control groups further limits confidence in the results, as does the general lack of follow-up studies beyond the immediate post-testing.

RESULTS FOR REALITY THERAPY

A summary of studies of Reality Therapy (RT) can be found in Table 7.2. The most thorough evaluation of Reality Therapy was reported by Masters and Laverty (1977). In this research, five matched pairs of schools in a Pennsylvania school district were identified and randomly assigned to an experimental or to a control (delayed treatment) group. E teachers and their students were assessed after one and after two years of implementation, and then were compared to the control group teachers and students at the end of their first year, before this latter group participated in RT training. Effects on teachers were assessed by classroom observations, which identified important differences in some (but not all) classroom instructional behavior—for example, more questions and acceptance of student ideas, but no differences on acceptance of feelings. Two teacher scales measuring attitudes consistent with the RT philosophy revealed no significant group differences. Other data, however, indicated that many teachers were implementing some RT methods; for example, conducting class meetings. Effects on students were, for the most part, *not* found by Masters and Laverty. Student achievement and attitude scores (except one subscale for part of the sample) showed no between-group differences. An effect was found on referral rates, with the C group rate being nearly twice the E group's rate. This latter result has many possible interpretations. It could mean that a substantial improvement in behavior had occurred as a result of the use of RT methods. It could also mean, as the authors note (p. 43), that teachers became more adept at handling the problems in their own classes. It might also simply indicate an administrative difference in handling problem behaviors, rather than either an improvement in student behavior or an increase in teacher competence.

An evaluation of a long-term project using Reality Therapy is reported by the Johnson City (NY) Central School District (undated). Between 1972 and 1984 this district's programs were extensively redesigned, with RT as a part of the model, along with objectives-based evaluation and curriculum design and use of a mastery model for instruction. (Because RT was only one of several components in the model, this study is not listed in Table 7.2, in order to avoid the implication that all of the effects are mainly attributable to RT). Substantial improvement in math and reading achievement was found using both cross-sectional and panel data, between 1976 and 1984. How important a role Reality Therapy played in producing the effects cannot be estimated, because of the absence of control groups and the lack of documentation of implementation of the various components. However, the application is worth noting because it does suggest that RT can be combined with program renewal efforts so that, as a whole, the program produces positive effects.

Six other studies examined the effects of RT using a pre-post, E vs. C design, although none of these studies used random assignment to groups. Lynch (1975) found no effects on math achievement for students of teachers trained in RT (however, the training was shorter than usual and implementation may have been weak). Welch and Dolly (1980), in a study of elementary classes, found no evidence for effects on either teacher or student variables. Although the measured teacher behaviors did not seem to match very well with RT objectives and therefore might not have allowed a good test of program effects on teachers, the student behaviors were very appropriate (i.e., on-task behavior, discipline referrals, absence rate). Browning (1978) conducted a study in eighth grade classes and obtained mixed results. RT-trained teachers developed more positive attitudes toward school and discipline concepts than comparison-group teachers; students of RT-trained teachers also developed more favorable attitudes, and also gained more in GPA over the course of the study (a six-week period). This latter result could be a function of changes in teachers' grading policies during the study rather than of improved achievement. Contrary to expectation, there was a slight increase in disciplinary referral rates in the E group and a substantial *decline* in referrals in the C group.

Matthews (1972) studied the effects of Reality Therapy in four elementary classes over a five-month period. Treatment implementation was monitored by taping class meetings. No significant differences between classes of RT-trained and untrained teachers were found on either the Metropolitan Achievement Test or on subscales of the California Test of Personality. Fewer behavior problems were reported by teachers in the trained group; however, the lack of independent validation (for example, via direct observation) and the fact that the teachers were aware of the nature of the study weaken the finding. Houston-Slowik (1982) found a moderate reduction in anxiety and an increase in academic interest for students in two junior high classes whose teachers utilized Reality Therapy for eleven weeks, compared with two classes in a "matched" school. However, the small number of teachers and the lack of randomization are limitations. Cady (1983) found substantial increases in MTAI scores and in measures of knowledge and ability to use RT concepts in groups given RT training in a summer course. A follow-up assessment three months later showed that much of the effect persisted. No assessment was made of whether classroom behaviors of the teachers or students were affected by the training.

Most of the other studies examined the behavior of a single group of RT-trained teachers or their students across baseline and treatment implementation phases. Moede and Triscari (1985) found evidence for a substantial drop in disciplinary referrals in four elementary schools whose teachers were given Reality Therapy training. However, it is not clear whether these results were a function of RT or of other programs in the schools; in addition, it is not clear whether the drop in referrals represents a change in student behavior or if it was a result of an administrative change in the way the schools handled student behavior problems.

Other positive evidence was obtained in several studies that used RT components to address specific problem students and their behavior. These focused applications appeared to be effective, at least in terms of producing immediate effects. Marandola and Imber (1979) demonstrated a sharp reduction in student arguing after a series of class meetings focused on this issue. Gang (1974) showed that using RT strategies with highly disruptive students was effective in substantially reducing their problem behavior and increasing their desirable behavior; the effect persisted for at least several weeks after the end of the direct treatment phase. Brandon's (1981) study of the effects of RT on absence rates was conducted using counselors instead of teachers. It is worth noting for several reasons. First, by using random assignment of chronically absent students to E and C groups, the design permits more confidence about causal inferences. Second, the results showed a significant effect on absence rates, which persisted one month after the end of the group meetings (but not for two months). However, no effect was noted on students' locus of control, which may help explain the loss of effect two months after treatment. A similar study by Atwell (1982), not shown in Table 7.2, also used RT as the basis for counseling four highly disruptive students. Follow-up classroom observations of these students indicated significantly improved on-task rates.

In summary, many of the studies of Reality Therapy that assessed effects on student variables had at least one student outcome variable that differed significantly for the E and C groups or from pre- to postassessment. Only a few of the studies attempted to assess effects on teacher behavior or attitudes. Findings from these studies were mixed, with two indicating large effects on various attitudes, and two others finding little or no effect on teacher behavior. In general, monitoring of implementation after training was weak, with numerous studies providing no evidence of teacher use. Applications of Reality Therapy ranged from its use in the modification of disruptive behavior of selected students to its incorporation as a component in a longitudinal design of a school district's programs. The two evaluation studies that suggest long-term effects (Johnson City, undated, not in table; Moede and Triscari, 1985) did not use control groups, nor was Reality Therapy's effect separated from other program components. A better-designed and more extensive evaluation (Masters and Laverty, 1977) found *no* effects on student achievement and very little evidence for effects on student attitudes. Although the RT schools in this study did have substantially lower numbers of disciplinary referrals, the finding, as noted earlier, has multiple interpretations.

RESULTS FOR ASSERTIVE DISCIPLINE

Studies of the effects of Assertive Discipline (AD) training are summarized in Table 7.3. Ten of these studies included teacher variables, although these were mostly assessed by questionnaires rather than by direct observation of classroom behaviors. Barrett (1985) found no change in student teachers' pupil control emphasis, anxiety, or concern level as a result of AD training. However, Henderson (1982) found that AD-trained teachers had less custodial concepts of pupil control and a more internal locus of control, although he did not find that these teachers had more positive self-concepts or assertive personality characteristics. Other studies (Allen, 1983; Bauer, 1982; Ersevas, 1980) found effects on teachers' perceptions of various aspects of discipline problems. Only one study of teacher perceptions found no effects: Kundtz (1981) reported no significant differences in the self-reports of management skills of teachers trained in Assertive Discipline, compared with those of teachers who had little exposure to AD.

Effects on teacher *behavior* were assessed in only two studies, both of student teachers. Furthermore, these studies used ratings rather than direct assessment of specific behaviors. Barrett and Curtis (1986) found small, though significant, effects; and Smith (1983) noted moderate effects on supervisor ratings of student teacher performance in the area of management and discipline. Unfortunately neither of these latter two studies examined student behavior, nor did the studies identify what specific teacher behaviors were affected by AD training.

The ten studies that included measures of student behavior produced results which were decidedly mixed. Only two studies assessed student attitudes or perceptions. Ersevas (1980) found no change in students' opinions of their classroom climate after implementation of AD throughout a school; however, students' perceptions of *school* climate improved. A negative finding was reported by Bauer (1982), whose ninth grade subjects in a school using AD had significantly *lower* school morale scores than their non-AD school counterparts.

Student suspensions or referrals were a frequently used criterion variable, but these results, as a whole, are equivocal. Terrell (1984) carefully matched eleven schools using AD (generally for two years) with eleven other schools. Comparisons of the schools on several student variables showed no significant differences for truancy rates, referrals, detentions, and suspensions, except for a significant drop favoring the AD schools in the number of in-school suspensions from 1983 to 1984. However, a moderate (but nonsignificant) effect favoring the *non-AD* schools was noted in the post-only number of disciplinary referrals and detentions. Parker (1984) found a *greater* number of referrals in grades seven through nine after implementation of AD, and no change in grades ten through twelve. Bauer (1982) compared effects for teachers in a school using AD with effects for teachers in other schools and found no overall differences in student absence or suspension rates. However, fewer boys, but a greater number of girls, received disciplinary referrals in the AD school. Finally, Vandercook's study (1983) found no significant *reduction* in referrals for discipline problems after teachers received AD training.

Two other studies produced no support for AD. Sharpe (1980) found no significant between-group differences in the achievement scores of students whose teachers had received AD training, compared with those of students of teachers who had not received it. Kundtz (1981) found no significant change in the number of teacher-reported student behavior problems of teachers who had more extensive AD training, compared with that of teachers with less exposure to AD.

Generally positive effects on students were reported in three studies. Allen (1983) examined changes in discipline referral rates after an AD program was implemented in a junior high school and found a significant reduction in referrals for class disruptions; the magnitude of the effect was small, however, and equivalent to approximately 0.2 fewer referrals per student per year. Ward (1983) found a significant pre-post decline in the frequency of teacher-reported disruptions after teachers received AD training. The absence of a control group and the lack of validation of the measure of teacher-perceived disruption make conclusions based on these data tenuous. The best evidence for positive effects of AD on students comes from McCormack (1985), who found lower rates of off-task behavior in AD-trained teachers' classes, compared with classes whose teachers did not use AD. Statistical controls were used to equate the groups on several variables, including student reading ability and teacher qualifications. However, no observations of the teachers occurred before they received AD training, and without random assignment it is possible that the AD teachers initially were better managers. Certainly the result needs replication. More generally, studies of AD would do well to use direct observation of both teacher and student behavior to assess effects.

In summary, studies of Assertive Discipline show consistent evidence of effects on teachers' *perceptions* of various aspects of discipline, including reduced problem behaviors. However, the evidence suggests only a small effect on teacher behavior itself. Evidence for effects on *student* behavior and attitudes is *not* very supportive of AD training; that is, more studies found no effects, or mixed and negative effects, than found that AD training resulted in improved student behavior and attitudes.

DISCUSSION

Considered as a whole, the research on the three models provides some evidence for positive effects on various *teacher* attitudes, beliefs, and perceptions, such as are assessed by the Minnesota Teacher Attitude Inventory, the Pupil Control Ideology inventory, and teachers' self-perceptions and reports of classroom behavior problems. The studies of Teacher Effectiveness Training are most convincing with regard to teacher attitudes, because all of those studies which included such a measure obtained a significant result for at least one (and often more than one) attitude scale or dimension. Several studies of Assertive Discipline also found evidence of changes in teacher attitudes and perceptions following training, although some did not. Studies of Reality Therapy did not often include measures of teacher attitudes and perceptions, so little can be said about the effects of this approach on teachers.

When the outcome measures were teacher *behaviors*, results again tended to be mixed, although TET studies, particulariy—and to a lesser extent, Assertive Discipline—did find at least short-term changes. Overall, fewer studies attempted to assess teacher behavior, and when they did so, smaller effects, or nonsignificant ones, were found. The relative paucity of results for teacher behavior indicates, at the very least, a need to monitor teacher implementation more closely and to study those factors that may impede or facilitate program adoption and use. The fact that several of the studies of TET found significant effects for some teacher behaviors (e.g., empathy, I-messages) must be viewed with caution, because the assessments were usually not done under normal classroom circumstances. For example, assessments were made of tape-recorded conversations with children, or were done during a specially designated treatment phase. Thus, it is possible to conclude only that teachers had an increased capability for exhibiting particular behaviors, but not that they necessarily would do so in their normal classroom environment. In the case of Assertive Discipline, the assessment of teacher behavior was limited to global ratings, and the significant effects tended to be small. Therefore, it is not clear from this research what types of teacher behaviors were changed by the AD training, nor whether the changes occurred on aspects most central to the AD model.

Studies of effects on students produced variable results across the models. For TET, some small but significant effects were noted on pupil evaluations of their teachers and on self-concept. Generally, however, little attention was paid in TET research to changes in student behavior, and when it was included among the dependent variables, effects were inconsistent. For Reality Therapy, the strongest and most consistent effects on students were noted in several studies that were directed at specific students who were exhibiting inappropriate behaviors. Evidence with regard to effects on long-term student behavior change and on student achievement is less convincing, in part because relatively few studies examined these outcomes and also because studies reporting positive results tend to be methodologically weaker than studies reporting no effects.

Studies of Assertive Discipline's effects on students did *not* show a consistent pattern of positive results for either attitudes and perceptions or for behavior. A few studies obtained positive results, but others found negative or no significant effects on students. Neither was there a tendency for moderate but nonsignificant effects favoring the AD-trained groups, reducing the likelihood that small sample sizes might account for the lack of positive findings. Thus, in spite of teacher and administrator perceptions that are often positive, there is not much evidence that AD training results in improved student behavior.

A difficulty in interpreting much of the research on these models is determining whether a given study is a reasonable test of a model's effectiveness. To do so, one must be able to answer the question, "Effective for what?" and the answer is likely to depend on a set of values and assumptions about what constitutes educationally desirable outcomes. Differences in value orientations are evident among the studies when one considers the range of variables used as outcome measures. For this reason, our review has grouped variables into several categories. It is assumed that readers will select or weight those most central to their purposes when evaluating the effectiveness of a particular model.

Another difficulty in dealing with this body of studies is that most failed to use any explicit model or theory base for predicting what effects would occur and why. As a consequence, there are often rather startling gaps in the chain of assessment that would enable the researchers to understand and interpret their findings. A relatively simple model for understanding how an in-service training program might affect student behavior could include (1) a description of the training process, (2) a determination of whether and to what degree the participating teachers accepted or made a commitment to use the model presented in the program, (3) observation and verification of the teacher's attempts at implementation of various components of the model, (4) the teacher's evaluation of implementation after trial use, and (5) assessment of student response during and after implementation. Although many studies contained adequate descriptions of the training procedures, few included assessments of mediating links to outcome measures. Nonsignificant results could therefore be the result of the inability of the model to produce the intended effects, an ineffective training program, and/or inadequate implementation of the model. Another unfortunate consequence of the lack of formative evaluation is that no empirical basis exists for identifying which *components* of a program were effectively used, why they might have been effective, or how the teacher might have altered the approach during the process of implementation. Another limitation is an absence of theory undergirding the conception of most of the studies. For example, many of the studies focused on teacher attitudes without considering how changes in attitudes might result in behavior change (e.g., use of a particular discipline approach). In spite of the widespread use of measures of teacher and student attitudes and self-reports, little use was made of the substantial body of social psychological theory on attitude development and its relationship to behavior change (e.g., Feather, 1982; Fishbein and Ajzen, 1975).

Nearly all the research reported on the impact of a *total* program, whereas only a few studies examined the effects of specific program components (e.g., I-messages, classroom meetings). The global approach has the advantage of providing an estimate of overall impact, but it offers no information on how various aspects of the program contribute to the total effect. Neither does it offer insights that might be helpful in program improvement. An alternative research strategy is to examine effects of specific program components. Consider, for example, if more research had been conducted of the same type as Thompson's (1975) study of the TET I-message component. Thompson found that, for elementary students emitting high levels of inappropriate behaviors, the I-message strategy was only marginally effective in reducing their rate of occurrence. Follow-up studies might have led to the development of modifications of I-messages or to alternative procedures that would be more effective, and to a greater understanding of contextual dimensions that enhance or interfere with I-message effects.

The emphasis on evaluating the effects of the total programs has also inhibited the accumulation of data that would lead to their redesign. Thus, there is a static quality to these models, and the user is left with the option of electing or discarding the whole approach, or "free-lancing" a variation without a substantive base for the modification. An alternative research strategy would be to assess both the global effects of a program *and* its specific components. For example, researchers could observe teachers during early and later phases of implementation, using naturalistic observations and interviews to identify and document those program components that teachers and students are able to utilize easily and those which are problematic and in need of modification.

The contents of the training programs themselves have received very little attention in this research. The studies did not usually report the teachers' perceptions of different training activities or model components (see Detmer, 1974, for an exception to this generalization) nor were variations of a model compared. Also, the context in which the approach was used was given scant attention. For example, studies of student teachers did not consider the effects of the cooperating teachers' perceptions or use of the model under study, a factor that would surely have important effects on the student teachers' ability to implement a program. Another contextual feature that needs greater consideration is the school setting, including factors such as the degree of administrative and collegial support for adopting an approach, the type of school organization, and characteristics of students attending the school.

The absence of comparative studies and the great variety of teacher and student outcome variables that were used make conclusions about one or another program's superiority tenuous. Examining the results for the total set of studies, it is apparent that the net effects of Reality Therapy and Teacher Effectiveness Training are positive for certain types of outcomes, although adoption of either approach would depend upon whether the types of outcomes for which the approach is effective are consistent with the user's objectives. It is also the case that except for some of the Assertive Discipline research few studies indicate negative effects. Thus an optimistic conclusion would be that these programs are at least equal to and probably represent a net improvement over "traditional" classroom discipline methods. The danger in acting on such an inference and in using these "packaged" approaches is that they may be viewed (incorrectly, in our opinion) as a solution for the many problems that teachers and schools face in the area of discipline, when in fact any given approach addresses only a limited set of problems and offers strategies that are effective, at best, only in some cases. Thus, a school district planning in-service work for new teachers or teacher educators planning a preservice teacher education program should view any one of these approaches as no more than supplemental to a more comprehensive treatment of the knowledge and competencies necessary for teachers to acquire in this domain.

In varying degrees, these models focus on guiding student behavior through rule clarity, use of consequences, and a variety of communication strategies to gain student commitment to behavior change. To a considerable extent, they are concerned with managing and correcting student behavior, solving problems, and so forth. Although this focus is an important one, it does not encompass the full range of the teacher's role in creating and preserving order (Doyle, 1986). Effective discipline requires that considerable attention be paid to classroom management, to instructional functions, and to preparation and planning. To cite two examples, research (Emmer, Evertson, and Anderson, 1980; Evertson and Emmer, 1982) has highlighted the importance of the initial phases of the school year in establishing a classroom setting that facilitates appropriate behavior and that prevents problems. Also, Kounin's research (1970; Kounin and Doyle, 1975) shows the importance of the degree to which a teacher keeps activities on track and prevents interruptions from slowing down lessons in order to promote high rates of student on-task behavior and freedom from deviancy. These examples suggest that discipline will be enhanced by teacher attention to planning, preparation, and the conduct of activities at the beginning of the year, and by conducting activities in efficient, interesting, and comprehensible ways throughout the year. Such concepts are *not* addressed by the models, except in very limited ways. Yet it is through such concepts that teachers can *prevent* much misbehavior and thus reduce the need for "disciplining" students. Therefore, this review's inability to demonstrate strong evidence for effects on student behavior results not so much from weak research designs and limited measures of student outcomes as from the failure of these models to address the day-to-day classroom management skills needed to engage students in productive activities and to prevent minor problems from becoming major ones.

Teachers or school administrators considering the use of any one of these models and its associated training program should carefully consider what function it will have in their overall scheme of instructional and behavioral management. If a program's goals are consistent with theirs and the summary of research evidence supports the program's efficacy in the goal area, then adoption would be reasonable. At the same time, it is important to realize that none of these models adequately addresses the complex set of preventive and supportive functions necessary for effective management and discipline. Thus the overall plan for classroom management and discipline will need to be analyzed carefully in order to ensure adequate coverage of areas not included in a chosen model.

These systems *do* provide teachers and administrators with some strategies for dealing with major threats to school and classroom order, and some provide rational, systematic means of communicating with students about expectations and consequences. These features may help explain the positive effects sometimes obtained when specific types of student behaviors were targeted for treatment. Therefore, these models might play a limited though useful role in a comprehensive system of classroom management and discipline.

Table 7.1

Summary of Teacher Effectiveness Training Studies

STUDY	SUBJECTS	PROCEDURES	DESIGN	TEACHER MEASURE	SIG.[a]	EFF.[b]	STUDENT MEASURE	SIG.	EFF.	COMMENTS
Walker (1982)	84 STs (elem)	E groups received a 24-hour TET course at the beginning of student teaching. The C groups received variations of traditional student teaching supervision and seminars.	E: Pre-Post; C₁ & C₂: Pre-Post (not random)	Teacher attitudes: MTAI / Dogmatism	NS / +	– / L	NONE			E group STs were volunteers. Pretest differences among the groups on the outcome measures were small and nonsignificant.
Dennehy (1981)	18 Ts (elem)	Two groups (n = 9) received 30 hours of TET training over 10 weeks. Classes were observed using Flanders' Interaction Analysis (IA) and Spaulding's Coping Analysis for Educational Settings (CASES).	E₁: Pre-Post, Follow-up; E₂: Pre-Post	Flanders' IA. Observed behavior: Accepts feelings, Praises, Accepts Ideas, Gives direction (less), I-messages, You-messages (less)	+/0, +/0, +/0, +/0, NS, +/0	L, L, L, L, –, L	Spaulding's CASES. Observed behavior: Self-directed, Pays attention, Sharing and helping, Social interaction, Seeks/receives support	NS, NS, NS, NS, +	–, –, –, –, L	Significant effects observed only in E₂. Tendency toward opposite effects in E₁.

Table 7.1 *(cont'd)*

Summary of Teacher Effectiveness Training Studies

STUDY	SUBJECTS	PROCEDURES	DESIGN	TEACHER MEASURE	SIG.[a]	EFF.[b]	STUDENT MEASURE	SIG.[a]	EFF.	COMMENTS
Laseter (1981)	22 Ts (7th, 8th)	Teachers received 30 hours of TET training; an unspecified number of teachers were untrained. For each student, the number of classes taught by a TET-trained T was the predictor; adjusted student gain on the Cal. Ach. Test (CAT) over a year was the criterion.	E: Pre-Post	NONE			Student achievement: CAT reading CAT math	+ +	NA NA	Statistical controls for entering achievement, grade, race, sex, and SES.

Study	Sample	Treatment	Design	Teacher outcomes	Results	Mag.	Student outcomes	Results	Mag.	Comments
Ewing (1980)	30 Ts (elem)	E group received 30 hours of TET training over 7 weeks. Post-tests were given one week after training concluded.	E, C: Pre-Post (not random)	Teacher attitudes: State Anxiety / Trait Anxiety / Tennessee Self-Concept / Teaching as a career / Toward Coworkers (post only)	+ / NS / NS / NS / +	L / – / – / – / L	NONE			Control teachers were volunteers from the same district, similar to E group in sex and age, but with more teaching experience.
Chanow (1980)	28 Ts, 140 Ss (7th, 8th)	E group received 8 weeks of TET training, 2½ hrs per week. Teacher outcomes were the MTAI, Attitude Toward Children (PARI), Attitude Toward Education (ATE). Student outcome was their evaluation of their teachers: III. Tch. Eval. Quest. (ITEQ).	E: Pre-Post C: Pre-Post (not random)	Gain on teacher attitudes: MTAI / PARI / ATE	+ / + / +	M / M / M	Gain on student attitudes: 4 of 5 subscales of the ITEQ	+	S	Ts in the E group had significantly higher means than the C Group and 4 of 5 subscales of the ITEQ.

Table 7.1 *(cont'd)*

Summary of Teacher Effectiveness Training Studies

STUDY	SUBJECTS	PROCEDURES	DESIGN	TEACHER MEASURE	SIG.[a]	EFF.[b]	STUDENT MEASURE	SIG.	EFF.	COMMENTS
McBee (1979)	198 Ts (K-12) in 14 schools	All Ts received a 2-day workshop on TET. Teacher knowledge of TET content and Pupil Control Ideology (PCI) were assessed before and after the workshop.	E: Pre-Post	Affective knowledge Pupil Control Ideology	+ +/0	L S	NONE			PCI scores became less custodial after some workshops; no change after others. No control group.
Nummela (1978)	6 Ts, 104 Ss (elem)	E Ts received TET training before school began. S measures were obtained in early Sept. and in March.	E, C Pre-Post (not random)	NONE			Student attitude scale (Battle) How I See Myself Questionnaire IAR Questionnaire	+ + NS	S S –	Groups did not differ on the Sept. pretest. All classes were taught in a campus lab school.

Study	Sample	Description	Design	Outcome measure			Outcome measure			Comments
Blume (1977)	73 pre-service Ts	The E group received four 1-hour sessions on active listening skills. Tapes of the Ts' conversations with children were scored for empathy.	E, C: Pre-Post, Follow-up (random)	Rating of empathy	+	L	NONE			Effect size was moderate on the 6-week follow-up assessment.
Huck (1975)	Ss of 20 Ts (7th-12th)	E teachers received 30 hours of TET training. Student perceptions of classroom environment were assessed in Oct. and in May.	E, C: Pre-Post (not random)	NONE			Student perceptions: Classroom Environment Index (multiple scales)	NS	–	Absence of significant differences was consistent in both junior high and senior high classes.
Thompson (1975)	2 Ts (elem), 6 Ss	Both Ts were given 6 hours of training in the use of I-messages. Ts then attempted to reduce high rates of inappropriate behavior of target Ss.	E: Pre-Post, Double-Reversal	Observed behavior: I-messages and reprimands	+	L	Observed behavior: Disruption	+/0	S	Failure to achieve control of disruptive rates during reversal indicates weak effects on student behavior.

Table 7.1 *(cont'd)*

Summary of Teacher Effectiveness Training Studies

STUDY	SUBJECTS	PROCEDURES	DESIGN	TEACHER MEASURE	SIG.[a]	EFF.[b]	STUDENT MEASURE	SIG.	EFF.	COMMENTS
Dillard (1974)	16 graduate students in education	All Ss participated in 12-week TET course, 3 hrs. /wk. Outcomes were assessed using the MTAI and by analyzing tape recordings of interviews.	E: Pre-Post	MTAI Tape analysis: Facilitative responding (more) Nonfacilitative responding (less)	NS + +	– S S	NONE			Interviews were conducted with individual pupils in non-classroom settings.

NOTE: The following abbreviations are used: Teacher (T), Student (S), Student teacher (ST), Trained group (E), Comparison group (C).

a Significance level: NS = not significant; + = p<.05; +/0 = significant differences for only a subset of variables or groups; NEG = p<.05 but the effect favors the control group; NA = significance test not reported.

b Effect size symbols: L = large; M = moderate; S = small (see text for explanation). NA = effect size could not be calculated. Unless otherwise indicated, differences favor the E over the C group, or Post over Pre.

Table 7.2

Summary of Reality Therapy Studies

STUDY	SUBJECTS	PROCEDURES	DESIGN	TEACHER MEASURE	SIG.	EFF.	STUDENT MEASURE	SIG.	EFF.	COMMENTS
Moede & Triscari (1985)	Ts and Ss at 4 schools (elem)	All teachers received RT training; schools began using ISS rooms with instructional monitors. Program effects were assessed by monitoring disciplinary actions over 3 years.	E: Pre-Post Follow-up	Teacher perceptions of effects on Ss	NA	NA	Number of "disciplinary actions"	NA	L	Discipline actions declined from 142 before the program began to 23 after 3 years.
Houston-Slowik (1982)	4 Ts 74 Ss (7th, 9th)	After participating in an 8-hour workshop, two teachers used class meetings twice a week for 11 weeks. Effects were assessed on self-concepts and locus of control of Mexican-American students.	E, C: Pre-Post (not random)	NONE			Self-concept Aspiration Anxiety Academic interest Leadership Identification Locus of control	NS + + NS NS NS	– M M – – –	MANOVA indicated sig. post-test effects. E and C classes were in two different schools; groups were matched on "pertinent socioeconomic, ethnic, and academic characteristics" (p. 52).

Table 7.2 *(cont'd)*

Summary of Reality Therapy Studies

STUDY	SUBJECTS	PROCEDURES	DESIGN	TEACHER MEASURE	SIG.	EFF.	STUDENT MEASURE	SIG.	EFF.	COMMENTS
Cady (1983)	142 Ts (K-12)	Teachers in summer workshops received 8 one-half-day training sessions on RT, Adlerian, or subject matter topics.	E1, E2, C: Pre-Post, & 3-mo. Follow-up (not random)	MTAI Test of knowledge of RT, Adler concepts Case study analysis	+ + +	L L L	NONE			After 3 months, effects were still significant. RT group had significantly higher means than the Adlerian groups, but the differences were generally small.
Brandon (1981)	14 counselors, 110 Ss (9th-12th)	Counselors were trained to use RT with chronically absent Ss, during 8 or more group sessions. Effects were assessed on absence rate and locus of control.	E, C: Pre-Post, Follow-up (1 & 2 mo.) (random)	NONE			Absences Loccus of Control	+/0 NS	L/S –	Sig. differences for absenteeism favored E on post-test and 1 mo. follow-up. Effect was smaller and nonsignificant for the 2-mo. follow-up.

Study	Sample	Description	Design	Dependent variables			Comments
Welch and Dolly (1980) and Welch (1978)	16 Ts (elem)	8 Ts received 24 hours of RT training and 8 matched comparison-group Ts did not. Classroom observations were made during 3 weeks pre-training and 3 weeks post-training.	E, C: Pre-Post (not random)	Teacher affective behavior	NS	–	
				On-task	NS	–	
				Discipline referrals	NS	–	
				Absences	NS	–	
Marandola and Imber (1979)	1 T, 10 Ss (elem)	Ten learning disabled boys participated in classroom meetings held on 8 consecutive days. Intervention focus was always related to argumentative behavior. Effect was assessed using observations of arguing behavior.	E: Pre-Post	NONE			
				Classroom observation: rate of arguing	+	NA	Compared with baseline observations, substantial reductions occurred in the amount of arguing.

Table 7.2 *(cont'd)*

Summary of Reality Therapy Studies

STUDY	SUBJECTS	PROCEDURES	DESIGN	TEACHER MEASURE	SIG.	EFF.	STUDENT MEASURE	SIG.	EFF.	COMMENTS
Browning (1978)	28 Ts, 668 Ss (8th)	After receiving 20 hours of RT training, the E teachers used RT procedures for the last 6 weeks of school. Effects were assessed on T attitudes and on S attitudes, behavior, and grades.	E, C: Pre-Post (not random)	Teacher attitudes: various semantic differential items (e.g., rules, school, discipline)	+	NA	Student attitudes: (same as teacher) Discipline referrals Grades	+ NEG +	NA NA M	ANCOVA used to equate groups on pretest variables. E and C teachers were selected from different schools. Discipline referrals declined in C group, and showed little change for E-group students.
Masters and Laverty (1977)	150 Ts, 3,500 Ss (elem)	RT was adopted at 5 schools. Extensive training provided for Ts. Effects were assessed by comparing E and C schools after 1 and 2 years of implementation, using a variety of T and S outcomes.	E: Pre-Post 1 and 2 yrs. C: Pre-Post (random)	Classroom observation: (Modified Flanders, Reciprocal Category System) Teacher attitudes (questionnaire)	+/0 NS	L –	Disciplinary referrals Student attitudes Student achievement	+ 0/+ NS	L – –	C-group schools received RT program after 1 year, i.e., delayed treatment. Post differences of attitudes between E and C students on one subtest, but only for the intermediate grade level.

Study	Sample	Description	Design	Measure			Comments
Lynch (1975)	11 Ts, 240 Ss (9th)	E teachers received 5 hours of RT training at the beginning of the school year. S achievement was assessed in Sept. and Jan.	E, C: Pre-Post (not random)	Supervisor rating of use of RT	NA	NA	Ratings of teacher use of RT components did not indicate much treatment impact.
				Mathematics achievement test	NS	—	
Gang (1974)	2 Ts, 6 Ss (elem)	The teachers, concurrently enrolled in a seminar on RT, were given additional instruction. Ts also selected 3 Ss who were serious behavior problems. Effects of teacher application of RT were studied by observing the target students.	E: Pre Post Follow-up	NONE			Significance tests comparing percentages of outcome behaviors during baseline, implementation, and follow-up periods were not conducted; however, change percentages were large.
				Student behavior: Sustained Schoolwork	NA	L	
				Oppositional	NA	L	

Table 7.2 *(cont'd)*

Summary of Reality Therapy Studies

STUDY	SUBJECTS	PROCEDURES	DESIGN	TEACHER MEASURE	SIG.	EFF.	STUDENT MEASURE	SIG.	EFF.	COMMENTS
Matthews (1972)	8 Ts, 221 Ss (4th, 5th)	E-group teachers received 5 1&½ hr. workshops. Class meetings were taped twice monthly. Treatment period: Jan.-May.	E, C: Pre-Post (not random)	NONE			Metropolitan Ach.	NS	–	Treatment implementation was monitored. Because the Behavior Checklist was completed by the teachers, potential bias may have occurred favoring the treatment group.
							Calif. Test of Personality	NS	–	
							Walker Problem Behavior Checklist	+	S	

NOTE: See Table 7.1 footnotes for abbreviations.

Table 7.3

Summary of Assertive Discipline Studies

STUDY	SUBJECTS	PROCEDURES	DESIGN	TEACHER MEASURE	SIG.	EFF.	STUDENT MEASURE	SIG.	EFF.	COMMENTS
Barrett and Curtis (1986)	536 STs	E teachers participated in a 6-hour AD workshop prior to student teaching. Program effects were assessed by comparing ST evaluations of training and supervisor's evaluations with the prior year's ST assessments.	E, C: Post only (not random)	ST rating of preparation for discipline Supervisor's rating of ST's discipline	+ +	S S	NONE			
McCormack (1985)	36 Ts (elem) (3rd)	Off-task rates in classes taught by 18 Ts using AD were compared to 18 Ts not using AD.	E, C: Multiple observations (not random)	NONE			Off-task rate	+	L	Presence or absence of AD use was a stronger predictor of off-task rates than student ability level. Use of AD was verified via questioning of the Ts, Ss, and principals.

Table 7.3 *(cont'd)*

Summary of Assertive Discipline Studies

STUDY	SUBJECTS	PROCEDURES	DESIGN	TEACHER MEASURE	SIG.	EFF.	STUDENT MEASURE	SIG.	EFF.	COMMENTS
Barrett (1985)	102 STs	E teachers received a 6-hour workshop on AD prior to student teaching. Effects were assessed on Pupil Control Ideology (PCI), Teacher Anxiety, and Teacher Concerns.	E, C: Pre-Post (random)	PCI Anxiety Concerns	NS NS NS	– – –	NONE			Part of the E group received follow-up supervision and feedback based on AD concepts, but no effect of supervision on outcomes was detected.
Parker (1984)	46 Ts, 36 Ss (7th-12th)	After 3 years of use, AD was evaluated by administering questionnaires to groups of administrators, teachers, students, and parents.	E: Post only	Questionnaire: Multiple items	NA		Referral rates (change from prior yr): Grades 7-9 Grades 10-12 Questionnaire: Multiple items	NEG NS NA	S –	Ts, Ss, and parents were mixed in their assessment of AD. Less experienced Ts were more positive in their evaluations of AD.

Study	Sample	Description	Design	Measure		Outcome			Comments
Terrell (1984)	22 schools (sec)	Eleven schools using AD were compared with 11 other schools, matched on SES, enrollment, ethnic mix, and location. Outcome variables were assessed by administrator responses on questionnaires.	E, C: Pre-Post (not random)	NONE		Change from 82-83 to 83-84			Matching process was carefully done. Most AD schools had used the procedures for 2 years. Moderately greater numbers of detentions and referrals occurred in AD schools, although in-school suspensions declined, compared with non-AD schools.
						Truancy rates	NS	–	
						Discipline referrals	NS	–	
						Detentions	NS	–	
						Suspensions from school	NS	–	
						In-school suspensions	+	M	
						Post only: 83-84			
						Truancy rates	NS	M (NEG)	
						Discipline referrals	NS	M (NEG)	
						Detentions	NS	M (NEG)	
						Suspensions from school	NS	–	
						In-school suspensions	NS	–	
Allen (1983)	353 Ss, all Ts (8th)	E teachers received AD training. Referral rates were compared before and after one year of implementation.	E: Pre-Post	Questionnaire: Perceptions of AD effects	NA	Changes in discipline			Teacher perceptions of AD effects were positive. Average number of referrals declined by about 0.2 per student per year.
						Referral rates for class disruptions	+	S	
						5 other categories	NS	–	

Table 7.3 *(cont'd)*

Summary of Assertive Discipline Studies

STUDY	SUBJECTS	PROCEDURES	DESIGN	TEACHER MEASURE	SIG.	EFF.	STUDENT MEASURE	SIG.	EFF.	COMMENTS
Ward (1983)	22 Ts (elem & sec)	After receiving AD training, Ts recorded the frequency of disruptive behaviors for one day. They then used AD for 4-6 weeks and recorded disruptive behaviors one more day.	E: Pre-Post	NONE			Student disruptions	+	M	Use of teacher reports of disruptions, without a validation check, is a serious limitation.
Vander-cook (1983)	25 Ts (elem)	All Ts received 15 hours of AD training. Effects were assessed by a questionnaire on attitudes toward discipline and by comparing referrals with previous year's	E only: Pre-Post	Attitude toward discipline	+	L	Referrals: Discipline problems	NS	—	Referrals declined from Pre to Post but not below prior years' level.

Study	Sample	Treatment	Design	Outcomes			
Smith (1983)	98 STs	E group received a 6-hour AD workshop. Outcomes assessed using the Rathus Assertiveness Schedule (RAS) and supervisor ratings.	E, C: Pre-Post (random)	Attitude: RAS	+	S	NONE
				Supervision ratings:			
				Assertiveness	+	S	
				Overall evaluation	NS	–	
				Classroom management	+	M	
Henderson (1982)	75 Ts (elem)	E group received a 6-hour AD workshop. Effects assessed after 1 yr. of implementation using teacher questionnaires.	E, C: Post only (not random)	Teacher attitudes:			NONE
				Pupil Control Ideology	+	NA	
				Locus of Control	+	NA	
				Self-Concept	NS	–	
				Assertive Personality Characteristics	NS	–	

Notes:

Smith (1983): Classroom management rating was taken from a subscale of a statewide assessment form.

Henderson (1982): Assertiveness was assessed using subscales of Cattell's 16 PF Questionnaire. E and C groups were matched on T age, sex, grade taught, and certification status.

Table 7.3 *(cont'd)*

Summary of Assertive Discipline Studies

STUDY	SUBJECTS	PROCEDURES	DESIGN	TEACHER MEASURE	SIG.	EFF.	STUDENT MEASURE	SIG.	EFF.	COMMENTS
Bauer (1982)	68 Ts (sec) (9th)	Ts in a school using AD were compared with other Ts in other schools over a 1- and 2-year period. Assessment based on referral rates, suspensions, T perceptions.	E, C: Post only (not random)	Teacher perceptions: Multiple items assessing degree of problems	+/0	NA	Referrals Suspensions Student morale questionnaire Absences	+/ NEG NS NEG NS	S – L –	Fewer boys, more girls referred at the AD school. Absence of preassessment of T perceptions limits the interpretation of differences. S scores on school attitude were lower in AD school.
Kundtz (1981)	62 Ts (elem)	Teachers in two school districts were compared. In one district all Ts had 1 or more years of experience using AD; in the second district, Ts had much less or no exposure to AD.	E, C: Post only (not random)	Self-report of various management skills	NS	–	Behavior problems	NS	–	S behavior problems were assessed by T reports. A majority of Ts in both groups reported that behavior problem frequencies had decreased.

Study	Description	Design	Measures	Results	ES	Measures	Results	ES	Comments
Sharpe (1980)	7 Ts, 83 Ss (Title 1, Ss only, elem, 5th, 6th)	Achievement scores of Ss whose Ts had received 6 hrs. of AD training were compared with scores of Ss of Ts who had not been trained.	E, C: Pre-Post (not random)	NONE		Metropolitan Achievement Tests: Reading Mathematics	NS NS	– –	Pre-Post testing was one year apart. ANCOVA was used to control for pre-achievement.
Ersevas (1980)	57 Ts, 169 Ss (elem)	Ts at 4 schools received AD training. Pre and post survey questionnaires assessed T and S (5th grade only) perceptions.	E only: Pre-Post	Assertive Discipline T Survey: About your class About your school	+ L + L	Assertive Discipline S Survey: About your class About your school	NS +	– M	Survey of parents found no changes in their perceptions of discipline at the schools.

NOTE: See Table 7.1 footnotes for abbreviations.

8

Improving Pupil Discipline and Character

Edward A. Wynne

Readers will discover that this paper takes a relatively pro-tradition perspective on pupil discipline and character development, a perspective which might also be called commonsensical. The traditional posture regarding pupil discipline and character has generally assumed that human institutions "know" a great deal about rearing children into effective adults. True, the "evidence" and theories supporting the traditional posture have not necessarily been refined to the degree necessary to satisfy some rigorous empiricists. However, the arguments for "tradition," as I hope to show, are not insubstantial.

A pro-tradition approach may represent a novelty for some professionals. Thus, a brief synopsis of the succeeding themes may be of help. First, there is some definitional discussion: readers must realize that not everybody agrees about what is good or poor discipline, and these difference have important effects on actual school policies. Next, a variety of immediate issues affecting pupil discipline and character are considered, for example, the collective life of pupils, courses particularly aimed at pupil character development, various proposals to "democratize" schools and classrooms, and modeling conduct for pupils. After establishing such principles, the paper examines how teachers can apply them in their classrooms. In particular, it focuses on the communication of values—either good or bad—and the establishment of systems of consequences. This discussion, incidentally, touches on the usually controversial matter of corporal punishment. The paper then addresses the relationship between pupil discipline

and character and popular values; although that discussion is incon-
clusive, it notes that one traditional support for in-school discipline
has been formal religion. This resource, because of shifting public
policies, has become steadily less accessible to educators. The concluding sections touch on the following issues: parents and pupil discipline; tactics for attaining consensus in particular classrooms,
schools and communities; and finally, implications for administrators and policymakers.

SOME DEFINITIONS

Before tuning to large issues of policy and theory, we must first consider some definitional issues. From that consideration, readers will
be reminded that much of the current discussion of these issues is
distressingly obscure. We can only move toward greater clarity and
precision after first confronting that obscurity.

The meaning of terms such as *good discipline* and *character* seems
self-evident. However, this is not necessarily the case, and definitional
differences, and the value judgments underlying them, are one important source of whatever discipline problems our schools confront
(Englehard, 1986). The relevant judgments about what is good and
bad discipline are made by innumerable persons and institutions —
ranging from individual teachers in classrooms, through school systems and organized groups of parents or educators, on to legislators
and appellate courts. If such diverse and scattered parties apply different definitions, it is understandable why much uncertainty reigns.
To provide clarity for analysis, this paper proposes basic definitions
for the key concepts of "discipline" and "character". Then, we can
consider their implications.

"Discipline" means making students observe rules of conduct congruent with the norms prevailing in social gatherings and work sites
in mainstream adult society. This definition is rather similar to that
proposed by Durkheim (1961). Indeed, it may appear self-evident.
However, consider this contrasting definition sometimes offered: "discipline" is the avoidance of student conduct which is *disruptive* to
the learning process.

To be explicit, are the following forms of conduct "disruptive to
learning": abusing drugs or alcohol, and sitting quietly (but bombed
out) in class; various forms of individual cheating; threatening during free play to "get" another pupil after class; hand holding, or more
intimate touching, between classes; individual pupils sitting in class

staring out the window during instruction; adolescent males wearing single earrings throughout the school day; or tardiness, class cutting, or unauthorized absences? The point of my listing is that many pupil actions which may not clearly disrupt learning violate typical adult norms.

The simple answer to the question posed by the preceding hypothetical list is "Whether particular things are disruptive depends . . . . " In other words, different readers of this paper are likely to give different answers to particular items in a list of potential forms of indiscipline. Such conflicting perspectives are found not only in society at large, but also in particular schools. The research has demonstrated, with some consistency, that diffuse and conflicting organizational goals are associated with less effective schools (and vice versa) (Hallinger and Murphy, 1985). The implications of diffuseness should be briefly examined.

If we hope to improve school discipline, it is important that school policies be made somewhat more clear and focused. (Note: This is not a counsel of perfection; some degree of compromise is usually essential; however, as the literature suggests, too many schools now err on the side of ambiguity.) If schools hope to identify and pursue clearer goals, then researchers and intellectuals must be more precise and prescriptive in their writing and analysis. Proposals for "applying consensual approaches," or "being sensitive to individual needs," or "exercising leadership," no matter how nice they sound, inevitably leave readers uncertain and confused.

This paper, especially when evaluating discipline practices which exist (or have existed) in many schools, takes a relatively definitive tone. Admittedly, the research support for some of these practices is often unclear. However, if practices have been applied for many years, to hundreds of thousands of pupils, and plausible arguments can be offered in their behalf, such arguments are entitled to be articulated with some emphasis. For instance, there is very little hard data to show that vigorous control over pupil dress is significantly related to improving discipline. However, there is an enormous mass of human experience which discloses that vital human organizations, in all cultures, have given deliberate attention to different forms of dress codes. Given this vast pool of experience, we are not being fair to educators if we say, in a tentative fashion, that the idea of rigorously controlling student dress—and even requiring pupil uniforms—should be "explored." The "truth" is that it is hard to imagine a significant human organization which has not subjected its members to important formal or informal dress restrictions, consonant with the major aims of the agency. Furthermore, if there is substantial discrepancy between dress practices and organization norms, the discrepancy will be a source of significant tension.

Acts inappropriate in most adult environments are tolerated around too many schools because they do not clearly disrupt the learning process for *other* students. Or perhaps one should say that teachers fool themselves into believing that certain forms of conduct are nondisruptive when they really cause disruption. The sharply contrasting perspectives of pupils and teachers regarding incidents of indiscipline are partial evidence to this point. Thus, a national sample survey of students and teachers reported that 26 percent of the students perceived of violence as a serious problem, but only 1 percent of the teachers saw it as a matter of concern. Again, 48 percent of the students saw student drug use as a serious problem, but only 18 percent of the teachers were concerned (Harris, 1988). Other recent surveys have reemphasized the matter of contrasting perspectives, by finding that even teachers were likely to perceive higher levels of discipline problems than administrators (Office of Educational Research and Improvement, 1987).

In sum, we have a distressing continuum: administrators see things as fine, teachers are somewhat concerned, and students are (apparently) seriously distressed. Logic would suggest that the student perspectives are most accurate: discipline violators may be able to hide their misconduct from administrators and teachers, but it will be evident to other pupils. One cause for the apparently ostrich-like posture of many responsible adults is that ignoring incidents of indiscipline which stay below a certain level of disorder lowers the work demands on adults: the adults do not have to become engaged in arduous acts of suppression if they believe no trouble is occurring.

Such toleration is also partly fostered by conflicting definitions of the goals of the "learning process". Is the main goal to transmit certain cognitive knowledge to pupils or to make them able to hold jobs? If cognitive knowledge is the aim, then should we be surprised when many young males from disadvantaged environments have trouble obtaining or holding jobs? Often they go to interviews wearing earrings, horse around on the job, or tease and make approaches to female workers. Where did they learn such self-destructive conduct? Partly in their schools. There, learning to realistically pursue and hold a job is too often not a goal of the educational process.

A key aim of the discipline process should be to teach students to conduct themselves like responsible adults—since such adults willingly accept an elaborate body of conventions and constraints. Schools and classrooms which fail to transmit such virtues do students a grave disservice.

As for defining "character," it is the affirmative side of discipline. Discipline is refraining from doing bad things; character is performing observable good actions. Discipline and character are inextricably related. It is impossible for a pervasive social system focused solely on repression to persist or be effective. Thus, good discipline policies must simultaneously be concerned with encouraging students to engage in affirmatively good actions—"prosocial conduct," observable acts or words of immediate, self-evident help to others. Such acts (plus observing discipline) constitute good character.

GENERAL PRINCIPLES RELATING TO PUPIL DISCIPLINE AND CHARACTER DEVELOPMENT

Pupil discipline and good (or bad) character are learned patterns. Like other forms of learning, they are affected by an enormous number of variables. These variables can be initially divided into two basic sets of factors: macro and micro.

Macro factors are developments which have pervasive effects on youth environments throughout the whole country, or some other large area. They encompass direct forms of intervention—such as laws—or more indirect patterns—such as broad shifts in public values. Some examples include applicable court decisions; popular norms about youth/adult relations; technological forces, such as the media; and many other elements. Such factors, in diverse, sometimes subtle ways, shape youth and adult conduct in different environments. Micro factors are the variables peculiar to a particular school, classroom, or even individual pupils: the innate (or genetic) disposition of specific learners; the pupils' home backgrounds; the local social and ethnic environment; the mix of other pupils surrounding the learners; the age levels of pupils; and the forms of organization of particular schools and classrooms.

Macro factors affecting pupil discipline and character development are usually beyond the control of particular schools or teachers, but all is not lost. Children and adolescents have a natural bent to respond positively to purposeful and well-conceived directions from adults who regularly exercise authority over them. And so educators still have powerful resources at their command—if they use them wisely.

One such micro factor under educator control is the subject matter of each particular lesson. Pupils are disposed to become engaged with their subject matter and work at learning, if it is properly presented. If such engagement occurs, discipline problems will diminish, since pupil energy is directed at wholesome ends. Furthermore, as we will see, many forms of subject matter lend themselves to helping pupil character development. Thus, subject matter can be mobilized to teach the subject per se, to lessen the temptations for pupils to practice indiscipline, and to stimulate the practice of good character.

Teachers, and other school adults who shape pupil conduct, must also identify and apply certain basic strategies—beyond the proper presentation of subject matter—to foster desirable pupil learning. In the area of discipline, they must clearly articulate what adults regard as good and bad discipline. This paper began with a general definition of 'discipline'. However, in an operating school, that definition must be subdivided into many components. The components will translate general principles into prohibitions relevant to the school situation. The prohibitions must be clear, related to the age level(s) of pupils, and aimed at the overt and covert discipline problems occurring in the classroom, school, and community.

Similar analysis and clarity are appropriate for pupil character development. Adults must identify the forms of affirmative good conduct they hope to see pupils practice in classrooms and the school, or while away from school but under school sponsorship, such as on field trips or in community service projects. Some of these forms can occur incidentally—saying "Please" or "Thank you." Others, like community service projects, can occur only after deliberate adult planning and decision making.

In conducting such acts of analysis and definition, the judicious use of pupil input can be useful—making allowance for the different age levels of pupils. However, this input should not be confused with the determination of basic principles. This must be an adult responsibility. Pupil input should be likened to (1) a suggestion box approach, where the class, school, or system can better advance its ends by considering a variety of insights, or (2) a learning exercise, where pupil good conduct is facilitated through increasing rule acceptance via pupil participation. But only adults can be blamed or fired for failing to maintain good discipline, or to develop pupil character. Therefore, the solicitation of pupil input should not be confused with the application of some form of primitive "democracy," where pupil opinion can be allowed to overrule adult judgment in significant matters.

The Collective Life of Pupils

One micro factor which warrants careful consideration is school policy about student assignment to classrooms. In particular, where do the school's class formation policies stand on a spectrum extending from traditional self-contained classrooms to highly fluid forms of departmentalization? (The succeeding discussion will not touch on another assignment issue—whether and when classes should be ability grouped. That issue is controversial, and cannot be given a balanced examination in the confines of this paper.)

Systems of pupil grouping are important because they determine whether and how pupils can form stable peer groups. In schools—to put the principle in a semisimplified fashion—such groups are either under wholesome adult direction, or prone to pursue antiinstitutional goals, such as drug use or delinquency. Or, sometimes, the school environment is so unstable that almost no forms of student groups centered around the school evolve. Presumably, such unrootedness is one of the precursors of the development of delinquent gangs away from and near the school.

Wise educators recognize the inevitability (and even desirability) of student groups, facilitate their formation, and direct their activities toward wholesome ends. Thus, the application of sound principles to the formation and management of pupil groups is a key element of directing pupil discipline. Incidentally, research has also shown that similar principles of group management can have beneficial effects in the area of cognitive learning (Slavin, 1980).

The range of class grouping or organization policies applied by schools varies considerably. The options range from one group of pupils with the same teacher for the whole day (or year), to different teachers for each subject area throughout the day, with the group of pupils before each teacher being reaggregated for each separate subject. Furthermore, there are intervening forms of adaptation, for example, continuing groups of pupils, with a succession of different teachers throughout the day. (And there is also the practical matter of ensuring that all "problem pupils" are not reflexively assigned to the same class.)

The form of adaptation applied, of course, partly depends on pupil age and school size. Still, there is often room for variations, depending on the vision of administrators. Individual teachers, beyond the effects of such schoolwide policies, also often have some room for discretion in forming students into groups in individual classes. One such group is the class as a whole. Classwide corporate expectations can be articulated, and classwide rewards and punishments provided for appropriate conduct and learning, for example, a special field trip, if the class attains a certain goal. Beyond the whole class, there are also the smaller, in-class groups (e.g., teams, rows, or other forms of groups). Such groups typically can be used for well-designed academic projects, class and community service activities, and other school-related purposes. Intergroup competitions can also be organized to encourage group strivings toward constructive ends. Such activities must be assisted by appropriately designed assignments and systems of reward and punishment.

There is a long line of American research about forms of pupil grouping in schools and the ways adult policies affect this process (Barker and Gump, 1964; Bronfenbrenner, 1970; Coleman, 1961; Klapp, 1969). Furthermore, many practicing educators are concerned with the comparative merits of approaches such as self-contained classrooms, homerooms, or divisions, houses, departmentalization, or extra-curricular groups. But too many contemporary education theorists and researchers have given inadequate attention to this important topic.

Courses for Developing Character

Sometimes it is proposed that teachers use didactic materials to teach discipline and character, for example, a course called "character education." The matter is complicated, and requires some analysis of general principles. To some observers, it will seem that such a didactic approach may be efficient. It saves class time and gets directly to the point. After all, there is a long tradition of using such materials—like the memorization of the Ten Commandments—to foster desirable learning ends.

Theoretically, we should assume that didactic materials can be useful. Unfortunately, theory and research also suggest that this judgment must be highly qualified. Schools which seem to have effectively applied such materials have usually integrated them into a total program, which has pervaded the school, and the school day. Thus, Allan Peshkin (1986) studied a contemporary Christian evangelical school. Student conduct in that school was subtantially different—and oftentimes better—than in the local public school. And the school placed heavy emphasis on character-oriented and didactic readings, discussions, and sermons. But such materials—which were a substantial element of the curriculum—were still only one portion of an environment pervaded with such principles. For example, all of the teachers were dedicated members of the sponsoring church, attended several prayer meetings a week, and worked for salaries several thousand dollars per year less than in the local public schools.

Furthermore, there is the matter of the design of such materials. Traditional religious didactic materials have been refined over hundreds and even thousands of years to attain certain institutional ends. For instance, almost all American Catholic schools formerly used the *Baltimore Catechism* as a tool for teaching pupils morals and character (1943). The questions and answers in the text reflect a considerable clarity and internal logic, which undoubtedly has persuasive effects. But basic doctrines in the *Catechism* were articulated in the Council of Trent, in 1563, and have been undergoing refinement through the intervening centuries. Undoubtedly, equivalent examples can be drawn from the Jewish tradition. It is no simple task for some contemporary author or publisher to produce some body of pro-virtue materials which (1) can win general adult acceptance, (2) clearly articulates a body of desirable values, (3) is appropriate for pupils, and (4) will regularly be used in a wholesome fashion by a comparatively diverse body of teachers in varied classroom situations (for some background, see Yulish, 1980).

The nub of the matter is that both research and theory—as well as the history of previous didactic learning practices—suggest that deliberately setting aside prescribed time for "character education" (or some like topic), can only, at best, be moderately effective (Wynne, 1985 and 1986). Indeed, such a measure might even be harmful by leading people to believe that an important constructive step has been taken. If some such set-aside exercise is adopted, the efficacy of the exercise will be strongly affected by (1) the care taken in designing the materials, (2) the cumulative length of time the materials are presented to particular students (e.g., fifteen minutes a day, every school day for eight years), (3) the quality of training in the materials provided teachers, (4) whether teachers using the materials basically sympathize with its premises, and (5) the integration of the material's values into the other components of the school's curriculum and general policies.

Still, one should concurrently recognize that there are even now some examples of apparently successful didactic materials commonly used in our schools. The traditional flag salute is one example, and that example reveals both the strength and weakness of didactic approaches. The contents of the salute are clearly defined. It is regularly reiterated in many classrooms. It is treated by many teachers and pupils as a matter of importance. And the patriotic elements of the salute are congruent with certain curriculum materials. As for problems confronting the salute, it is notorious that some courts have propounded principles undermining the vitality of the practice, many contemporary curriculum materials place little emphasis on patriotism (Vitz, 1986), and lastly, some education intellectuals (and high school teachers?) have mixed feelings about the propriety of regularly practicing or requiring the salute.

Other Principles

Role modeling is another principle affecting pupil discipline and character development. Such modeling involves adopting the conduct of older, or simply more prestigious pupils, and also pupils modeling the conduct of adults in school. The powerful influence of models has long been recognized— from Plato and the *Book of Wisdom* onward. However, we sometimes forget the stressful demands modeling situations place on the models. Because of this stress, too many youth-serving adults try to avoid the modeling responsibilities inherent in their work; such responsibilities require them to transform teaching into less of a job and more of a calling. A graduate pupil of mine reflected on her learning about modeling in the following moving terms:

> My attitudes about teacher responsibilities have changed over the years. This change came as a result of my becoming a teacher. Working on the inside, I have become more stringent in my expectations of myself and other teachers. In terms of appropriate conduct, before I didn't think it was necessary for teachers to set good examples. Now, that seems more important to me. Students really look to, rely on, and need teachers' guidance, examples, understanding, and help. We have to be cautious in how we deal with these extremely fragile people.

A system of rewards and sanctions must apply to students to enhance the norms of discipline and character. The system should comprise both informal and formal elements, and be appropriate to the pupils' age levels. Informal elements might include the traditional teacher's stare, encouraging words, smiles, and words of criticism or praise, or other incidental forms of approval or disapproval. At a more formal level, many acts of recognition and punishment— badges, pins, stars, detentions, informative report cards, corporal punishment, notes to home, mention in the school paper—are applied in different classrooms and schools to foster discipline and character, as well as academic learning. Research has demonstrated that many effective schools maintain elaborate systems of pupil recognition (Wynne, 1985).

Since we should be concerned with group reward and management, as well as with individual conduct, some of the rewards and punishments should apply to groups—teams, classrooms, or other units—as well as to individual pupils.

Passing reference should be made to the pop psychology proposition that we should not reward good conduct, since that may teach students that they should not do well unless an external reward is evident. This anti-reward proposition is belied by all research in behavioral psychology, as well as by reflective analysis of diverse learning environments. People always pursue the forms of learning which are rewarded. Sometimes the rewards are subtle and diffuse—smiles, pats on the back, or even the withholding of potential punishment. And on other occasions, the rewards are dramatic and blatant—Nobel prizes, the attainment of academic tenure, the right to some conspicuous symbol or title. And, sometimes, after thorough socialization, a person may learn how to "enjoy" some seemingly arduous activity without apparent external rewards. But all of these variations merely underline certain basic principles: learning, especially at its early stages (or where complex material is involved), is critically motivated by the provision of valuable external rewards; what things are valuable varies from one situation to another; scarcity is a common attribute of valuable resources; and systems which do not provide learners with valuable rewards will have low capabilities for teaching.

IMPLICATIONS FOR TEACHERS AND CLASSROOMS

Recommendations to teachers regarding discipline and character development must be implicitly related to the age levels of the pupils involved, and the form of school and classroom organization. Thus, it is not coincidental that, in Japanese elementary schools, each teacher remains with the same pupils over several years—and the excellence of the Japanese pupils' discipline as well as their academic learning is notorious. And so the following general principles must be adapted to particular operating situations.

Teachers should have clear personal visions of their own discipline and character standards. Are they concerned essentially with avoiding gross disorder in their classes, or do they apply broader and higher criteria of good conduct? Assume that a teacher—either personally, or in compliance with explicit school policies—accepts the definitions proposed earlier in this paper. Now, consider the problems of implementation.

First, there must be a well-organized and well-presented academic curriculum so that students are encouraged to be engaged in cognitive learning. Such engagement diminishes discipline problems.

Next, with reference to character, the typical standard curriculum has to be considered for its character development implications. Many areas of the curriculum lend themselves to such emphasis: history, social studies, reading, health education, and literature. These subjects invite teachers and pupils to consider, in a sympathetic light, character-relevant themes, such as loyalty, politeness, delayed gratification, law-abiding conduct, and gratitude. Teachers should highlight such themes in teaching, and select materials to facilitate this end.

Teachers also have many occasions to deal with pupils in areas beyond the formal curriculum. Teachers may monitor various extracurricular or sports activities, plan assembly presentations, oversee pupil fund-raising, conduct regular or occasional in-class ceremonies (daily flag salute, holiday celebrations), or supervise students in lunchrooms or halls. These activities have important implications for both discipline and character development. It should be recognized that some contemporary authorities recommend that teachers be allowed to divest themselves of many such nonteaching responsibilities, on the theory that such activity demeans the centrality of teaching. This matter should be directly considered.

Such divestment probably represents the general current trend. Thus, we have security guards, lunchroom attendants, and other noneducators working as monitors. It is understandable that teachers, during the school day, need some time to relax or to become engaged with colleagues. But the plea for relaxation is different from the plea that teachers should not perform monitoring functions. It is theoretically probable that the influence of teachers on pupils increases when teachers act before students in a variety of roles and display consistent patterns of conduct (with minor variations appropriate to the situation). Thus, teachers should strive to create such occasions and to manage them according to the principles underlying their basic discipline and character development policies, for example, clarity, consistency, the upholding of adult values, and a concern with maintaining wholesome group integrity.

Communicating Values

Teachers must communicate to pupils the discipline and character policies which apply in the school, in general, and in their classrooms in particular. Such principles must be explained to students and justified in a clear, polite, and firm fashion. Where appropriate, students can be invited to assist in this process of justification. However, as mentioned earlier, such involvement should not mask the fact that, ultimately, adults are responsible for defining the values which prevail in the school.

The policies may be posted in the classroom, and/or listed in instructions distributed to pupils (and with receipts signed by parents). In-class policies should be designed to be congruent with the more general principles applying throughout the whole school.

To communicate values by being good role models, teachers must deliberately examine their own pedagogical goals and conduct. This conduct can touch on such matters as dress, commitment to the work, forms of address and speech, patterns of collegial relations, fairness and politeness to pupils, firmness and good humor, and their preparation for each class. Teacher conduct in such matters communicates powerful messages to students about character and discipline. Indeed, many teachers can recall teachers in their own past whose exemplary conduct inspired them toward their current profession; contemporary teachers should conduct themselves so as to communicate equivalent messages to students.

Consequences for Student Behavior

Teachers must finally be concerned with the matter of consequences — rewards and sanctions — within the class for affecting pupil discipline and character. As with most other issues relating to discipline and character, this concern must be integrated with schoolwide (and system-wide) policies. These superordinate entities articulate certain systems of rewards and punishments which prevail throughout the whole school or system. But individual teachers are still required to adopt forms of consequences which complement the prevailing arrangements.

The basic principles governing positive and aversive reinforcers (punishments) are simple. They must be graduated. Many of them must be capable of speedy application: for example, you will not have recess today. They must generally be desired, or feared or disliked by pupils. They must be capable of application without making severe demands on teacher time or energy. They must be acceptable to the external adult community. In many instances, the application of such rewards and punishments should be supplemented with explanatory remarks, or even a counseling-type dialogue—perhaps in private. However, raw deterrence is one part of any effective system of discipline (van den Haag, 1975; Zabel, 1981, p. 200). Once some punishment has been clearly threatened, there should be no reluctance to administer it to guilty pupils. The key occasion for reflection is the warning— the design and announcement of potential consequences. If certain pupils have profound emotional problems, outside help for those pupils or their teacher may well be appropriate. However, in the great proportion of situations, the wholesome assumption is that pupils will properly respond to moderate, appropriate, forewarned punishment.

There is a body of literature which strongly deprecates the merits of what is traditionally called "punishment" as a means of shaping behavior (see, for example, Krumbholtz and Krumbholtz, 1972, p. 183; Skinner, 1971, p. 58). This literature points out that, after release from the punishment, or the threat of effective punishment, the suppressed undesirable conduct often revives. Furthermore, the literature contends that the act of punishment—whatever its form— provides pupils with poor models, that is, of persons engaging in hurting behavior. In general, these contentions are abstractly correct. However, they apply an unduly harsh test to measure the efficacy of punishment—as if there is any relatively simple and absolutely reliable system of changing undesirable human behavior. Actually, all such systems—whether or not they apply punishment—simply achieve varying degrees of efficacy; none of them are foolproof. Furthermore, much of this antipunishment literature is insensitive to normal class situations.

In passing, we should note that some authorities (e.g., Purkey, this volume), contend that "traditional" forms of discipline via "suppression" have never worked, since education history has been replete with complaints about student indiscipline. However, the most careful study documents that between about 1965 and 1975 pupil discipline actually changed for the worse: it did not stay at one point (Rubel, 1977). Furthermore, informed persons would largely agree that those particular years were an era of generally permissive values in education. None of this is to suggest that there is a simple one-to-one relationship between strictness and pupil good discipline; an enormous variety of factors undoubtedly affect levels of pupil discipline. But contending that "strictness has never worked" fails to recognize the multidimensionality of the challenge, and of the shifting definitions of "good discipline" which have evolved throughout

American history. Probably our definitions of discipline have been as mutable as our definitions of what constitutes an adequate education.

Another defect in the antipunishment literature is its insensitivity to normal classroom challenges. The literature focuses largely on acts of individual misbehavior; however, teachers almost never deal with isolated learners. Teachers are concerned with the effects of their conduct on (1) the particular disruptive child, and (2) the rest of the class or other group, which is usually watching. It is even possible that an act of punishment may, in some complex way, "fail" for a particular child, but deter the rest of the class from similar misconduct. Furthermore, the antipunishment literature attributes to teachers, or other adult managers, inordinate time and other scarce resources. In probably half the disorder situations confronting teachers, the basic need is to quickly suppress conduct that generates a variety of costs, such as stimulating other pupils to mimic the conduct, interfering with pupils' attention to learning, and taking the teacher's energy away from instruction. Thus, teachers necessarily have a much lower level of tolerance of misconduct than adults in experimental, transitory, one-to-one situations.

The preceding remarks make no reference to corporal punishment, and that matter probably warrants some explication. Although in most states the moderate use of corporal punishment by teachers is unquestionably lawful, some educators and many academics are critical of such practices (see, for example, American Psychological Association, 1975; Forness and Sinclair, 1984). However, a recent thorough study in schools (Gottfredson and Gottfredson, 1985), concluded that "clear, firm and fast discipline" was strongly related to good discipline in schools. Furthermore, in the study there was some correlation between such discipline and the practice of paddling students for serious rule violations. An interview with one of the study's authors disclosed that he did not believe the study definitively settled the pros and cons of the effects of paddling. But he did believe that the available research on the topic is so mottled that carefully designed studies on the efficacy of paddling compared with nonpaddling would be fully warranted (personal communication, 1988). In other words, the merits of corporal punishment are still an open issue.

Such open-mindedness about corporal punishment will not necessarily lead to dramatic changes in many peoples' opinions. Furthermore, corporal punishment—like every other form of human control over other persons—is capable of abuse. However, it is also important to recognize that corporal punishment contains many of the elements of an effective deterrent: it is generally disliked by pupils; it is easy to apply; it does not absorb much teacher energy; and so on. Perhaps those who oppose corporal punishment should accept the responsibility of designing equivalently effective alternatives—and recognize that maintaining an effective in-school detention system in a small-size elementary school, where a teacher must (and probably should) be retained as a monitor, can cost at least $30,000 a year— the average one-year salary of a Chicago public school teacher.

It is true that there is a considerable body of research which is often cited to show that corporal punishment doesn't work (American Psychological Association, 1975). But such research is afflicted by the defects just noted. Thus, the research typically focuses on the pupils who receive corporal punishment, or compares those pupils to certain other pupils who were punished by other means, or who just received counseling. There are innumerable limitations to such research:

1. It is extremely difficult to compare discipline patterns between schools which license corporal punishment and schools which prohibit it. The very fact that a school uses—or prohibits the use of—corporal punishment is probably related to many other variables which affect its total discipline level; for example, the anticorporal punishment school may be in a more stable, middle-class community.

2. The research rarely examines the total discipline levels of the compared schools (an extremely difficult fact to measure), but usually just compares the effects of different treatment on specific pupils. But one of the main virtues of any vital punishment is its effect on the *overall* environment.

3. Counseling, and other forms of noncorporal punishment, take staff time and resources. The research rarely considers the cost-effectiveness of different approaches.

DISCIPLINE AND VALUES

Many of the measures just proposed are affected by matters of opinion, interest group positions, and profound philosophical divergences. For example, one common traditional means of transmitting good character to young people—in America and elsewhere—was through the identification of divine sanctions and punishments. Thus, George Washington, in his farewell address, made some remarks he thought self-evident:

Of all the dispositions and habits, which lead to political prosperity, religion and morality are indispensable supports. . . . The mere politician, equally with the pious man, ought to respect and to cherish them. A volume could not trace all their connections with private and public felicity. Let it simply be asked, where is the security for property, for reputation, for life, if the sense of religious obligation desert the oaths, which are the instruments of investigation in courts of justice? And let us with caution indulge the supposition that morality can be maintained without religion. Whatever may be conceded to the influence of refined education on minds of peculiar structure, reason and experience both forbid us to expect, that national morality can prevail in exclusion of religious principles.

Some people have raised questions about Washington's actual level of religiosity. But, regardless of that level, like most prominent citizens of his era, he strongly believed that formal religion was an important resource in character formation. The "active" secularists, in fact, formed only a minute fraction of the Founders.

Washington's magisterial statement is largely supported by the findings of current research. Thus, a 1982 national survey of a sample of American high school seniors disclosed that 37.3 percent of the respondents reported they attended church once a week or more, and 49.5 percent of these attenders reported they have "never used" illegal drugs. The comparable figures for the "never" attenders were 9.6 percent and 8 percent. Another question asked respondents about the importance of religion in their lives. Here, 28 percent said "very important," and 39 percent of these were nonusers of illegal drugs. The comparable figures for the "not important" responders were 10.7 percent and 8.5 percent (Bachman, Johnston and O'Malley, 1984, p. 18).

Interestingly enough, despite such data, American policy has progressively moved toward heightening the distance between religion and education. Thus, in 1962, a Supreme Court decision *(Engel v. Vitale)* finally precluded prayer in public schools. At a later date (1980), this line of separation was extended to prohibit the display of the Ten Commandments in public schools as an exhortatory device *(Stone v. Graham)*. Without commenting on the legal correctness of these interpretations, one can still recognize one technical effect of the decisions: they have diminished the pool of inhibitors provided to public school educators. After all, traditional acceptance is one of the most profound arguments humans have offered on behalf of social norms. But, for many purposes, those traditions are embodied in explicitly religious references, "Thou shalt not. . . ."

I know that more than one educator has displayed a poster in his class or office mentioning that God did not offer "Ten Suggestions." In other words, they used the precedent of the Commandments, and their peremptory tone, to justify certain basic school perspectives. But such a precedent is valueless if students do not know what the Commandments are, or are not urged to revere them.

Again, apropos of diverging values, reference has already been made to the apparent efficacy of corporal punishment as a form of deterrence. Yet, despite this data, one should not expect many prominent educators to take a clear stand on behalf of this practice.

Probably the most powerful force eroding the quality of pupil discipline and character in contemporary American public schools is the ambivalence many adults have about matters such as: the role of religion in public life; the application of relatively stern and effective punishment; the legitimacy of punishment systems which, in operation, produce disproportionate levels of punishment of certain groups of pupils; the rightness of holding young people to relatively traditional standards of conduct; and the feasibility of requiring teachers to act as fully admirable role models, with the heavy responsibilities such modeling entails. (See Holmes, 1984, for a broad critique of these trends.)

Readers should not assume that the many controversies subsumed by these phrases will be speedily resolved via discussion, or the discovery of definitive pieces of ingenious evidence. Indeed, it is likely that efforts to collect relevant evidence will be severely handicapped and that the evidence itself may well be ignored. To be explicit, several years ago I was one of a panel of advisors to a national survey of public opinion on schools. A question was proposed about public preferences among different discipline techniques. I suggested that the list of the ten possible alternatives be revised to include corporal punishment. My suggestion was disregarded. And so we do not "know" the public's opinion on this widely applied technique of apparent efficacy. My guess is that the pollsters were reluctant to ask, just because they thought the public might register approval. And so the pursuit of truth goes on.

PARENTS AND PUPIL DISCIPLINE

Much of the foregoing discussion has obvious implications for the role of parents. Still, some direct remarks may be helpful.

Whenever possible, schools should rest their authority on parent consensus and assent. Such support can greatly increase the vitality of school discipline and character development. Pursuit of such assent can be assisted by well-articulated definitions, typically developed in consultation with parents, or at least with a careful sensitivity to parent values. Parents should be informed of school and classroom policies in writing, and their assent explicitly solicited (via some form of signed acknowledgement or agreement). This recommendation does not imply that all parents will agree with such definitions, although support will oftentimes be quite high. However, the process of consensus development can provide a powerful base if and when confrontation arises between the school and one or more dissenting (or "irresponsible") parents. Furthermore, it is often easier to win parent support for written discipline principles during the "quiet times," such as the beginning of the school year, than when rules are being directly enforced against some parent's unruly child. Thus, definition, good draftsmanship, fence mending, and dedication to parent-school communication can both avoid parent-school controversies, and moderate those which eventually do occur.

Another element of parent-school relations is the matter of school of choice. In such situations, considerable thought must enter into the development of relatively unusual (for public schools) goals which are morally justifiable and attractive to an appropriate group of parents. And here the input of parents can obviously be helpful in planning.

Something must also be said about the element of parent-school confrontation. Whether contemporary parents, as a group, are more irresponsible than their predecessors is difficult to determine; however, it is evident that many educators face problems related to parental disengagement from wholesome school concerns. One example is the difficulty involved in maintaining school-parent communication between educators and two working parents or single parent families. Of course, educators should display some sympathy for the stress facing such families. However, there is simultaneously a need for schools to sometimes press to hold parents to basic responsibilities.

A story told by one of my teacher interviewees nicely illustrates this principle. The interviewee was assigned to an elementary grade. She regularly gave her pupils significant homework. On the second day of school, as could be predicted, a good proportion of her class came in minus homework. The teacher had arranged (in advance) with the office to have her class temporarily covered. Then, she went down to the office phone, accompanied by four or five of her erring pupils. She phoned each child's parent(s) in succession. If there wasn't a parent home, she tried their work numbers. She reached most of the parents—often at work—on the first day the tactic was applied. She politely introduced herself over the phone, said she was sure the parent wanted to cooperate with the school in ensuring his or her child's homework completion, and so forth. Almost all of the parents, after a little grumbling, ended by thanking her for the call. Many of them, especially those called on the job, were probably quite upset at their children. Even the children whose parents were not reached in the first calls were properly intimidated. For the rest of the semester, homework completion rates were high. One might say that parent-school cooperation was a strong point with this teacher. But she realized she had to display initiative—and a little determination.

ATTAINING CONSENSUS

Consensus, both in the school and with its immediate external community, is important in developing pupil discipline and good character. If it cannot be attained at a macro level, then it must be pursued by more discrete groups. And many efforts in this direction are now under way. A number of public school systems have developed various patterns of parent (and pupil) choice. Such choice can permit parents to enroll children in certain schools (or even subschools or houses) which deliberately maintain clear, coherent systems for pupil discipline and character development. These focused entities can also establish more relevant criteria for the hiring and supervision of faculty.

A variety of forms of voucher (and tax forgiveness) systems have also been proposed to advance equivalent ends. The financing of such systems can be facilitated at the national, state, or local level. These systems all assume that parents will be provided with some fiscal empowerment to make education choices, just as they choose their child's doctor, summer camp, or other service. Presumably, the philosophical tone of the school will be an important component underlying that choice.

Some readers familiar with such proposals are distressed at the idea that our precious "common" schools are becoming less common. There is no doubt that this is one meaning of such proposals. It is not that most proponents of choice are inherently hostile to racial or socioeconomic integration. However, the proponents basically resist the idea that fostering racial or social integration is the critical criterion for evaluating a school's philosophy. Many proponents of choice prefer philosophic coherence compared with simply collecting a group of parents and pupils with disparate values under one common roof.

But the root cause for the current tendencies toward disintegration in many schools is not largely the drives of "parochial" parents. Instead, it is the failure of many ideologues to apply commonsense traditional criteria to the design of youth environments. Too many adults have become dedicated to fostering, or tolerating, an extraordinarily high degree of so-called pluralism in society. The inevitable concomitants of such pluralism are equivalent demands that individual schools tolerate similar diversity. Actually, there is a certain hypocrisy to many such pluralism pleas. In practice, "pluralism" in education is defined to clearly exclude explicit sympathy with religion—although high proportions of parents and pupils avow religious beliefs, and religious practices are important elements of the everyday life of many people.

IMPLICATIONS FOR SCHOOL MANAGEMENT AND HIGHER POLICY LEVELS

The formulation and publication of appropriate definitions of good discipline and character are important responsibilities of school managers. Conflicting opinions about such definitions persist in many areas of society—especially among too many education administrators. Given such ambivalence, teachers often feel uncertain and unsupported. Thus, principals and higher-level educators can provide teachers with important help by taking appropriate definitional measures, such as by publishing well-written documents and making clear statements on public occasions such as pupil assemblies (Schrag, 1979).

Pupil discipline and character are more than the prevalence of apparent tranquility in school. Thus, administrators must maintain in-school feedback systems which are probing enough to reveal what is going on. Undoubtedly, this is why the effective schools research has put so much emphasis on the matter of principal "visibility"—for, by being visible, a principal concurrently makes sure he or she is receiving a variety of forms of information about pupil conduct (Wellish, 1978). But, in addition to visibility, there are other complementary feedback systems which can be applied: receiving prompt and accurate information about reported discipline incidents and pupil cuts, tardies, and unauthorized absences; maintaining systems to monitor exams to detect and deter cheating; conducting anonymous, periodic surveys of pupils to estimate levels of pupil alcohol and drug abuse; and making ample informal and discreet contacts with representative pupils and parents to provide alternative sources of information.

Apropos of pupil character formation, enumeration systems can be designed and maintained to count and monitor levels of appropriate activities. Numbers of students engaged in extrarcurricular activities can be counted (just as we calculate class attendance), and group advisors can provide periodic written reports of the activities involved. Award systems, established to stimulate such activities, can also provide useful monitoring information; the data collected to justify awards can help measure the quantity and quality of activities involved.

Educational administrators, at all levels, can play an important part in the shaping of class subject matter (Hallinger and Murphy, 1985). They determine textbook buying policies. They articulate minimum requirements for lesson plans and monitor the plans applied by teachers. They establish systems to provide teachers with in-service training and to encourage collegial consultation about instructional matters. Because of such varied responsibilities, administrators play a critical role in structuring the curriculum to foster discipline and improve pupil character.

In every school, there is obviously considerable potential for overlap and confusion among the many different educators concerned with pupil discipline and character development. Some teachers may go too far and adopt an extremely intrusive role, whereas others may mistakenly say the whole matter is the responsibility of the family, the church, or possibly the guidance counselor. The traditional and proper answer to such uncertainty is that *all* adults in contact with the young have a shared responsibility for positively affecting discipline and character. But the degree and form of this responsibility vary according to many particulars. Administrators must emphasize this basic responsibility and clarify its application to school staff members. For instance, it may be necessary to adopt a schoolwide definition of cheating. Then, pupils are confronted with a consistent anticheating policy in all classes, and teachers know what norm to enforce. However, at the same time, it may be appropriate to ask each teacher to determine the sanctions against pupils who fail to complete homework on time. Still, unless different responsibilities are clearly allocated, both teachers and pupils will become resentful.

Teachers who act as role models for pupils subject themselves to strenuous demands. Such demands must be iterated and rewarded by administrators with consistency; otherwise some teachers will act appropriately while others may unfortunately drag their feet

(Rossman, Corbett, and Firestone, 1985). Thus, administrators must clearly specify what being a "good role model" consists of: avoiding clock-watching, always being prepared for classes, dressing professionally, treating colleagues respectfully, and so on. Teacher applicants must be informed of such expectations, and hired and evaluated (before receiving tenure) on the basis of their acceptance of such requirements (Bridges, 1986). And tenured teachers must maintain those standards. Finally, administrators themselves must concurrently display, to teachers and pupils, the same patterns of modeling they require of teachers.

Administrators as well as teachers have authority to affect the patterns of pupil grouping applied throughout whole schools or school systems. There can be greater or lesser subject specialization among teachers. Individual teachers can be assigned to work with persisting groups of pupils for longer or shorter periods of time per day, or over longer calendar periods, for example, two or three years compared with one semester. Pupils can be formed into groups which persist for diverse periods of time, for example, over a number of years. Administrators, and school boards, can also determine whether to break up students' progression through twelve years of school into a K-8 and 9-12 division, or into three or more stages, via junior high or other means. The three-stage division obviously makes for far less continuous pupil-pupil and pupil-teacher contact, and has implications for discipline and character.

In departmentalized schools, so-called homerooms or divisions can be formed. This can allow for some teacher-pupil continuity. Alternatively, "houses" or other subdivisions may be formed in schools to create groups somewhat smaller and more coherent than the entire school. Or vigorous extracurricular programs may be designed and maintained which enlist all, or almost all, students into vital, persisting, and closely adult-monitored groups. Teachers who act as advisors for such groups oftentimes need support and counsel about the policies which should guide the groups. And so these adults must be provided with directions and monitoring.

CONCLUSIONS

Some of the proposals and tacit criticisms that have just been recited are ambitious; others, to a degree, confront elements of the prevailing academic and intellectual zeitgeist. But readers with sympathy for some of the measures proposed still have grounds for encouragement.

There has been a persisting body of public dissatisfaction with the discipline and character environment surrounding American youths. And there is a substantial body of data showing that such dissatisfaction is warranted (Wynne and Hess, 1986). Furthermore, other research indicates that many contemporary public schools, in a variety of ways, still strongly adhere to many traditional values (Wynne, 1986). Thus, we have elements of public dissatisfaction and support plus actual educator "good practice." Given this medley, it is not unreasonable to conclude that the values and practices I have identified will persist and will have a growing influence on American public education. Reality can only be kept out for so long—and then it thrusts itself back into our lives and institutions.

PART III
School-Community Strategies

INTRODUCTION:
School-Community Strategies Section

This third section on school-community relationships and strategies encompasses a wide variety of topics. The first two have become areas of great concern in recent years: the influence of the courts on school policies and procedures, and school relationships with local police agencies. Many have argued that court decisions on discipline-related cases, particularly in the 1970s, have undermined the authority and ability of teachers and administrators to preserve order in schools. The 1960s and 1970s were also a period of growing cooperation between schools and the police, in part because of unrest from the period of extensive school desegregation and youth protests of the Vietnam War.

The first chapter, by Henry Lufler, examines the link between court decisions and changes in school discipline practices, especially the question of whether school personnel enforce discipline rules less than before for fear of lawsuits. He reviews key court decisions, the scant body of research on their effects, including educators' knowledge of school law, and the role of legal and educational commentators on court decisions. The paper notes that key decisions did not open a floodgate of litigation, and argues that changes in the behavior of school personnel come more from the impact of commentaries than from the court decisions themselves. Lufler proposes various studies to increase our knowledge in this area, and suggests ways that current research findings can be used to enhance the legal education of school personnel.

At the conference where these papers were first presented, Lufler's statements drew extended comments from prepared reactors. James Rapp (1986) pointed out that misinformation is commonplace, but that ill-placed fear of litigation is not the only plausible factor restraining school administrators. Fear of personal harm and professional reprisal, minimizing discipline problems to avoid appearing incompetent, and misgivings about forms of discipline like expulsion or corporal punishment may also limit administrators' actions. Rapp also called for research on the discipline of handicapped students because federal law (the Education for All Handicapped Children Act) imposes uniform national standards for their treatment. They are sometimes treated more leniently than nonhandicapped students (Simon, 1984).

The second reactor, Ivan Gluckman (1986), cited a legal memorandum from the National Association of Secondary School Principals (NASSP) advising its members that the Supreme Court did not intend to hamper the administrator's ability to maintain order in schools. The NASSP has also provided group professional liability insurance automatically to its members since the late 1960s in another move designed to strengthen the resolve of school administrators, in contrast to legal commentary from other sources advising extreme caution in disciplinary actions.

In the next chapter, on school-police cooperation, Robert Rubel examines strategies aimed at prevention, the response to chronic problems, and control of acute student misbehavior and crime. National programs sponsored by the U.S. Departments of Education and Justice are reviewed, followed by local police agency and school system projects. These include a school team approach, incident profiling, classroom education, police liaisons, school security procedures, and alternative education programs. Noting that little research has been done on the programs reviewed, Rubel calls for more research on promising programs and on working relations between school administrators and police officials. He suggests that a school team approach to planning and problem solving, coupled with a police-developed method of collecting and analyzing offense data, offers a model with broad applicability to serious school discipline and crime problems.

This school team approach has been tested in forty-four schools in Anaheim, California; Jacksonville, Florida; and Rockford, Illinois in a multiyear joint demonstration project of the U.S. Departments of Justice and Education. Key activities at the school level included analysis of the problem, organizing an action team, selecting and implementing appropriate intervention strategies, and monitoring the activities and results. A similar program is now under way in other cities, and a handbook has been produced describing the strategy (Rubel and Ames, 1986). The chapter by Sang in this section includes information on a Jacksonville computerized system to track discipline code infractions developed in conjunction with this project.

The final three chapters are on model programs: university-based training of school teams, a community service proposal, and descriptions of various innovative programs one school system has created to handle different kinds of discipline problems. The first paper describes a program to train various members of the school community. The Texas Classroom Management and Discipline Program began in 1983 to train school teams throughout the state. Margaret Dunn, the director, describes the training, technical assistance, publications, and conferences of the program. Participants learn how to build team solidarity, develop school-community relationships, select disciplinary techniques, and develop action plans. Those requesting technical assistance frequently ask for help to counteract school crime and substance abuse, to establish alternative education programs, and to help at-risk students. Most teams implement their action plans, sometimes in several locations. Specific team activities in various school districts are discussed.

This Texas program was modeled on the long-standing Alcohol and Drug Abuse Education Program (ADAEP) of the U.S. Department of Education. Since 1972, the ADAEP has trained over five thousand school-community teams across the country out of regional training centers. Teams composed usually of a school administrator, teachers, counselors, and other members of the school community spend a week or more at the centers learning to work together, and then receive ongoing technical assistance to implement their action plans (U.S. Department of Education, 1986). The efficacy of this approach for dealing with school crime and disruptive behavior has been tested in a three-year study of over two hundred teams. Students and teachers reported any personal victimization and fear of crime, classroom disruptions, and school safety concerns. The evaluators concluded that effective teams can reduce school crime, and the longer a team works effectively the greater the reduction (Grant and Capell, 1983). Thus the Texas program is building on a strong foundation of research and practice.

In Jacksonville, Florida, the Duval County public school system has instituted a student code of conduct with three classes of offenses, and a sophisticated system to record and act on infractions. Herb Sang, the former district superintendent, describes these and sixteen different programs designed to redirect behavior rather than to remove students from the system. These programs represent prevention, intervention, and discipline strategies in both elementary and secondary schools. They emphasize guidance and counseling, even in unlikely areas such as helping students handle grief, and developing interpersonal skills especially important for adolescents.

This chapter nicely describes the progressively more serious offenses and consequences in the Jacksonville code of conduct, and how the code is presented to the student body. Thirty-one states require their school districts to develop and distribute discipline codes to students (Jann and Hyman, 1988), and a handbook has even been published to help schools construct such codes (Foster, 1980). Conduct codes typically include school rules, consequences for disobedience, the school's discipline philosophy, and general disciplinary procedures, and are publicized widely (Duke, 1986). In view of all this activity, it is surprising how little study there has been on the development and disciplinary consequences of codes of conduct. Sang mentions a test of how well students comprehend the Jacksonville policies, and other school systems may also test for comprehension. But effects of codes on student behavior, though difficult to determine, are more important, and they deserve more attention.

In the final chapter, Jackson Toby and Adam Scrupski lay out a new strategy, coerced community service, for handling serious school offenders. Reviewing practice and research on suspension and alternative schools, they note that suspension has fallen into disrepute, and that in-school suspension is often meted out for lesser rule infractions. Toby and Scrupski outline the nature of coerced community service, and how it would be supervised. They weigh its benefits, whether it would be chosen by offending students, and whether it would prove practical for school systems. As with many of the others, this paper also contains research suggestions: ideas for testing aspects of coerced community service.

These chapters on school-community strategies span many areas. They cover various aspects of the school's environment and linkages with community agencies. They range from preventive measures with young children to the treatment of serious offenders. They contain more description of programs and practices than the other sections, but research is also summoned where it is available. As seen before, no one best strategy emerges for a given situation. But many components presented can be selected, shaped, and tested to create strategies most appropriate to local circumstances.

9

Courts and School Discipline Policies

Henry S. Lufler, Jr.

This paper examines what we know about the link between court decisions and changing school discipline practices.[1] Little research has directly addressed this question, though the preponderance of academic commentary, as distinct from research findings, suggests that school personnel enforce discipline rules less than they did in earlier times, in part because of the threat that someone will file suit. Because of the lack of research looking at this important question, the paper also proposes a variety of studies to supplement our knowledge in this area. The paper's final section contains suggestions on ways that existing research findings can be used to improve the ongoing legal education of school personnel.

At the outset, the paper reviews the literature, mostly from the field of political science, that has looked at the impact of education decisions. This literature yields a variety of testable hypotheses useful to contemporary impact researchers and to those debating the appropriate role of courts.

TRADITIONAL IMPACT STUDIES

Research projects studying the impact of U.S. Supreme Court education decisions were conducted in the 1960s. Made possible by substantial grants, these studies had a methodological complexity not seen in the last ten years. This research offers evidence that the key to changed behavior lies not so much in what court decisions have said as in how they have been interpreted by school personnel.

Local interpretations are derived from legal and education commentators who filter information from courts to education practitioners. To the extent that these intermediaries are overly pessimistic about future court intervention in education, it can be argued that these commentators have caused school personnel to become overly cautious when dealing with discipline and other issues. This paper, then, will suggest that the contention by some educators that courts have too much to do with schools is, in part, a self-imposed phenomenon.

In today's discussions about the impact of courts on discipline or other education issues, little reference is made to early judicial impact studies conducted by political scientists and sociologists. Most earlier studies focused on the impact of Supreme Court decisions concerning three topics, two involving education: school prayer and school desegregation. The third area focused on the rights of criminal defendants, such as the impact of *Miranda v. Arizona*[2] on the behavior of police and prosecutors.

This impact research began with the simple, testable proposition that Supreme Court decisions in these controversial areas might be ignored or evaded. As is often the case with new lines of research, research questions became much more complicated when social scientists discovered that there were shades of compliance or noncompliance and that many individuals whose behavior was expected to change, such as police officers or principals, had no idea what the Supreme Court actually had said about the matter at hand.

Early impact research (Wasby, 1970; Becker and Feeley, 1973) determined that numerous variables, such as the nature of the decision and the parties at whom it was directed, affected short-term compliance. It was also learned (Dolbeare, 1967; Barth, 1968) that educators had an incomplete understanding of what was required by the school prayer[3] and other Supreme Court education decisions of the 1960s. Compliance with decisions, especially in the short run, was found to depend in large measure on the activities of third-party groups, such as civil liberties associations, which worked to see that distant court decisions were complied with locally (Scheingold, 1974). Such groups also played a key role in transmitting information about the content of decisions, since few individuals read Supreme Court decisions and fewer still presume to understand their local impact. It was in the 1960s, then, that the role of intermediaries in shaping local responses was first studied.

Researchers found that some administrators who understood the content of decisions decided to avoid changing their behavior until told to do so by school boards or until threatened with lawsuits. Others, however, moved to comply with instructions to end school prayer or Bible readings shortly after a Supreme Court ruling. Resistance to or acceptance of the early prayer decisions was found to be related to geographic region. Dolbeare and Hammond (1971), for example, surveyed elementary school teachers and found that, before 1962, 87 percent of the teachers in the South and 93 percent of the teachers in the East had morning prayers. Two years after the prayer decision, the figure had fallen to 11 percent in the East but only to 64 percent in the South (Dolbeare and Hammond, 1971, p. 32). Resistance or compliance also was found to be related to the actions taken in neighboring school districts and to an individual administrator's respect for the Court as an institution. Researchers hypothesized that resistance to Supreme Court prayer decisions in the South was related to a lower level of respect for the Court and to a pattern of resistance seen in desegregation cases.

Two key variables were found to be helpful in predicting local response to the school prayer decisions—the personal attitudes of school administrators and the role of community elites in deciding how to respond. Frank Sorauf (1976), after studying all 67 cases involving church-state separation decided between 1951 and 1971 in federal and state high courts, found that personal attitudes were the key factor in determining compliance once a school district lost a court decision. Community elites, such as school board members, also played a significant part in determining whether their school district would comply in places when it was not a direct party to the litigation (Rodgers and Bullock, 1976).

The early impact studies, taken as a group, led to a number of findings useful in today's debate on the role of the courts in reviewing discipline or other educational practices. Some of these conclusions, which could be hypotheses for further study, are the following:

1. Decisions requiring changed behavior in large bureaucracies, such as school systems or police departments, require active support from administrators if compliance is to occur.

2. Compliance is easiest to obtain if changed behavior is required of only a few actors in a bureaucracy.

3. State and local school boards and community political elites help determine which court rulings will be followed.

4. Local compliance to a Supreme Court ruling is more likely to occur if a local group demands its implementation.

5. Intermediary organizations, such as national teacher unions, associations of school boards, administrators, and legal groups, transmit the content of court decisions.

6. Information about court decisions often is garbled and misinterpreted when it is absorbed at the local level, especially when the message is received by those not having a direct responsibility to comply.

7. The behavior of individuals in large, bureaucratic organizations may change as the result of misperceptions of legal requirements.

8. Positive attitudes about the Supreme Court, or courts in general, increase the likelihood of individual compliance, whereas negative attitudes more likely result in resistance (Muir, 1967).

9. Individuals are more likely to comply with decisions with which they agree.

10. Administrators in large organizations may use the court decisions as the justification for establishing new policies or procedures actually unrelated to the decision (Cuban, 1975).

11. Social groups may use a court decision in one area to push for changes in other unrelated areas (e.g., the generally unsuccessful attempt to link desegregation and the suspension of minority students) (Bennett, 1979).

Compared with recent education research on the law that has focused on legal knowledge, employing true-false quizzes about the content of court rulings, or mail surveys about perceived court impact, these early impact studies had a methodological richness that far surpasses current efforts. They also were more substantially funded, making it possible to conduct surveys combined with on-site data acquisition and observations. There was a former willingness, as well, to gather data through in-depth case studies in a single location.

It is important to note that more recent research on courts and schools has addressed a larger question untouched in earlier studies—the cumulative impact of all education cases. A key issue today is the increased control of school operations by administrative rules and legal decisions generally, rather than the impact of single cases.

THE CONTENT OF CONTEMPORARY EDUCATION DECISIONS

Early impact research employed relatively simple measures of compliance, such as whether defendants were read their rights or whether schools began the day with a prayer. Today, however, we are interested in studying the impact of more complex decisions, or the effect of groups of decisions within unsettled areas of the law. Contemporary cases involving religion in the public schools illustrate this point. Early research asked whether or not schools still had Bible readings or prayers. Today's cases involving religion in schools focus on such issues as holiday observances, after-school prayer groups, or invocations before ceremonies. Case law in these areas is still unsettled, with conflicting decisions as yet unaddressed by the Supreme Court. Lower court decisions in these cases, however, still have both a direct and indirect effect on school policies.

Assessment of compliance or the impact of decisions is made more complicated by such decisions as *Tinker v. Des Moines*,[4] *Wood v. Strickland*,[5] or *Goss v. Lopez*.[6] Although *Tinker* applies to a constitutional right of free expression, the nondisruptive wearing of a protest armband, it is impossible to survey principals with regard to compliance. *Tinker*, after all, is more than a case about armbands; it establishes the principle that students do not "shed their constitutional rights at the schoolhouse door." There is a great distance, however, between saying that students have a limited right to free expression in school and determining what the boundaries of that right might be. It therefore is no surprise that one legal commentator (Flygare, 1986, p. 165) referred to *Tinker* as marking "the emergence of school law as a discipline." Legions of school lawyers and academic professionals have made careers out of advising schools on a reasonable interpretation of cases like *Tinker*, and in following and reporting on lower court decisions as judges wrestled with the same question.

Wood v. Strickland held that school officials may be liable for denying students their constitutional rights, but does not and could not elaborate what those rights might be or what would constitute a "denial." The case was made even more difficult by the conclusion that school officials would be liable for damages for the denial of constitutional rights, even if they "should have known" those rights but did not. It is helpful to remember that the earlier studies on impact found that compliance was most likely if a court directive spoke clearly about intended behavior.

Goss v. Lopez found that students had property and reputational rights that must be protected in even a short suspension from school. Therefore, the Supreme Court required schools to conduct a brief "hearing" before a suspension. The Court reasoned that students would be less likely to be suspended erroneously if principals gave the student a chance to learn why the suspension was occurring and to tell his or her side of the story. As will be detailed below, calling this brief exchange between the principal and student a "hearing" caused numerous educators to wonder how much due process might be extended to students in other school-student exchanges.

A number of important Supreme Court education decisions in the 1970s, then, created constitutional rights without offering clear signals as to how those rights might be defined or where the Supreme Court was leading. This opens up a question only touched on in contemporary research. "Legal uncertainty," and its impact on school operations, remains a fruitful topic. One study, for example, found that teachers felt they engaged in less discipline of students than they used to because they thought that courts had gone further in advancing student rights than was actually the case (Lufler, 1979). In case law areas where decisions conflict or the law is unsettled, the role of school law "experts" in offering interpretations became more important.

THE ROLE OF COMMENTATORS
AND LOCAL RESPONSES

Following *Tinker, Wood,* and *Goss,* there was no shortage of predictions by commentators discussing where court decisions might lead, or decrying the unhappy state of affairs that necessitated the speculation in the first place. This created what now should be seen as a new impact research question, the effect of legal commentators on the behavior of school personnel. Commentators not only wrote about a particular decision but, using crystal balls of varying clarity, also predicted future decisions based on the case they described.

The cases that commentators discussed were directed at school administrators, requiring, for example, that principals give students a pre-suspension hearing. In addition, it was found (Hollingsworth, Lufler, and Clune, 1984) that commentaries had an impact on the way teachers behaved, even though teacher behavior was not the subject of the court decisions. This phenomenon created a new level of impact analysis, the study of the secondary or unintended consequences of court decisions. It is important to remember, then, that there is a difference between studies of *compliance* with education court decisions, generally focusing on administrators, and studies of the *impact* or *aftermath* of decisions, which is a much broader question.

Writers in legal publications also used cases like *Goss* to debate larger issues, such as the appropriate role of the judiciary in hearing public school cases. Some argued, for example, that *Goss* was an unnecessary intrusion into the operation of educational institutions (Wilkinson, 1976). In a similar vein, courts were seen as an ineffective vehicle for bringing about social change in large-scale social organizations, such as schools (Horowitz, 1977). It was even suggested (Graham, 1970) that courts had a finite degree of public acceptance and that the ability of courts to bring about social change was limited. Under this theory, courts have political capital that must be expended carefully. Finally, some wrote about what future cases might look like if the decisions in Goss or other cases were extended to other school practices (Kirp, 1976; Yudof, 1979; Hazard, 1976).

Educators writing in publications distributed to administrators and teachers also wrote about these decisions (Nolte, 1975a; 1975b; Brothers, 1975)). They generally adopted the philosophical perspective that courts had gone too far in regulating the in-school behavior of education professionals. They also argued that courts were likely to go further.

Although many commentators had predicted that *Goss* and similar cases would open a floodgate of litigation leading to a further intrusion into school administration, this did not, in fact, occur. A number of post-*Goss* cases involving due process were heard by lower courts, but these generally resulted in rulings favoring no expansion of hearing rights (Lufler, 1982). In addition, the Supreme Court itself limited *Goss* by ruling that only nominal damages would be available to suspended students who had not received a hearing, absent any proof of actual injury.[7] Likewise, the Court ruled that corporal punishment, even in a case where injury had resulted, was not cruel and unusual punishment in violation of the eighth amendment, nor was a hearing of any sort required before its imposition.[8]

Awareness of decisions that regulate school administrator autonomy, however, seemed to travel more quickly than information about cases that did not (Hollingsworth, Lufler, and Clune, 1984). In general, the alarmist arguments about an over-aggressive judiciary, common in the 1970s, received greater attention at national school conventions and in the popular press than the news about decisions that supported school personnel. In the 1980s, however, there were some exceptions to this observation, with pieces bearing this positive theme appearing in popular publications (Menacker, 1982; Gluckman and Zirkel, 1983; Bartlett, 1985).

The nature of some of the Supreme Court education decisions in the late 1960s and early to mid-1970s, then, led to two related phenomena. First, the role of legal commentators in exploring and interpreting complex decisions became more crucial. For better or worse, commentators began to suggest where the courts were headed, often offering disquieting predictions. Second, from a research perspective, it became more difficult to design judicial impact studies because what needed to be studied could not be addressed effectively by the simple compliance study methodology used in earlier research. "Impact" became a broader concept and one more difficult to limit for analysis.

THE LITIGATION EXPLOSION

At the same time that writers were discussing the increased number of court cases directed at public schools, there was a general discussion in the popular and academic press concerning the "litigation explosion" that was occurring in all areas of the law (Fleming, 1970). It was argued that many aspects of society were moving toward overregulation by the judiciary and that the use of the courts to resolve disputes threatened traditional modes of political and social discourse (Glazer, 1975). Both *Time*, in 1963, and *Newsweek*, in 1973, established "Law" feature sections, and the filing of cases involving such issues as educational malpractice and even "malparenting" was popularly reported.

While the discussion of unusual education cases proceeded in the popular press, school lawyers and administrators meeting in conventions also discussed such cases as challenges to National Honor Society selection practices, attempts by students to secure advanced places in the school band, and other litigation with unusual fact situations. Professional education groups began offering liability insurance to their members, further contributing to the feeling that lawsuits were an immediate threat to educational professionals.

Unusual education cases were widely publicized, but what was heard less often, especially in popular publications, was information on final outcomes. That the plaintiffs in novel cases invariably were unsuccessful was less well publicized than that the cases were filed in the first place. This point seems to apply most to popular newsmagazines, such as *Time*, or to daily newspapers, and less so to journals, such as the *Kappan*, that describe decisions themselves.

What also went largely unchallenged during this debate was the assumption that increased litigation was a permanent state of affairs. One critic of the litigation "explosion" literature observed, "[a]ppearing in prominent law reviews, publications in which, notwithstanding their prestige, there is no scrutiny for substantive as opposed to formal accuracy, these polemics were quickly taken as authority for what they asserted" (Galanter, 1983, p. 62). At the very least, the contours of increasing litigation needed to be studied (Galanter, 1986).

Though the increasing number of lawyers as a proportion of the population leads to the suggestion that they may be increasing marginal or frivolous lawsuits to advance their practices, it is less clear that the increasing number of attorneys actually had resulted in a proportional increase in litigation.[9] The number of court cases filed per thousand people has increased only in some jurisdictions, including federal district courts, but the number going to trial per cases filed apparently has diminished (Grossman and Sarat, 1975). It may therefore be useful to view lawyers as participating in "supervised bargaining," rather than as agents who seek a resolution of issues in courts (Lampert, 1978; Zirkel, 1985, a). Studies examining the impact of courts on schools therefore need to expand their research agenda to include a larger focus—the impact of the legal profession as one group that bargains on behalf of students.

Regardless of whether attorneys actually file suit, school officials increasingly reported in the 1970s that they worried about litigation. Threats of lawsuit, often made by parents having little understanding of the probability of prevailing with such challenges, combined with uncertainty about the actual content of education decisions to make life more complicated for schoolteachers and administrators.

Research conducted in the 1970s focused on the narrow question of legal knowledge. The surveys, however, did not seek to measure the consequences of a lack of knowledge or of the fear of litigation. Nor did research in this period consider the broader question of how the law was used in bargaining to obtain changes in behavior from school personnel.

SURVEYS ON SCHOOL LAW KNOWLEDGE

Research in the 1960s on the impact of courts found that the public did not have a particularly clear understanding of the areas in which the Supreme Court had rendered major decisions (Kessel, 1966). Perry Zirkel (1977, 1978), the leader of the education law survey movement in the 1970s, again found a low level of awareness with regard to the content of major education court cases. Of the twenty questions he asked concerning Supreme Court decisions, the average teacher respondent answered ten correctly.

Other research (Hollingsworth, Lufler, and Clune, 1984), conducted in 1977, found that more than half of the teachers in six Wisconsin schools believed that students had more rights than courts actually had conveyed. For example, 53 percent of those surveyed believed that students had the right to legal counsel before being suspended. It is not surprising, therefore, that 45 percent of the teachers thought that "too much interference from courts" was an important cause of discipline problems.[10] The same study found that the students responsible for most of the schools' discipline problems, the 10 percent of the student body responsible for 90 percent of the rule infractions, also believed that the courts had gone further in protecting them than was actually the case.

A study of 125 Chicago area schoolteachers (Ogletree and Garrett, 1984), found that having had a school law course increased correct response percentages, but that significant percentages of respondents did not know the provisions of state law and the basic elements of court decisions. In another questionnaire study concerning ten Supreme Court decisions, researchers (Menacker and Pascarella, 1983) found that administrators generally were better informed than teachers, but that the results for both groups were "disappointing."

A much more involved "Survey of Children's Legal Rights" was administered to university sophomores, seniors, and practicing teachers (Sametz and McLoughlin, 1985,). The authors found that "teachers and education students alike appear to have only a limited knowledge of children's legal rights." The respondents did better in some areas (exclusionary discipline, juvenile criminal rights, and school attendance) and less well in others (child abuse, special education, and corporal punishment). It is important to note that teachers did better in understanding the law in areas where they might be expected to have more personal responsibility and less well in areas where administrators or specialized education personnel, such as counselors, might be expected to take the lead. A failure to match case content with typical job responsibilities is a shortcoming in much of this survey research.

Research conducted in fifteen Indiana high schools in 1981 found that 71 percent of the principals, but only 30 percent of teachers and counselors, were able to list all the rights granted to students in short suspensions (Hillman, 1985). As might be expected, principals were also much more informed about expulsion cases, since they were more likely to have firsthand experience with them. About two-thirds of the teachers and administrators felt that procedural rules governing discipline imposed restraints on their actions (Teitelbaum, 1983).

The most recent and broad-based of this research involved a stratified national survey of nine hundred junior and senior high school administrators. It was conducted by the Center for Education Statistics in 1985 and addressed the question of compliance with the *Goss* decision presuspension hearing requirement, among other issues. The survey revealed that almost all schools (more than 99 percent) followed the procedures. Many schools went further, by allowing parents to attend a hearing if the charges were denied (88 percent), by providing an appeal process (95 percent), or by allowing some questioning of witnesses (73 percent). Only 3 percent of the respondents thought that the *Goss* hearing requirement placed a significant burden on schools.[11]

In a companion report on the same survey (Center for Education Statistics, 1986b), "teacher fear of being sued" was reported by fewer than 10 percent of the administrators to be a significant factor in limiting the school's ability to maintain order. In a later report (Center for Education Statistics, 1987), fear of being sued for disciplining students was seen by only 18 percent of teacher respondents in a national survey as being "very much" or "much" a factor in limiting teachers from maintaining order. These data suggest that fear of litigation may have been overstated as a source of changed teacher behavior, that "change" in discipline practices should be made a research hypothesis, or that fear of litigation may be ebbing in the 1980s.

NEEDED RESEARCH

Recent knowledge surveys of school personnel still show some uncertainty among respondents with regard to the holdings of key court cases. Not all these surveys, however, have used specialized questions for teachers, administrators, and counselors. There is no reason why a knowledge of the same legal areas, however, should be expected from each group. Likewise, there needs to be a stratification of survey questions based on the grade level of teachers.

The legal issues that arise in secondary schools are significantly different from those present when children are in the early grades (Rodham, 1973). Most educational materials on the law, however, have been written with secondary schools in mind.[12] In the research area, we do not know whether elementary schoolteachers have the same level of concern about lawsuits and their personal rights as secondary teachers. Unresearched changes also may have occurred in the way elementary teachers use discipline as a result of this concern.

A research project involving teacher surveys, stratified by grade level, could be conducted at relatively low cost. Beyond questions related to substantive legal knowledge, such a survey also could begin to probe the question of the origins of legal understanding. In designing new forms of legal information for teachers—whether inservice programs, courses, or written materials—it would be useful to know how teachers currently acquire information. Information may also be acquired in different ways, depending on the subject area. Some areas may have a higher salience for teachers based on their personal situation.

This paper has discussed the role of "intermediaries" at several different points. Our understanding of the transmission of legal knowledge, however, is incomplete. We need to know, for example, how administrators receive legal information, both in the general sense, such as what they read or study, and in more specific cases, such as how they relate to their school district's legal counsel. Almost nothing is known about the frequency of such contacts, the content, the extent to which the counsel is more risk averse or more assertive than the administrator, and the effectiveness of various forms of client-attorney relationships in reducing the overall cost of litigation. We also need to develop theories to guide this research (Yudof, 1986), since there is little research on attorney-client relationships, generally (Sarat and Felstiner, 1986).

We need to know more about contacts between attorneys and school districts. In general, we can imagine a variety of legal system contacts, starting with "threats" of lawsuit, often hollow and without substance, to more serious cases where some injury to a student has occurred. As was discussed, we need to know more about the ways attorneys "bargain" on behalf of clients with school districts. Whether attorneys for plaintiffs represent individuals or special interest groups may also be important.

Similarly, we have little knowledge of the actual contours of litigation in school districts. In fact, there are very few formal, written opinions in the case law areas discussed in this paper (see Table 9.1). We also know that school systems are the more frequent "winners" in published cases (see Table 9.2). But we know nothing about the litigation "iceberg" below the published opinions — the number of cases initiated and settled out of court or dropped.

Research in a few selected school districts, using records and data generated contemporaneously, could begin to address the actual boundaries of public school disputes. It would be useful at the outset to distinguish among types of cases in such research: injury-based tort cases, probably the largest group; issues regarding handicapped students, arising either out of the federal Education for All Handicapped Children Act or related state laws; cases asserting federal or state constitutional rights, usually involving Title 42, Section 1983 of the U.S. Code; and employment cases.

It is also important to focus on case outcomes, with special attention to the cases settled. We do not know, for example, how many cases are compromised as a function of case type. At the very least, it would be useful to discover how many cases a school district settles just to avoid litigation and whether this was done when the facts suggest the district would prevail.

New research should also consider a return to the hypotheses and the methods of earlier impact studies, as detailed previously.[13] A number of subject areas could be used for this intensive, community-based research. The impact of school discipline procedural requirements is an obvious possibility.[14] Such a study could examine intensively the link between court decisions and teachers who report that they engage in less discipline. A number of conflicting hypotheses related to the decline in discipline are present: (1) teachers discipline less because they know the law in this area and find it to be an impediment; (2) teachers don't know the law and imagine, incorrectly, that courts have limited their power to control discipline; (3) failure to discipline because of legal threat is an alibi allowing teachers to reduce their level of involvement in an activity they didn't like anyway; (4) there really has been no significant change in the way teachers discipline students, but only a change in what people have written about the subject; or (5) there's been a change, but it has nothing to do with subsequent increases or decreases in student misbehavior.

It would also be possible to do a before-and-after impact study of some new law or court decision in a particular jurisdiction. It would be useful to focus on a particular school group, such as teachers or administrators, in such a study. As with the litigation study just proposed, substantial funds would be needed because an in-depth study in the field would be needed. Some flexibility also would be needed to focus on a recently decided case because research would need to start quickly. A new avenue of school law, such as the right of students to a safe educational environment, might also be the focus of research (Sawyer, 1983).

Whatever the subject area, further large-scale research on school discipline and the law would be helpful. This is an area where there has been much national concern and much written that makes major assumptions about linkages among the courts, schools, and individual behavior. It is also an area where there has been almost no social science research.

CHANGES TO IMPROVE
DISCIPLINARY CLIMATES

This paper argues that the existence of an "explosion of litigation" should be rendered a research hypothesis rather than accepted as fact. It has also suggested that we don't really know whether teachers or administrators have changed their behavior regarding enforcement of school discipline rules and, if they have, if this change can be attributed to court activity. However, regardless of one's positions on these issues, or the outcome of future research, there should be agreement on the need need for additional exposure to school law issues for all school personnel.

School law materials need to be specialized. Doctors are not specialists in every major medical issue; likewise we should not expect teachers to know or be interested in all areas of school law. Materials especially need to be tailored to meet the special issues that are common to particular positions, such as superintendents, principals, counselors, or special education teachers.

At the same time, the assumption is too often made among teachers that knowledge of school law is "someone else's job." This assumption contains an element of truth, insofar as administrators have the major responsibility for handling difficult cases. But teachers cannot ignore the fact that a significant percentage of lawsuits involve staff members. This means that teachers should not be able to avoid learning basic principles of school law. Likewise, public school students would benefit from a similar discussion, perhaps in the context of a social studies class. To the extent that students have a greatly exaggerated sense of their legal rights, such instruction could reduce disorder.

Although there are a large number of education law texts, some written for teachers, almost no study has been undertaken to determine those courses of instruction or approaches that are most effective. Neither do we know the extent to which disorder is reduced in a school where both students and teachers have been exposed to legal issues, though such projects were funded recently by the U.S. Office of Juvenile Justice and Delinquency Prevention.

Although there are other steps a school can take to reduce disorder, remaining outside the purview of this paper, there is one final perspective on legal education worthy of note. It is necessary that school personnel learn of the outcomes of controversial cases involving such issues as educational malpractice. The dismissed case never seems to receive the same attention as the big settlement, or the preliminary outrageous demand. Popular publications should make a systematic effort to report the cases in which the plaintiff's request is held to have no merit.

Table 9.1

Federal Courts and State Courts of Appeal Cases Reported, 1979-87, Search and Seizure and Discipline

	YEAR DECIDED								
	1979	1980	1981	1982	1983	1984	1985	1986	1987
Search and Seizure									
Sniff Dogs	1	0	2	1	1	0	0	0	0
Strip Searches	2	0	0	0	2	1	0	1	0
Lockers and Cars	1	0	0	1	1	0	0	3	0
Possession Searches	1	1	1	4	5	2	4	1	3
Drug Tests	0	0	0	0	0	0	0	0	2
Total	5	1	3	6	9	3	4	5	5
Discipline									
Expulsion	2	1	5	8	1	4	6	9	2
Substantive Rule Issue	1	3	2	2	2	0	2	0	2
Grade/Credit Reduction	0	0	0	0	2	2	0	2	0
Suspension	4	1	0	3	2	4	2	6	6
Discipline of Handicapped	5	0	2	3	1	1	2	1	5
Corporal Punishment	4	4	1	1	0	3	2	2	2
Total	16	9	10	17	8	14	14	20	17

Source: *"Pupils"* and *"Handicapped"* chapters, *Yearbook of School Law*, published annually by the National Organization on Legal Problems in Education (Topeka, Kansas).

Table 9.2

Prevailing Parties, Search and Seizure and School Discipline Cases, 1979-87, Federal Courts and State Courts of Appeal

	SCHOOL DISTRICT PREVAILS	PLAINTIFF PREVAILS	REMANDED
Search and Seizure			
Sniff Dogs	4	1	0
Strip Searches	2	4	0
Lockers and Cars	4	2	0
Possession Searches	14	7	1
Drug Tests	0	2	0
Total	24(58.5%)	16(39.0%)	1(2.4%)
Discipline			
Expulsion	23	9	6
Substantive Rule Issue	11	2	1
Grade Reduction	4	2	0
Suspension	22	6	0
Discipline of Handicapped	10	7	3
Corporal Punishment	12	6	1
Total	82(65.6%)	32(25.6%)	11(8.8%)

Source: *"Pupils"* and *"Handicapped"* chapters, *Yearbook of School Law*, published annually by the National Organization on Legal Problems in Education (Topeka, Kansas).

10

Cooperative School System and Police Responses To High-Risk and Disruptive Youth

Robert J. Rubel

This chapter reviews research on police-school strategies and techniques to alleviate discipline problems in public schools. More specifically, it examines strategies developed between police agencies and school systems aimed at preventing, reducing, or controlling serious student misbehavior and crime, especially programs and projects that demonstrate police-school cooperation. The discussion also includes programs or projects that apply a crossover technology; for example, school projects using police-like contingency planning or police projects using classroom curricula.

At the outset, it is important to draw distinctions between disciplinary violations and crimes. In this chapter, disciplinary violations represent only violations of school rules; they are rightfully censured solely by school district employees. Crimes, on the other hand, represent violations of federal, state, or local laws and concern law enforcement agencies as well as school system officials. Usually, when projects share areas of interest and concern they also share communication and planning. In this chapter, research into this sharing is examined.

There is not a great deal of formal research about police-school agreements and projects. There are any number of anecdotal accounts of projects, a lesser number of descriptive accounts, and very few formal evaluations. Thus this chapter concentrates on program descriptions and research deemed to be something more than merely

213

anecdotal. In addition, distinctions are drawn between conclusions based upon experience and those based upon research.

STRUCTURE OF THE REVIEW

Throughout this presentation, descriptions of a particular strategy (including the assumptions that underlie it and its relative importance in discipline improvement), precede discussion of the particular approach used to implement it. Finally, research relating to individual projects is discussed. The following model is used: a strategy leads to an approach that leads to a project. For each strategy, four questions are addressed: What is the strategy? Why should one be concerned with it (rationale)? What is known about it (point of origin, duration, type of evaluations available)? and What else might one want to know about it?

Both for the police agency projects and for the school system projects, three primary strategies are considered: prevention, response, and control. For the purposes of this chapter, *prevention* refers to actions taken in advance of a problem, designed to increase the probability that the problem will never develop. *Response* refers to projects aimed at limiting the chronic recurrence of similar events. *Control* covers projects designed to stop some acute action that has occurred or that is occurring.

Before beginning this review of research on national programs, local police agency, and school system projects aimed at improving student discipline, a study on school-police working relations is explored.

Perhaps the most interesting and useful study of police-school relationships is to be found in Fox and Shuck (1964). One of Fox and Shuck's key research questions asked whether police agencies and education agencies even use the same basis for judging their mutual working relationships. Fox and Shuck discovered that once professionals from both lines of work begin to think about it, they agree that they use four key factors to evaluate their relations with others: information, assistance, individual contact, and interagency activities.

Fox and Shuck found important differences in responses by police and educators regarding the aspects of their working relationships that met with greatest success and failure. Whereas educators report the greatest occurrence of both good and poor working relationships in the area of police providing assistance in times of need, police report the greatest occurrence of good working relationships in the area of information and the greatest number of poor experiences in the area of individual contact during times of need. This implies that, within a single strategy, planners may have to tailor projects to meet the needs of individual school systems and police jurisdictions to fit into existing patterns of their historical working relations.

The balance of this chapter examines the research and evaluation literature as it deals specifically with projects aimed at addressing serious student misbehavior and crime in public schools. In this first section, two federally sponsored programs that present school district responses to severely disruptive and criminal youth are reviewed. Unlike projects in the two sections that will follow, these programs developed a workable model for change and then implemented that model in selected sites nationwide.

NATIONAL PROGRAMS

The first of these two programs to be examined has been sponsored by the U.S. Department of Education since the mid-1970s. This model calls for *cooperation* to promote *planning* to achieve an *improved learning environment*. The second program is sponsored by the U.S. Department of Justice. This model has taken some lessons from the Education Department program and added a twist: exploring the success of using *information* to motivate *planning* to produce *improved management* of disruptions and disruptive youth.

U.S. Department of Education

Since the early 1970s, the Alcohol and Drug Abuse Education Program of the U.S. Department of Education has provided training to school officials and educators nationwide in the "school team approach" to solving problems of drug abuse and disruptive behavior in schools. During the late 1970s, the Office of Juvenile Justice and Delinquency Prevention (U.S. Department of Justice) supported a large study to investigate the success of this model for achieving reductions in school-based crime and disruptive behavior. In part, the model called for intensive training for members of the school's community (teachers, administrators, students, and parents) in order to build a team of skilled planners. By the time a school team leaves training, they have a well-developed plan for combatting drug dealing, drug abuse, or other disruptive school-based problems.

The study reached the following conclusion: "The findings suggest that such an effort can decrease the amount of victimization reported by students and may also decrease the level of tension, fear, and danger perceived by students in the school." This evaluation exposed a general weakness of all training programs: without strong and dedicated local leadership, the excitement and drive that develop in an intensive workshop setting soon dissipate along with the intended impact. Many of the school teams never implemented their written plans. But for those who did, the experiences were rewarding, for they were able to achieve demonstrable progress toward reducing their target problems (Grant, 1981).

This School Team Approach is both sophisticated and complex. In combatting school-based crime and disruption, it provided three major thrusts: a discipline strategy to change the school's way of handling discipline, attendance, and school security; increased communication within the school and between the school and the community; and increased self-understanding and ability of students to relate to other people.

Among the principal findings were these:

1. "Schools in crowded inner city situations need to have a strong academic focus [in order to provide a tangible purpose for being in school]."

2. "Once the school is stabilized (academic programs in place, and meeting *expected* traditional standards, students perceive themselves as safe, etc.) then innovative projects can be attempted."

3. "Teacher morale is an important factor in a school that is effectively reducing crime and fear of crime."

4. "Leadership is not only vital to a school, it is vital to the success of the teams." (Grant, 1981, p. 121)

U.S. Department of Justice

Responding to widespread concern that serious disruption and crime were harming American public education, the National Institute of Justice (NIJ) in 1981 began to explore approaches to assist school principals and district education officials better to understand the nature and extent of student misbehavior as the step preceding planning or implementing specific projects (Rubel and Ames, 1986). Quite early in this exploration, NIJ entered into an agreement with the Department of Education that involved cofunding and also sharing elements of the School Team Training approach.

As noted, the Education Department's School Team Approach used a model of cooperation to lead to planning to help improve the educational setting. The Justice Department's program incorporated that same strategy and expanded it. In this instance, the model is testing the assumption that "information is power," and as such, that computer-aided analysis of data on the nature and extent of school-based misbehaviors must precede planning, and that planning based on this solid information will lead to improved management of student crime and misbehavior. It is also a fundamental premise of this program that crimes (violations of laws) must be carefully identified and catalogued separately from discipline violations (violations of school rules). The program, called the School Management and Resources Team (SMART) Program, has four phases: safety audit (an analysis of the district's existing policies and practices regarding the handling of youth who commit crimes in schools); data collection and analysis (a computerized process that records what happened, the degree of seriousness, date, time, and location, actions taken, and so forth); data interpretation (by teams who then write action plans); and command-level interdepartmental coordination among education, police, and other criminal justice professionals (essentially agreements to agree to work together against youth who commit crimes in the schools).

As the model developed, it was ultimately tested in a total of seventy-seven schools in four school districts nationwide from 1983 to 1986. These research questions were posed:

1. Will local school districts accept and benefit from a program that addresses crime and discipline problems in school through partnerships between education and law enforcement?

2. Will a data-based analysis process be effective in helping schools identify and reduce recurring problems? (Rubel, 1986a)

Based on case study evaluations, the program has shown promise in these areas:

1. *Helps Students*
   a. Brings troubled youth to the assistant principal's and counselor's attention for early intervention.
   b. Reduces fear of crime and disruption to increase students' attention to the business of education.

    c. Communicates consistency within the school for both policies and practices (rules and consequences).

2. *Helps Principals*
   a. Enables principals to *target* their energies to attack one problem at a time.
   b. Shows precisely who and what is going wrong throughout the school (students or teachers).
   c. Checks whether the specific intervention is working, as planned (on-line feedback loop).

3. *Helps Central (District) Office*
   a. Evens out the districtwide application of policies (e.g.: handling drug sales; weapons; gang activity).
   b. Ensures consistent districtwide application of dispositions (e.g.:degree of censure for theft of property worth $50 or $200; prosecution for battery).
   c. Helps the superintendent to build bridges of communication and cooperation to police and youth-serving agencies (memoranda of understanding).(Rubel, 1986)

The initial evaluation of this program covers the first two years of the field test in forty-four secondary schools in three sites (Tremper, 1985). Since then, the program has been implemented in thirty-three secondary schools in one additional site, and that activity has also been evaluated (National Institute of Justice, 1988).

Among the principal findings from the first two years were these:

1. The more that principals took an active leadership role in supporting the program and empowering the teams to create intervention plans, the better and more effective were the plans.

2. The higher the administrative rank of the participant, the greater benefits they perceived from the program. That is, superintendents and their assistants appreciated the benefits of the program the greatest; assistant principals appreciated it the least.

3. The program area thought to be most beneficial for improving school safety was that of interagency cooperation.

Three of Tremper's major findings concerned interagency agreements between the school systems and the police departments.

1. The project emphasis on interagency coordination addressed a strongly felt need for better responses to serious and repeat criminal offenders.

2. Interagency groups favored informal arrangements over written agreements. They did, however, make substantial progress toward undertaking joint endeavors and strengthening informal ties.

3. The partnership between the federal Departments of Justice and Education served as a valuable model of cooperation to spur local efforts.

The second evaluation only examined the question of the program's effectiveness in reducing discipline incidents. In a statistical test of program interventions compared with controls, it was established that the School Management and Resource Team Program succeeded in reducing disciplinary infractions.

The aspect of the overall program tested in this second evaluation was the utility of the computer-aided incident analysis system that calls for recording certain information from every teacher's referral of a student into the office of the principal or assistant principal for discipline. The data are entered daily and processed by a school district's central computer on a routine basis.

The district's computer produces tables and charts displaying key elements of information relating either to individual students or to groups of incidents. For example, it would be possible to produce a table of the students most frequently referred by teachers to the main office, teachers most often referring students out of their classes, or the kinds of dispositions a particular administrator is making for a particular kind of offense. Or it is possible to produce a chart displaying the period of day, day of week, and zone of the school where any type of incident is occurring (fights, battery, vandalism, locker thefts, tardiness, etc.).

Once the data are returned to the principal and assistant principals in a useful form, that administrator begins to develop an action plan that proposes specific strategies to reduce particular problems that were highlighted by the data. This system enables the central office of the school district continually to monitor—with only a few weeks of lagtime—not only the wide range of misconduct that is continually present in modern American schools, but also the success or failure of individual principals to redress problems they proposed to address in their monthly action plans.

Now the discussion will turn to projects and practices of local police and education agencies who must deal with severely disruptive and criminal students. These projects share a common theme: they have evolved locally to meet local needs; there has been little, if any, attempt to develop a shared structure with similar projects nationwide.

LOCAL POLICE AGENCY PROJECTS

"In the high school the police officer's role is similar to that of an American military advisor overseas," wrote Vestermark (1971 p. 86). "His presence may be unwelcome, his advice only grudgingly heard. When needed to respond to a serious fight, for example, he may insist on resolving it in ways that are contrary to the principal's wishes." This is because, as a commissioned officer of the state, the police officer is sworn to intervene in any crime committed in his or her presence. Indeed, in certain instances the principal may actually be threatened with arrest for obstruction of justice if the orders of the police officer are not followed. In a phrase, police on school grounds often present something of a mixed blessing; although they are undoubtedly capable of resolving crises, their presence may have the unintended consequence of triggering a different kind of crisis even while resolving the first one. Police on campus can be provocative.

To counteract and defuse many of these feelings and situations, law enforcement professionals nationwide have for years endeavored to work with educators to improve relations even while helping local school principals reduce crime and delinquency. The first strategy they have used is that of prevention.

Prevention Strategies

Prevention strategies call for thinking about and planning for events before they become problems. Over the years, police planners have developed a range of approaches that fall into a prevention strategy and a variety of projects that use one or more approach. Two approaches will be discussed that are reasonably well documented; within each, available research about selected projects will be reviewed.

Classroom Education.   Many projects fall within this approach. These projects assume that disruptive behavior results in some part from a combination of defiance of authority and unfamiliarity with the consequences of actions. In general, these projects evolved in the late 1960s as a generation of our nation's youth began to demonstrate against almost everything, everywhere. Police, in one effort to counter this social turmoil, turned to the public schools with curriculum-based educational projects.

The earliest attempt to describe this range of educational projects appeared in a book titled *Police Programs for Preventing Crime and Delinquency* (Pursuit et al., 1972). This volume explores the underlying bases for educational projects, and describes those that showed the most promise. Their analysis of the programmatic rationale is valid today:

1. To promote a better understanding of the law, judicial processes, and the role of law enforcement as it affects the youth in the community

2. To offer the youth an opportunity to ask questions and express their views related to law enforcement, thereby to create a better understanding between youth and law enforcement personnel

3. To inform the youth of laws that affect and guide them

4. To inform the youth of the crime and narcotics problems among young persons (Pursuit et al., 1972, p. 316)

As might be expected, projects begun in the late 1960s and early 1970s have changed with the times, but many of the projects that Pursuit and his coauthors described remain today. These include the "Citizen and the Law Program" that later evolved into the sophisticated and much publicized "Law Related Education" (LRE) program sponsored at times both by the U.S. Departments of Justice and Education (see, for example, publications of the Constitutional Rights Foundation in Los Angeles, and of the Public Education division of the American Bar Association in Chicago). From their inception, police-taught education courses were designed both for elementary and for secondary students.

Projects in the early 1970s, such as "Adopt-a-Deputy," "Police-School Cadet Program," "The 'Be A Good Guy' Plan," and "Officer Friendly," appear to have been principally designed to overcome the wave of anti-authority sentiment that then appeared to sweep school-aged children. These early projects were not educational in the sense that there was a curriculum. They were educational in the sense that they were designed to build friendship through familiarity (Pursuit et al., 1972). Officers were assigned to schools—particularly elementary schools; their job was to visit classrooms in uniform and to speak with students about police, policing, and the law.

As fear and animosity toward law officers subsided, educational projects based on a set curricula began to emerge. Begun in Los Angeles by the Constitutional Rights Foundation, and eventually adopted widely, these courses slowly grew from short units within "civics" courses to stand-alone units that taught younger children about right and wrong, and taught older children about the finer distinctions between civil and criminal law. The central assumption of these projects was that youth needed clearly to understand the consequences of actions in order to be able to choose correct over incorrect behavior.

The principal research on modern-day LRE, as it relates to delinquency prevention, is found in Johnson and Hunter's 1984 study covering a three-year period. Based on a comparison of 61 classes using LRE and 44 classes not using LRE, the authors found that while "LRE can improve students' attitudes, perceptions, and behavior ... these favorable outcomes do not follow automatically from adopting an LRE textbook and offering a course by that name." Indeed, the researchers found that "the capability of LRE to improve citizenship and behavior is highly dependent on the way in which the course is implemented." For example, classes where the LRE curriculum was seen to be better used shared these characteristics:

1. A second round of formative feedback provided by the evaluators to trainers

2. Greater emphasis on strong support by the building administrators as a criterion for including classes in the study

3. More prevalent use of outside persons as coteachers (Johnson and Hunter, 1986, p. xii)

A review of other school-based police-initiated educational projects reveals that some of these newer efforts provide classroom instruction that focuses quite accurately on many elements of the overall LRE approach: that is, although the LRE model takes a wide-ranging approach to teaching students about law and justice, new projects have grown up that enable law officers and teachers to provide guidance and counsel in specific areas.

Perhaps the best current examples of projects that target a specific offense are Project SPECDA (School Program to Educate and Control Drug Abuse), developed by the New York City police department and school system and implemented in fifth and sixth grade classes in the Bronx and Brooklyn, and Project DARE (Drug Abuse Resistance Education), developed by the Los Angeles police department and school system and implemented in elementary and junior high schools in the Los Angeles area. Both SPECDA and DARE have common elements and common assumptions: both endeavor to equip children, through lectures, demonstrations, and audio-video materials, with "the skills for resisting peer pressure to experiment with alcohol, tobacco, and drugs" (DeJong, 1986, p. 2); both projects assume that today's school-age youth need strong and decisive adult leadership and counsel to help them overcome tremendous peer pressures to engage in illegal drug activity. SPECDA's goals demonstrate the focus and intensity of a new genre of program. The broad goals of earlier education projects have been focused; the general interest of education and police professionals in improving school-police relations has been usefully honed.

Perhaps the best example of a program that targets a specific population (rather than a specific problem) is the Youth Awareness Program cosponsored by the District of Columbia Public Schools and the D.C. Metropolitan Police Department. This program focuses on urban adolescents and employs forceful adult leadership to help these youth to make appropriate life-choices in the face of negative peer pressures and difficult socioeconomic circumstances. The sponsoring agencies work together to develop new policies, procedures, and instructional materials; to train liaisons and resource personnel; and so forth. The courses, taught by police officers, last one semester. Pre- and post-testing during the 1983-84 school year revealed that younger students (twelve to fourteen) gained significantly in knowledge of laws and police responsibilities and improved attitudes about police in general, but gains among older students (fifteen and older) were not significant (District of Columbia Public Schools, 1984).

Police Liaison. This approach grew out of a project within the Flint, Michigan, police department in the late 1950s and was funded by the Mott Foundation. By 1968, when the Law Enforcement Assistance Administration (LEAA) began promoting police liaison projects, the Flint model had already been replicated in Tuscon and was in various stages of development in some nineteen other cities nationwide (Pursuit, 1972, p. 306).

Although specific goals and objectives certainly differed between cities, the basic goals of police liaison projects were as follows:

1. To establish collaboration between the police and school in preventing crime and delinquency

2. To encourage understanding between police and young people

3. To improve police teamwork with teachers in handling problem youth

4. To improve the attitudes of students toward police

5. To build better police-community relations by improving the police image" (Shepard and James, 1967, p. 2).

Police liaison projects represent an early model of law enforcement intervention and counseling in informal school settings. Liaison officers are assigned to work in specific schools; their salaries are reimbursed by the school district. This "marriage" of education and law enforcement appears to be the earliest form of police-school interagency cooperation, a topic that is discussed in a later section of this chapter.

Unlike most of the police-school agreements that will be discussed later, police liaison projects appear to have been initiated by local police professionals rather than by local educators. It appears that an underlying assumption of these police planners was that by placing officers in secondary schools they could fulfill a "security" function and also have informal access to the very youth who were committing the preponderance of delinquent acts in the community.

Response Strategies

As previously discussed, these are approaches designed to curtail further occurrences of unwanted acts such as drug sales, gang activity, vandalism, or burglary. There are not many descriptions of projects involving the police that truly represent responses to particular problems. Most descriptions appear in three sources: in Surratt (1974); in *Violent Schools — Safe Schools* (National Institute of Education, 1978; hereafter, the Safe School Study); and in Vestermark and Blauvelt (1978). These works describe the range of police assistance projects for specific events: using police to help monitor after-school events; using police to monitor school arrival and departure safety; having officers work undercover to help curtail drug transactions; tailoring police nighttime patrol patterns better to monitor school buildings that might be subject to vandalism or burglary; and helping the district stop an employee theft ring.

Surratt's work, entitled *A Survey and Analysis of Special Police Services in Large Public School Districts of the United States* (1974), and the Safe School Study contain some quantitative findings, whereas Vestermark's is descriptive and strategic. The latter goes into much greater detail than the first two about when, why, and how to involve police in school matters.

Surratt surveyed 932 school superintendents nationwide and obtained 519 usable surveys. He found that "more than two-thirds of the large school systems . . . utilized the services of local police departments in the areas of protection at after-school events and school arrival/departure safety; [that] fewer than half of the large school systems . . . [used police] for protection of buildings and grounds after school hours, patrolling halls and grounds during the school day, and instruction or counseling; . . . [that while] a majority of the police departments paid for most of the police services reported in three of five areas of special police services, the question of fiscal responsibility for police services was unresolved" (Surratt, 1974, pp. 49, 170-171). Surratt did not relate variables to each other or try to explain such events.

The Safe School Study, a stratified random probability sample of the nation's secondary schools conducted during 1976, remains the only comprehensive national research into the nature and extent of crime in American schools, and a catalogue of what is (or was) being done about it. Among the lists of "things being done" is found *security office operations* and *police action*.

Although there is not a great deal of information on policing in schools in the Safe School Study, some of the findings are unusual enough to warrant further thought and discussion. For example, suburban areas, then small cities, next rural areas, and lastly large cities report "very much support" from local police (47, 41, 39, and 29 percent respectively). But one notes that the areas served by police appear in a different order. "Police on regular patrol"—infrequent at best, ranging from only 8 to 11 percent of responding schools—is most frequent in large cities, as would be expected. By juxtaposing these findings, it becomes apparent that although about 11 percent of all large city schools have police on regular patrol (and 5 percent of them also have police stationed in the schools), administrators of these schools are least likely to say that they receive "very much support" from local police.

The findings reported both by Surratt and by the Safe School Study are descriptive rather than explanatory and, as such, of little use to those endeavoring to derive conclusions about the utility and effectiveness of particular approaches and strategies. There does not appear to be any "impact" research or evaluation of these types of police-initiated school-based prevention projects. Furthermore, it appears that short-term interventions planned and carried out by policing agencies either succeed in meeting their intended purpose (and are then discontinued) or fail to meet their intended purpose (and are discontinued). Since the conclusions are the same, the only apparent difference is that if they succeeded in the eyes of the commanding officers, they will likely be tried again. Tried often enough, some report of them reaches the general public. Quite a bit of time can elapse before these experimental and practical projects do, indeed, reach the attention of the general public.

It may do well to provide an example of this point. Irving Spergel (1985), in his recent study of gangs and their handling by the Chicago Public Schools, does not mention projects and activities of any aspect of the Chicago Police Department, even though there is an active "Youth Gang Squad" division. This is only noteworthy because by 1985 the Chicago Police Department had for three years been developing specific programmatic guidelines *just for interdicting gang activity in schools.* To this date, then, special police projects and projects focused on responding to particular school-based problems appear not to have been subject to an impact evaluation.

Control Strategies

To this point, we have been examining police response strategies involving the school system. These strategies have grown out of the apparent fact that there are two conditions generally present when school district administrators turn to the police to control events: a sudden event that appropriately falls within the domain of law enforcement, and a problem that turns suddenly from chronic to acute. More simply, principals call the police either to handle criminal complaints or to manage a crisis. This section discusses approaches taken to work out relations in "normal times" to control particularly troublesome student behavior.

Research on normal school-police relations comes from Fox and Shuck (1964), who catalogue differences of perceptions between policing and educating agencies regarding each others' degree of cooperation. However, as previously described, Fox restricts his inquiry to the relationships of police officers to each other and to school administrators. He catalogues neither the nature nor the extent of contacts between these two agencies nor the police impact upon student crime. So again, there appears to be a gap in the research base—no studies of the most common forms of police responses in schools.

Information on acute school-police relations is somewhat more plentiful, but again mostly descriptive. Vestermark and Blauvelt (1978) describe how to manage bomb threats. Blauvelt (1977) tells how to handle hostage situations in public schools. Vestermark (1971), writing a general treatise on "collective violence" presents what remains to this day the definitive tactical procedural manual for dealing with situational (spontaneous) and guided (planned) riots on school grounds. Williams (1984) gives us a crowd-control plan for schools; Campbell (1982) authors a manual for police and school handling of street gangs; the Milwaukee Police Department's Gang Crimes Unit (1986) produces an annually updated directory of gang indicia, terms, and signals; and Mourning (1987) discusses current policies and practices regarding the use of metal detectors in schools. To restate: these are all program or activity descriptions, and the principal clue that they actually work is that they are being promulgated, even if only— in some instances—as "fugitive literature."

LOCAL SCHOOL SYSTEM PROJECTS

The next part of this chapter is devoted to projects initiated by local school systems. In the previous section, discussion focused upon projects developed and implemented by local police departments. Readers will note a substantial change in the content of the projects initiated by local school systems.

By the mid-1970s, the nation had begun to realize that students were actually committing crimes in the public schools. The Gallup Polls began reporting that "discipline" was the greatest educational concern in the country (Gallup, 1974-85), and the U.S. Senate held hearings in an effort to understand the phenomenon (U.S. Congress, 1975). By 1975, the then six-year-old National Association of School Security Directors had some 350 members; of these, all but a handful were commissioned law officers employed by school districts (Rubel, 1977).

But it is just as difficult now, as it was then, to grasp either the nature or the extent of crimes committed on campuses. Although it would be natural to expect that school districts with their own security departments would be able to keep track of the entire range of incidents occurring at local schools, that is—and always has been—far from the fact. For example, the Safe School Study explained in detail why and how certain kinds of offenses seem to be substantially underreported by educators (National Institute of Education, 1978). Perhaps the most thorough, recent treatment of the problems faced by the educational community in defining and fully reporting criminal incidents appears in the *School Discipline Notebook* (National School Safety Center, 1986). It points out that the general confusion over what is really a crime and what is really a violation of a school rule hampers educational planners (probably including local school principals) in their efforts to curtail their "discipline" problems.

That point now becomes central. It is apparent from this literature review that most school-based strategies involving police agencies or school security departments are general rather than specific in scope: that is, they appear to address general problems of delinquency rather than specific types of criminal or severely disruptive behavior. Only during the upcoming discussion of the roles of school security projects as part of prevention strategies is there a recurring call for a planning process that involves the clear separation of student crimes from disciplinary infractions as a precursor to developing and implementing truly effective projects.

Prevention Strategies

Within this first strategy, the research points to two types of law enforcement approaches open to educators when dealing with youth who present problems of serious disruption or crime. First, the district administrator may turn to the police in an effort to develop closer overall working relations; and second, if the school district has its own office of school security, district officials may look there for help in developing methods for improving "discipline" in their schools. In either case, the assumption on the part of the education officials is that those with law enforcement backgrounds have technical skills to offer that may well supplement the district's own planning or technical skills.

Working With Police.   When discussing ways police work with schools, it was noted that these projects usually brought law officers into schools as educators. When schools initiate the contacts, it appears that the projects are substantially different. Here, for example, there appears to be a decided concentration upon efforts at coordination and cooperation. This might be expected. Fox and Shuck (1964) noted that "contact with police" by school personnel represented the area of poorest perceived relations. It appears to be a central assumption of this approach that these meetings help to put police and education professionals clearly on one team, and in that, there is undeniable benefit.

School Security. About two hundred school systems in this country have their own divisions of school security (National Alliance for Safe Schools, 1985). Most of the directors of these divisions had many years of law enforcement experience before joining a school district. Usually, the director and his officers are commissioned police officers or special officers. They certainly have arrest powers on school grounds, and in some school systems they have arrest powers in the city as well. In many large urban centers, these school peace officers or school security agents are armed. Minimally, they carry handcuffs.

No research or evaluation studies were found on school security offices or officers. Two publications describe school security operations and personnel. The first is a doctoral dissertation by Melvyn May (1979) entitled "A Descriptive View of Security Services in Selected School Districts by Geographic Region and Student Population." The second is a national directory of public school security operations (NASS, 1985). Since these documents provide descriptive rather than explanatory information, neither will be discussed here. However, when a school district's strategy calls for using security operations, there are three separable approaches that can be explored: data collection and planning; physical security; and student-centered intervention projects.

Data Collection and Planning. This approach assumes that by defining acts clearly and by collecting accurate and current information about the nature and extent of problems, it will be easier to plan effective projects. Put another way, before program planners can hit a target, they have at least to see the target. Surprisingly, careful data collection and planning is by far the exception rather than the rule in delinquency prevention projects run by school districts. Frequently the process of collecting and analyzing data is omitted entirely from the planning cycle. This fact was tacitly acknowledged by the American Association of School Administrators in their 1981 publication *Reporting: Violence, Vandalism, and Other Incidents in Schools* when they wrote "In many cases, school districts still do not have clear records of incidents of school crime" and then went on to describe how to develop such records.

That school administrators are hampered in their planning of prevention projects because they often misname events (confusing disciplinary violations with law violations) is also discussed in detail in *School Discipline Notebook* (National School Safety Center, 1986). The need to separate discipline from crime is emphasized by Rubel and Ames (1986) in discussing a problem-solving strategy for school-based crime and discipline. Here, the authors push the need for naming events (distinguishing between a fight and a battery; breakage and vandalism; fire and arson, etc.) and tracking their occurrences through a computerized incident-profiling system that enables principals to easily see time and location clusters for any specified type of criminal or noncriminal offense. This appears to be the first instance when the law enforcement technology known as incident analysis has been applied in an educational setting. Another evaluation of the impact of implementing a comprehensive data collection and analysis system has been described earlier in the discussion of national programs.

Physical Security.   The second approach within the school security strategy has the security office conducting needs assessments and then purchasing, installing, and monitoring a wide range of physical security devices. The single existing objective analysis of the impact of intrusion detection devices upon crime prevention in schools was prepared by Murray (1980). The author finds that although intrusion alarms appear to have some capacity to reduce burglary, there appear to be no other statistically significant reductions in school-related crime and vandalism in an inner-city school district: that is, attendance did not change substantially, and daytime offenses were unaffected. One wonders, however, what else he expected to find; the usual assumption among security specialists is that intrusion alarms (burglar alarms) help prevent after-hours break-ins by electronically simulating a populated building. Put differently, the idea is that the type of person who declines to enter an occupied building to commit a theft will also be dissuaded from entering an alarmed building to commit a burglary because the alarm will, at least in theory, summon people who will discover his presence.

Student-Centered Intervention.   This approach to discipline improvement considers first the needs and the viewpoints of students. Proponents of this approach are quick to point out that many prevention projects only represent temporary solutions because the students feel no sense of ownership in them and work to subvert their intents.

Perhaps the most notable effort to present crime prevention options that at the same time are sensitive to students' self-image yet bridge the gap between a school district's security operation and the principals who run the schools is seen in the National Association of Secondary School Principals' book *Effective Strategies for School Security* (Blauvelt, 1981). Apart from its sensitive tone, this book offers a wide range of procedures for principals and their assistants to address battery, arson, theft, robbery, burglary, and so forth. Again, this work is descriptive, not analytical.

Blauvelt has authored many other works on school security and administrative management of crises, but one speaks to this section with particular clarity. "Interface: Security and Students" (Blauvelt, 1984) describes a program conducted for many years in the Prince George's County, Maryland, public schools whereby security office personnel worked as faculty sponsors for extracurricular clubs called Student Security Advisory Councils. This program enabled students to define and help to solve the problems of crime and criminality that most concerned them. Those who planned this program assumed that if high school students participated in identifying not only the problems that faced them but also the solutions to those problems, they would at least feel that the school district administration was on their side, cared about their concerns, and valued their advice and recommendations.

Although no studies of this project have been conducted, it does provide an important option for educators: an opportunity to apply some degree of law enforcement rigor to discipline and crime prevention practices that can be implemented in elementary or secondary school settings.

Response Strategy

As previously described, when law enforcement professionals initiated in-school crime reduction projects, these projects were designed to repulse specific events. In this same vein, once educational planners are moved to implement some program to address a particularly chronic problem, they tend to focus on the "intolerable behavior" that they want changed. Although volumes have been written about school-based prevention projects designed to encourage good behavior, improve the social climate of the school, or target slow learners with enriched curricula, these all fall outside the scope of this chapter. Indeed, this research survey has shown that there are few projects that feature highly focused, school-initiated responses to seriously disruptive and criminal youth. A possible reason for the paucity of evaluative research follows from the very nature of the projects that the educational planners must consider—quick and decisive responses to particular problems such as locker thefts, bicycle thefts, assaultive behavior, and drug dealing. Usually, the problems don't stay around long enough to enable the school to design a program, set up a research agenda, and seek money to fund it. But occasionally they do; there appear to be a few projects that are caught by the response strategy net that have been reasonably well described and evaluated.

Before presenting these individual projects, readers might wish to recall that the Office of Juvenile Justice and Delinquency Prevention (OJJDP), U.S. Department of Justice, has for years taken a keen interest not only in project development, but also in the theoretical basis for preventing delinquency in school settings. In 1979 OJJDP published *Delinquency Prevention: Theories and Strategies* to examine the range of strategies then available to school systems and communities to address severely disruptive youth. More importantly, this work discusses in detail the practical implications for each strategy. Put differently, the authors carefully catalogue each of the many theoretical approaches to delinquency prevention and explain why they would or would not succeed on the basis of findings from research.

In summary, the conclusions from the research show that school-based delinquency prevention and control approaches require the following:

1. Organization (or reorganization) of schools to improve the potential for educational success for all students

2. Development of a relevant school curriculum which is responsive to student needs and interests

3. Application of methods of instruction (including reward systems) that can increase student commitment to education (and to teachers)

4. Establishment of community linkages which promote youth interaction with nondelinquent peers and adults, and adoption of nondelinquent norms of behavior

5. Provision of fair and consistent school administrative policies and procedures (including disciplinary practices) which can enhance student sense of responsibility, maintain good morale, and provide a feeling of security among students and teachers

Although this chapter is generally limited to works that have more substance than simple description, two publications are noteworthy simply because of the wide range of project descriptions they provide. Both publications come from the Office of the Superintendent of the Los Angeles County Schools. These two works are *Strategies for Reducing Violence and Vandalism* (Los Angeles County Public Schools, 1980) and *Constructive Discipline:Building a Climate for Learning* (G. Roy Mayer et al., 1983). Together, they emphasize analyzing and improving the school environment rather than blaming and punishing students. They stress teaching students how to behave rather than merely teaching them how not to behave. Using this positive approach, these books develop and show how to enforce a discipline code for the classroom and school by employing a three-part framework for selecting behavioral procedures. This framework is envisioned as a triangle. The first leg involves punishing students for major infractions, the second leg calls for a variety of constructive alternatives to reduce minor infractions, and the third leg emphasizes positive procedures to strengthen students' appropriate and constructive behavior.

That, finally, brings us to the only identified work that actually evaluated response strategy projects designed by educational planners and implemented in public schools. These projects, known collectively as "Alternative Education Programs," were begun in late 1980. The Office of Juvenile Justice and Delinquency Prevention provided the funding for eighteen demonstration projects operating in 94 sites nationwide. The findings showed that of twenty-three significant differences for program goals, twenty were in the positive direction. These included goals for reducing delinquent behavior in and around schools, reducing suspensions, increasing school attendance, increasing academic success, and improving transition to work and postsecondary education (Gottfredson, 1983).

Control Strategies

School district strategies for dealing with acute problems of disruption are pretty well limited to crisis contingency plans: in other words, options open to a school principal when there has been a homicide, a rape, a bomb threat, or similar extreme situation. Again, there is a recurring theme: many examples of contingency plans and none researched or evaluated for their effectiveness. As with police control strategies, the best available test of success appears to be that the particular plan has survived the ravages of time and made it into print.

Examples of contingency plans for educators range from the U.S. Department of Justice's Community Relations Service publication "School Security: Guidelines for Maintaining Safety in School

Desegregation" (1979) through the National Alliance for Safe Schools's "Checklist for School Crisis Contingency Plans" (NASS, 1978). These plans share a root assumption: that the very process of planning puts educational leaders in control of events, rather than allowing the events themselves to control the decision makers.

Perhaps the best collection of contingency plans prepared in a form and format that school district administrators can use is seen in the National Alliance for Safe Schools's 1984 document "Guide for Creating School Safety Plans." This collection includes the document used by the New York City Board of Education to require such plans of their principals; the text of the Milwaukee Public Schools safety plan as it applies to rumor control, bomb threats, and intergroup conflict; and the Community Relations Service's overall recommendations for establishing conflict management projects for school systems.

CONCLUSIONS

The material reviewed in this chapter suggests, first and foremost, that there is a substantial difference between the kinds of projects that result from police wanting to work with school systems and school systems wanting the help of the police. It appears that when police agencies consider working in a school setting, the emphasis is upon education, either with primary or secondary school youth. This may take the form of informal classroom presentations (Officer Friendly) or a carefully planned curriculum (McGruff). On the other hand, when school district officials solicit the police for cooperative projects, the emphasis appears to be upon using police to help with special patrols or security-related assignments. In some cases, the emphasis is upon formal or informal agreements about how the police departments will respond in certain circumstances.

Another finding is that school and police projects that target specific chronic problems of youth crime have seldom been researched. From the school side, there has been very little research about curricula to prevent drug dealing, weapons possession, or battery. From the police side, there has been no real systematic research of the effects of the existing array of response or control options for common problems such as theft of school property or battery on school grounds.

Research Needed

A wide range of research questions arise from this review of the evaluation literature into school-based discipline improvement projects.

Among the national programs, for example, might the *SMART* Program model—which has been implemented only in limited settings—produce different results if implemented within an entire state, all at once? Also, how large or small a district can still find the program useful? Will it be of any use in a five-thousand-student district where the most serious problems are tardiness? Will it really be of any use in a three-hundred-student rural district with one high school where the principal is the superintendent and knows all the students by name?

Among the local police agency projects, some of the questions raised by Fox and Shuck suggest other avenues of inquiry. Fox and Shuck examined working relations of "line officers" (those who respond to calls for assistance) with "line school administrators" (principals and their assistants). The answers were useful, even though the research is now over twenty years old. Their study should probably be refined and replicated. For example, one might usefully explore current relations between juvenile officers (and school squad officers, where they exist) and school principals as well as the relations between precinct captains and departmental chiefs with their counterparts in the school districts. It would be important now to recognize areas where these professionals feel greatest and least amounts of cooperation, better to understand the dynamics of modern police-school stresses.

Little is known about the relations of the district superintendent and the chief of police. There is some evidence from the experiences of project personnel associated with the SMART Program that relations at the "line" level are controlled unilaterally by local precinct captains and may not reflect accurately a superintendent's working relationship with the chief of police. Of course, that too carries implications for policy and practice, and must be considered in any school district plan to work cooperatively with the police to curtail crime and disruption in the schools.

Perhaps some future research can be channeled into determining with greater clarity the capacity of ongoing educational programs to be implemented in diverse settings, addressing the entire spectrum of disruptive and criminal incidents.

Implications for Practice

Most of the major themes in this chapter carry some implications for practice. This chapter has reviewed how law enforcement professionals have developed many kinds of projects over the last twenty-five years.

The first projects were aimed at overcoming youth's antagonism toward authority. The next wave of projects were aimed at taking advantage of youth's capacity to learn about, and participate in, crime prevention activities. The current cycle of projects endeavor to instruct youth how to apply peer pressure to reduce specific problems, such as drug use. When planning projects that are meant to be cosponsored by police and schools, some of this history is useful. It would also be useful to recognize the increasingly sophisticated use by police departments and school districts of elementary and secondary school curricula, since this is a relatively recent development.

Throughout this chapter it has also been noted how education system professionals have turned to the police community for advice and counsel regarding crisis planning as well as planning projects to combat specific types of crimes occurring in the schools. Frequent references have been made to the wide disparity among school principals—from school to school and from district to district—when it comes to defining the parameters of acts they consider sufficiently serious to warrant calling the police.

Finally, this chapter has documented how, after many years of separate development within the U.S. Departments of Education and Justice, a program has emerged that appears to combine key elements of the approach of each. By combining the school team approach to planning and problem solving with the law enforcement method of collecting and analyzing data, there appears now to be a model with almost universal appeal. It is a model, moreover, that addresses the central theme of this chapter—school system and police agency cooperation and planning.

11

The Texas Classroom Management and Discipline Program

Margaret E. Dunn

Numerous studies indicate that discipline is a common problem in the schools and that discipline problems tend to escalate if not resolved. The Classroom Management and Discipline Program was initiated to help local school districts in Texas maintain and improve school discipline. It is a statewide university-school-community partnership, funded by the Office of the Governor, Criminal Justice Division and operated by Southwest Texas State University, and it is designed to promote the success of all students.

Throughout every aspect of the program there is a strong emphasis on the concept of the school community. The school community includes schoolteachers, administrators, and support staff; the students and their parents; and the multitude of community agencies and organizations operating within the district or providing services for those residing in the district. The schools are not seen as operating in a vacuum, but rather as an extremely vital component of the local community, affected by both the strengths and the problems of the area.

The program provides both leadership and resources for improving school discipline and academic achievement. Its goals are to help

The author wishes to thank E. Eugene Rios, John A. Wooley, and Cynthia Mott, key staff members of the Classroom Management and Discipline Program, each of whom read and critiqued this paper.

school districts maintain and improve school discipline; to reduce dropout rates, school disruptions, truancy, drug usage, and school crime; to develop alternatives to school suspensions; and to implement programs to enhance the overall learning environment.

PROGRAM SERVICES

Program services are provided to the entire school community: teachers, administrators, support staff, school board members, representatives from community agencies, and parents. These program services, aimed at improving school discipline, include providing training and technical assistance, developing and distributing relevant publications, and sponsoring conferences on timely issues. All services are provided at no cost to the local school communities.

Training

The program provides both intensive five-day courses on campus during the summer and short one- and two-day on-site, statewide courses for local districts' staff development training throughout the school year. All presenters have strong knowledge about their topics, practical experience in their fields, and expertise as adult educators.

Summer courses are offered yearly with participation limited to school teams of four to five members. At least one team member must be a school administrator; other team members can be drawn from all segments of the school community including teachers, counselors, board members, parents, and community representatives. Diverse representation on the team is encouraged; the only prerequisite is that all team members must be actively involved, with the school system representing either the entire school district or a single campus.

All 1,100 superintendents in the state are invited to send teams from their districts to the summer courses; however, space is limited. The week-long course in classroom management and discipline is offered four times, with each session open to a maximum of sixty participants constituting twelve to fifteen teams. Teams are selected by program staff so that each course will have an overall group of teams reflecting a balanced mix of large and small districts from geographically representative rural and urban districts. Regional training and technical assistance are also provided by this project upon request of local school districts or communities, subject to budget and time limitations. In accepting requests to provide on-site services, the program serves both large and small areas, reflecting a wide geographical distribution.

Throughout all training courses a variety of methods and formats are used. Presentations take the form of lectures, group discussion and problem solving, role-playing, simulations, demonstrations, debates, small group discussion, and project planning, as well as individual work. The team members are actively involved in learning new skills, polishing old ones, and personalizing the best of the old and the new. Many opportunities are provided for participants to practice new techniques and to be videotaped if they choose. The five-day course concentrates on four major areas: strategies to improve school discipline, legal issues relevant to school discipline, social problems affecting student behavior, and school-community networking.

Multiple strategies to improve school discipline are presented as part of an overall comprehensive and integrated approach. Topics include action planning, team building, selecting disciplinary techniques, and establishing alternative education and in-school suspension centers.

Presentation of legal issues relevant to school discipline includes a thorough discussion of both the juvenile justice laws and the school laws operant in the state. Distinctions in terminology and provisions in the legal codes are explained to minimize confusion. The legal component is very helpful to educators because there are many conflicts in definitions and procedures regarding children under Texas law, especially regarding attendance requirements and school expulsion issues.

Social problems affecting school discipline are considered in relation to student behavior. Procedures and programs to address such problems as teenage suicide, drug and alcohol abuse, truancy, and dropouts are presented. The presentations are made by professionals recognized as having expertise in addressing these complex problems. Model programs from community agencies and school districts are described.

School-community networking is facilitated through presentations that provide suggestions to improve school-parent cooperation, information about school-court liaisons, and model school partnership programs. The aspect of forming school partnerships is an integral part of the school community concept. School personnel are encouraged to link with the many resources in their own communities in order to maximize their own efforts and work toward common goals.

Many sessions are conducted concurrently, so that individuals can select the particular topics which interest them the most or promise the most benefit to them or their districts. Often school teams will send a member to each one of the offerings, then share information and materials with the other team members.

A particularly successful aspect of the training courses is action planning. Each team works together every afternoon Monday through Thursday to develop a plan of action that is tailor-made to address a discipline-related concern they have for their campus or district.

The Classroom Management and Discipline Program conducts regional training throughout the year, upon request and within program limitations. Each year approximately 1,200 people receive training in their local districts on topics of local concern. Requests for this training are made most frequently for scheduled staff development training days. The exact topics and presentation formats are decided jointly between the requesting school district and the program staff. Topics frequently requested include student motivation, disciplinary styles and techniques, legal issues in discipline, disciplining the special education student, child abuse recognition and reporting, school drug prevention, and effective classroom management. Often training is requested for a particular audience, such as new teachers, attendance officers, school bus drivers, vocational teachers, or staff from specific grade levels. Other times, the training sessions are open to most or all of the district personnel. The actual in-service format varies with the size of the group, the topic being presented, and the preferences of the school district. Most frequently, local in-service training addresses classroom management skills and various disciplinary approaches and techniques.

Technical Assistance

The Classroom Management and Discipline Program provides technical assistance upon request and within program limitations. The types of assistance requested most frequently focus on a need identified by the requesting school district, such as preventing substance abuse on school grounds and during school-sponsored activities, reducing school crime, establishing alternative education programs, or addressing the needs of students considered "at risk." The technical assistance usually takes the form of on-site consultation, identification of resources, and group facilitation. The program posture is one of support for district personnel, students, and community. The program itself does not dictate ideas or select specific programs but does provide a variety of ideas for the local districts to review and adapt to fit their own needs.

Publications

In addition to providing training and technical assistance, the program develops and distributes timely publications. These publications currently include the modular training notebook, a resource directory of services for youth and their families, and a booklet addressing teenage suicide and the school situation.

The modular training text is in notebook form and is updated each year in order to accommodate new topics of interest and reflect the most up-to-date research findings and legal requirements. The notebook is divided into five major sections. Section I, Classroom Management, includes the following topics: Organizing and Managing the Classroom, Selecting Approaches for Improving School Discipline, and Combining Disciplinary Approaches for Your School. Section II, School and Community, includes the following topics: In-School Alternatives to Out-of-School Removal, Improving School Attendance, Preventing Drug Abuse Through Education, and Prevention of Child Abuse and Neglect. Section III, Legal Issues, includes the following topics: An Introduction to Juvenile Justice, Selected Excerpts from the Texas Education Code, and Selected Excerpts from the Texas Family Code. Section IV, Special Issues, includes the following topics: School Crime Prevention and Security, Search and Seizure, Teenage Suicide, Dropout Prevention, and The Behavioral Individual Education Plan: A Disciplinary Tool. Section V, Additional Materials, contains the bibliography. During the first year of the Classroom Management and Discipline Program, each of the 1,100 school districts in Texas received a copy of the text and each of the 20 regional education service centers received five copies. Since that time an additional three thousand texts have been distributed during the training sessions or by request.

The resource directory is a guide to state and national organizations and agencies which provide services for children and youth, their schools, and their families. The entries are organized according to educational programs, service agencies, university services, state agency services, out-of-state or national agencies, and hotline listings. Each of the 250 entries gives a short program description; a listing of services provided; and the title, address, and phone number of the program's contact person. The directory is very popular and is already in its third printing, with more than seven thousand copies distributed to date.

The booklet, *Teenage Suicide*, prepared for the program by Dr. Eleanor Guetzloe, has been distributed to every school district, each of the 190 juvenile probation departments, each of the 20 regional education service centers, and all 20 councils of government in the state. An additional ten thousand copies have been distributed upon request. The publication, which deals specifically with the school's situation relevant to teenage suicide, is presently being reprinted because of the high demand for it. The booklet gives a discussion of the school's responsibility in suicide prevention; behaviors associated with depression; suicide crisis intervention in the schools; and components of a comprehensive school plan regarding suicide prevention, intervention, and postvention.

Two new publications are being planned, one dealing with gang activity and the other focusing on school-based substance abuse prevention. Both booklets will be available in the spring of 1989.

Conferences

The program sponsored a national conference in late 1986 on classroom management and discipline, during which nationally recognized authorities discussed effective and proven measures and helped participants explore successful programs and practices. Speakers included William Glasser, Thomas Gordon, William Wayson, Carolyn Evertson, Edmund Emmer, Robert Spaulding, C. M. Charles, and others.

The program also sponsored a conference addressing at-risk students during which a number of programs, ideas, and partnerships were presented. Although providing for the needs of at-risk students has always been a priority in Texas schools, recent state legislation has called for the development of specific programs to address these needs in every school district. The major thrust of this initiative is to provide for student success and to reduce the likelihood of students dropping out of school. Students considered at risk include multi-problem youth, as well as youth whose problems include academic, behavioral, environmental, familial, economic, social, developmental, and other psycho-social factors. Large corporations, including Southwestern Bell, International Business Machines, Tenneco, and Southland, explained their involvement with local schools and discussed ways for school personnel to initiate school-business partnerships.

PROGRAM FEATURES

The Classroom Management and Discipline Program provides a mechanism for obtaining and using information drawn from both research and successful practice to improve school discipline and to increase cooperation among the diverse populations of the school community. Key features of the program are the collaborative emphasis, the action-planning process, the change agent function, and the training-of-trainers concept. These are discussed in the following sections, along with some successful local action plans.

Collaborative Emphasis

The program is a true partnership involving the university, the school, and the community on both the state and local levels. Southwest Texas State University has an especially strong School of Education which has one of the highest enrollments in teacher education of any university in the country. The School of Education places a heavy emphasis on having students truly prepared for the classroom, knowledgeable in educational research, and confident from field experience. The Lyndon B. Johnson Institute for the Improvement of Teaching and Learning, of which the Classroom Management and Discipline Program is a part, includes a number of projects involving School of Education faculty directly in Texas schools.

The Criminal Justice Division, Office of the Governor, funds many alternative education projects and programs addressing the needs of students at risk of failure or of dropping out. A priority of this agency is early prevention of delinquency through the strengthening of positive school experiences for youth, especially high-risk youth. As part of this emphasis, the Classroom Management and Discipline Program is funded to provide training and technical assistance, not only to the schools in the funded special emphasis programs, but also to any interested school district. The criminal justice monies are being invested in the schools as a partnership because it is believed that many of the problems facing educators today originate outside the classroom and because of the high correlation between children with trouble at school and children in trouble with the law.

Clearly there is a strong need for community agencies to cooperate and collaborate with the schools in order for youth, especially multiple-problem youth, to receive needed services. Services provided to schools through criminal justice funds encourage and sometimes require interagency linkages, especially with juvenile probation, child protective services, drug abuse counselors, police, and mental health agencies. Training courses offered by the Classroom Management and Discipline Program include presentations by a number of social service agencies and organizations. The presentations describe the services that these agencies can provide for educators, the mechanics of establishing communication and cooperation at the local level, and the process for obtaining funds that may be available from the various community and social agencies for school-based projects. In Texas, state funds are provided for school-based programs and specific student needs by agencies as diverse as the Criminal Justice Division, Office of the Governor, the Texas Commission on Drugs and Alcohol Abuse, the Texas Juvenile Probation Commission, and the Texas Department of Human Services. More often than not, educators are not aware of the resources they can tap into from these agencies. Information learned from these presentations provides participants with better understanding of the roles of their own community agencies and a foundation for future cooperation.

Action-Planning Component

The action-planning process facilitates information sharing, group communication, and collaborative decision making. Each day the entire group meets together for a presentation and discussion of both the process and products of each step involved in action planning. Then the participants regroup by team. Program staff serve as facilitators for the teams, using a ratio of five teams per facilitator. The facilitator's job is to keep the teams on task, to clarify questions about expectations and procedures, and to secure specific information or expertise as needed for plan development. Through the group effort and emphasis on team building, unity and commitment to goals and objectives are shared. As the action plans develop, both resources and obstacles are identified and taken into consideration; from this process a realistic plan of action emerges.

Action planning is successful for many reasons. Respected professionals who truly believe in education and youth provide needed information. Time is provided daily for school team members to work together and jointly develop an action plan which incorporates new information and ideas gained from the training program. The values and personal needs of all participants are respected. The Classroom Management and Discipline Program may be counted upon for technical assistance during later implementation of the plans. There are two important stipulations in action planning: (1) whatever the team selects for its project must be an issue or concern over which members represented on the team have authority, and (2) whatever the team selects must be related to school discipline, taken in a broad sense. The action plans are presented on Friday morning, the last day of the training course. Each team walks the other participants through the steps of its action plan: problem identification, articulation of a realistic ideal (the degree to which the problem can actually be reduced or impacted), listing of obstacles to be overcome, composition of possible resources to be brought to bear on the issue, development of the plan addressing the problem, and a specification of all the activities and job responsibilities needed for implementation of the action plan upon the team's return to its home district. At this time the entire group of participants reviews the individual team plans and provides words of encouragement and caution as needed.

Change Agent Function

The Classroom Management and Discipline Program functions as an effective change agent mainly by guiding the development and assisting the implementation of each team's action plan. Throughout the week-long courses, the program deliberately and consistently promulgates the need to implement change for the better, change that will improve the school environment for both the students and the educators.

Since the program began, school teams have developed more than 400 action plans. The majority of plans were designed for implementation at a single campus. Many of these were expanded into other campuses or throughout the district as the plan of action proved successful at the original site. In total, more than 350 of the plans have been implemented by the school teams. Many action plans have been shared and implemented at more than one location, and the overall implementation rate is well over 150 percent, based on follow-up data supplied by the participants. The action plans developed during two recent years, many of which involved establishing local in-service training in classroom management and discipline, have achieved over a 300 percent successful implementation rate.

There are many reasons for the high rate of successful implementation. There is direct participation in planning the change by people who are going to participate in the planned change, are knowledgeable about the issues being addressed, and are in a position to implement the change. The benefits of the planned change are appreciated by those planning the change because they have selected their target for change on the basis of its perceived priority and practicality. A support base is built for the planned change because a variety of representatives from the school community constitute the team that developed the plan of action. The planned change is well thought out, targets a situation considered important by the team, and is subject to formative and summative evaluation by both the team members and the local school administration. Regarding the plans that were not implemented, the reasons given most frequently were that there had been personnel changes or budget cutbacks.

Through action planning, the Classroom Management and Discipline Program directly addresses real problems in the schools. It provides pertinent information, allows participants to select from a variety of options, and facilitates the development and implementation of programs tailor-made to meet local needs. A representative sampling of successful action plans developed and implemented by program participants addressed the following.

Student Referrals to the Office.   The Santa Fe Independent School District reduced the overall number of referrals for misconduct to the principal's office by involving teachers and parents in a cooperative project. Team members conducted local teacher in-service sessions using the Classroom Management and Discipline Program's notebook and training materials. The in-service program focused on disciplinary techniques they could use and helped teachers develop a classroom management plan. A system of parental contacts was established which called for teachers to contact all their students' parents prior to any problems.

Recently the Santa Fe Independent School District with Classroom Management and Discipline Program staff developed ten new action plans to establish and operate an innovative alternative for at-risk youth and school dropouts. The district, having received funding from the Criminal Justice Division, Office of the Governor, will provide an evening school with a heavy emphasis on individual counseling and tutoring.

Uniform Homework Policy.   The Smithville Independent School District wanted a uniform policy regarding homework for their junior high school. Some teachers were not giving homework assignments because many students were either cheating on assignments or not turning them in as required. The new homework policy called for all teachers to assign homework on a regular basis and to insist that assignments be done completely and individually. Students who failed to do so were subject to the school's disciplinary procedures. As a result of their action plan, not only was the assigned homework completed and turned in on time, but also their students experienced a significant increase in their standardized test scores.

Conduct in Cafeteria Before School Begins.   The Humble Independent School District team developed a cafeteria monitoring program for mornings between 7:00 A.M. and 8:15 A.M., when students waited for classes to start. Prior to the plan's implementation, there were many problems and supervision of the children was difficult. Teachers now rotate the early morning duty, assist students who need help on their assignments, and monitor quiet study groups and quiet socializing. The students bring study materials, and teachers award good-conduct tickets to well-behaved students for a drawing at the end of each six weeks for special prizes. The project has generated increased parent support, improved behavior, and strengthened study skills.

Increasing Attendance.   The Athens Independent School District implemented a plan to improve attendance which resulted in 2 percent increased daily attendance and a considerable increase in the state's funding based on the average daily attendance. The attendance improvement model included direct participation of students in competitions between classes for the best attendance and was supported by a variety of incentives donated by parents and school personnel. Additional privileges, such as passes for the cafeteria line, were won by students with good attendance. Parents were informed of the importance of school attendance and were contacted anytime their child was absent.

Increased Parental Involvement.   The Sharyland Independent School District wanted to motivate parents to be more involved in their schools. To improve motivation, they created a districtwide newsletter printed several times each year. This newsletter includes information that parents are interested in—anything from special programs to extracurricular activities to student honors. The newsletter has been well received by the parents and the general community. Many articles have been reprinted in the local newspaper, and parental support has been increased for the schools.

Student Discipline Handbooks.   The Hoffman Independent School District team members helped their district develop student handbooks that were distributed to all students. In these handbooks, the district outlined the specific procedures school personnel would take in dealing with discipline problems and the corresponding consequences for infractions. The handbook also helped the district staff to follow a consistent method for dealing with disruptive students.

The handbook was more successful in precipitating school improvement than many handbooks are because teachers, parents, and students had direct input in its creation. A concise description of responsibilities, policies, and procedures were clearly outlined.

Behavior On School Buses.   The Madisonville Consolidated School District team wanted to improve student behavior on school buses. They therefore developed a parent referral form to be filled out by the bus driver when a student misbehaved. After a referral a parent conference is held, at which time the parents' ideas are solicited for correcting their child's behavior. The program has resulted in greatly improved behavior on the bus, and the parents are pleased with the improved safety conditions which resulted from the improved behavior.

District Planning.   The Mission Independent School District has used the team concept and action-planning process to develop a number of initiatives, such as decreasing referrals to the office for disruptive behavior, implementing a dropout prevention project, and developing a life management course in which community members make class presentations. The school district has also initiated a monthly morning meeting with interested community and social service agencies to discuss common problems and improve service linkages. At times the group meetings use the action-planning process to identify and solve common problems.

Training of Trainers Concept

School team members who return from the summer courses are quite frequently asked to provide local staff development training for other teachers in their home districts. A follow-up study revealed that as many as 85 percent of the program's participants had in fact conducted such training and had relied heavily on the information from the modular text for the training sessions and various handout materials that they had received while in attendance. The program now includes specific information for presenting staff development on discipline and classroom management. Teams are given tips for successful staff development. They are reminded that the presentations should be meaningful and should include the direct involvement of the learner, especially in the planning stages. They should be ongoing and nonthreatening and, most important, specific and practical. Opportunities for coaching and feedback concerning the new skills should be provided. Through this "training of trainers" concept the benefits of the training program have been made available for thousands more than were able to attend the week-long course.

Program Development and Evaluations

The goals, activities, and curriculum for the Classroom Management and Discipline Program were identified by program staff with the assistance and cooperation of professionals from the university, the public school systems, and the juvenile justice system in Texas. An advisory board, composed of members from representative organizations and agencies directly involved in education or juvenile justice, was established to monitor program implementation and to assist in decision making regarding any modifications of the program. During its first twelve months the program was pilot-tested, and was closely monitored by board members and carefully evaluated. The determination to continue the program was based on the success of first-year evaluations. Evaluations were both formative and summative and included a needs assessment of participants at each training course, daily evaluations, speaker evaluations, overall course evaluations, and an outside evaluation. Decisions regarding program modification were and still are based on the information received through the evaluative process and yearly review by the advisory board. Through the years the program has been expanded and course content has been changed to reflect areas identified as needed, such as sessions relevant to suicide and child abuse. A stronger emphasis on disciplinary techniques and options has evolved.

Evaluations reveal a high degree of satisfaction with the program. Course context and speaker reviews are consistently rated above 4.5 on a scale of 1 to 5, with 5 the highest. In a study of past participants taken eight months after they had completed the week-long training course, 98 percent indicated that they felt more confident in their disciplinary skills as a result of their participation in the course, and 99 percent stated that they have found the information and materials they received during the training course to be useful to them during the school term.

The Classroom Management and Discipline Program has received three national distinctions: it was selected as a model program by the National Association of Secondary School Principals and was featured in their *National Directory of School-College Partnerships* (1987), and it was the recipient of both the Christa McAuliffe Showcase for Excellence Award given by the American Association of State Colleges and Universities (1986) and the Special Merit Award given by the Council for the Advancement and Support of Education (1984). The program was also commended in a resolution passed by the Texas legislature and has been selected by the Criminal Justice Division, Office of the Governor, as a model demonstration project.

New Directions

The Classroom Management and Discipline Program received funding in 1988 from the U.S. Department of Education to establish two demonstration projects: Schools Against Substance Abuse (SASA) and Project XL (Excel). SASA works directly with the thirty-six school districts and communities that currently participate in the student teacher training experience at Southwest Texas State University. This new component provides training and technical assistance to law enforcement officers, court personnel, educators, and representatives from community agencies to recognize and prevent student drug abuse. It fosters improved linkages between schools and communities in the region so that information and services to youth may be coordinated with proactive rather than reactive approaches. Communitywide systems of service coordination are being developed rather than piecemeal approaches that are often inconsistent and fragmented. Through this collaborative effort, it is hoped that substance use and abuse will be eliminated or greatly curtailed in these schools.

Project XL (Excel) is a dropout prevention program involving the Dallas Independent School District, the Dallas Communities in Schools, and the Classroom Management and Discipline Program targeting a district high school and its nine feeder schools. Project XL includes identification, prevention, and outreach services for at-risk youth and potential dropouts. It provides mentoring, tutoring, counseling, and childcare services. It accesses vocational and academic courses as well as job placement services, and networks with community resources and businesses to provide collaborative services for students and their families. Project XL conducts research and data analysis regarding dropouts and related problems, as well as provides technical assistance, staff training, and program development for more effective teaching strategies to be used with at-risk students. Aspects of the Effective Schools Model are being replicated through Project XL.

CONCLUSION

The Classroom Management and Discipline Program is an action-oriented program that has proven to be successful in improving school discipline. In an evaluation of the program's first five years, the Director of Training for the Texas Juvenile Probation Commission, Bernard Licarione, noted that the program's success rate is phenomenal. He reported that the evalutions, the action plan implementation rate, and the sheer numbers of participants and requests for services far exceeded expectations. The most exciting aspect of the Classroom Management and Discipline Program is that it works.

12

Jacksonville's Student Code of Conduct: A Balance of Rights and Responsibilities

Herb A. Sang

The Duval County School System (Jacksonville. Florida) is one of the twenty largest school districts in the nation, in terms of both population and geographic size. More than 104,000 students from across 827 square miles attend one or more of the district's 142 schools. Each year, the population swells by 2,000 children new to these schools and the academic and behavioral expectations of their educators.

Although Duval County's written code of behavioral expectations may not be unusual, its threefold approach to behavior management is. First, the district has clearly defined behavioral policies, and provides the incentive and instruction necessary for students, teachers, and administrators to operate successfully within the published guidelines. Second, the district monitors the actions and the conduct of the students to consistently reinforce expectations. Third, programs to retrieve and redirect students to more appropriate standards of behavior keep students in school.

We know that this clear approach to expectations and consequences is working. The incidence of serious offenses (alcohol. drugs, arson, robbery, explosives, criminal mischief) has been cut in half, and the costs of vandalism to schools has dropped 60 percent in the past four years. Although the reasons and circumstances surrounding student misconduct vary by case, Duval County's approach

253

to discipline is presented here to provide educators with a comprehensive framework for improving student behavior.

A STUDENT CODE OF CONDUCT

In any productive setting, it is essential for everyone to know where he stands, what is expected of him, and what he can expect in return. This is particularly important in a large school district, where unclear guidelines can result in a broad range of interpretation and inconsistent consequences. A strong framework of behavioral expectations, widely communicated and consistently enforced, provides students, teachers, parents, and administrators with a clear understanding of where they stand, what is expected of them, and what they can expect in return.

A Student Code of Conduct was developed and adopted by the Duval County School Board in 1978. This code provides a basis for all disciplinary decisions and a foundation for the administration's belief that students will rise to the level of expectancy. In a written handbook, the code defines the role of students, parents, and school personnel in maintaining an atmosphere conducive to learning, students' rights and responsibilities, types of activities which are considered unacceptable, and the procedures for administering formal disciplinary actions.

Three classes of offenses and consequences for each violation are clearly defined. *Class I* is composed of minor offenses, including class disruption, threats or harassment of others, gambling, tardiness, use of profane language, and so forth. Classroom teachers generally deal with class I offenses through in-class action or contact with the parents or guardian for subsequent offenses. *Class II* offenses include defiance of authority, fighting, vandalism, petty theft, trespassing, willful possession of stolen property, leaving school grounds without permission, and so forth. Parental contact, extended work assignments, detention, or in-school suspensions are generally used for class II violations. *Class III* violations are considered major offenses involving alcohol, drugs, arson, battery, robbery, grand theft, burglary of school property, possession of firearms or weapons, bomb threats, sexual acts, and so forth. Because of the seriousness of a class III offense, a disciplinary conference with the principal and parents or guardians is held to define the disciplinary action to be recommended by the principal, including suspension, special program referral (described below), or, lastly, expulsion.

Although parents may waive their involvement in this conference, they are clearly notified that such offenses are strongly dealt with in the Duval County Public Schools.

Students receive orientation to the code in a variety of ways. Large and small group assemblies are used to present the code. Each student receives a personal copy annually and must sign a signature sheet attesting to his or her understanding of it. In addition, a pre- and post-test is given to ensure student comprehension of the policies. Students who fail to demonstrate an understanding of any part of the code are given individual attention by school guidance staff. At the secondary level, the code is integrated into language arts and social studies classes during discussions of legal systems or reading comprehension exercises, and student newspapers often serve as a forum for discussion.

The rationale for establishing a student conduct code is apparent. Since the code is administered throughout the district, students and teachers know how infractions will be handled, and this knowledge eases transfers between schools. Students new to the district are also given clear, written expectations. A twenty-member review committee composed of principals, teachers, students, guidance staff, and others annually reviews the code and recommends modifications based upon disciplinary data and reports from the previous year. This review process has resulted in a clearer distinction between the disciplinary procedures for students who commit multiple class II offenses and are in need of intensive counseling, versus students who endanger others through a class III offense and warrant stronger discipline. Similarly, the review committee has added two categories to the code: students who forge signatures or falsely present notes are considered class I offenders, and students who knowingly conceal or present false information to school officials when questioned about a serious incident can be charged with a class II offense.

A MONITORING SYSTEM

The traditional approach to disciplining students who continue to violate conduct rules has been repeated suspension, expulsion, or forced withdrawal from school. The fallacy of such approaches is that the student is forced to operate outside of the system, and frequently considers the punishment a reward from a system the student refuses to accept.

In Duval County, expulsion is a last resort. Instead, each child's behavioral problems are monitored and addressed as appropriate on the basis of the youngster's personal needs. The school stays abreast of each student through an Individual Student Profile (ISP), which is a cumulative record of academic achievement, health information, and specific concerns that would impact the student's classroom behavior. For each teacher, it is a helpful way to become familiar with students; it becomes a useful record of effective as well as ineffective behavior management strategies (discipline).

At the district level, a computerized system is used to record code infractions of all students, but is most useful for tracking students who commit class III offenses (alcohol, drugs, arson, robbery, firearms). All secondary schools receive a monthly accounting of incidents in their schools, which includes the name, the offense, the discipline code, and the precise location in the building where the offense occurred. This incident-profiling system aids principals in pinpointing specific areas where security can be improved, as well as students who are at risk for more serious behavior problems.

Each week district security personnel review detailed reports that include the sex, race, and date of birth of the offender, the date of the offense, details on the offense, and the immediate disciplinary action taken. In this way, a full accounting is immediately available to help identify patterns that may not be apparent in one school but can be seen as a problem on a wider scale.

This districtwide approach has led to a new investigation procedure by police when responding to emergency calls after school hours (patrolmen were not entering locked areas even though trespassers had scaled the fence to gain entry), as well as the need for an improved security system (an increasing number of break-ins were not detected). Similarly, handguns have begun to pose an everincreasing threat at schools throughout the district—not just in a few troubled areas. The discipline policy adopted by the Duval County School Board in response to this threat has been directly credited with cutting the number of gun-related incidents in half. Students found in possession of firearms, including starter guns, are eligible for expulsion for the remaining school year plus one additional school year.

Although an effective deterrent to many students who consider carrying a gun, expulsion does little to help the student offender. This tracking and profiling system has uncovered a serious need for an intensive program targeted to young teens (ages thirteen to fifteen). At present, only two options exist: committing the student to a state-run institution or returning the student to the home environment. A residential academy is seen as the district's next step in providing twenty-four-hour counseling for youth who have committed a serious offense or have a history of behavior problems. During a ninety-day stay, students would attend academic classes interspersed with vocational and recreational activities and counseling. Parents or guardians would also be required to attend counseling and weekly follow-up meetings scheduled by the guidance counselor after the student returns to the home school.

REDIRECTING BEHAVIOR

Although a lack of consensus characterizes many aspects of school discipline efforts, there is one area where agreement is almost universal—the need for prevention programs. Students who have behavior problems can benefit from efforts to teach them self-control, to redirect their interests, and to heighten their self-esteem. To this end, educators are urged to communicate behavioral expectations, to enforce rules consistently, and to apply appropriate sanctions.

Although consistency is the premise of Duval County's Student Code of Conduct, there is an inherent flaw in this logic that must be addressed in other ways; not all students are alike. Directives to be consistent may lead educators to overlook crucial differences among students that cause misbehavior. Learning disabilities, emotional problems, health concerns, family upheaval, and more can result in negative attitudes about school, poor academic performance, increased absenteeism, and disruptive behavior.

Duval County's program can be grouped into three categories: prevention, intervention, and discipline. In all cases, an emphasis is placed on redirecting behavior through guidance and counseling instead of punishment.

Prevention

CARE (Changing Attitudes Regarding Education). Beginning in the early elementary grades, students who exhibit poor attitudes about school and their behavior are evaluated by an interdisciplinary team to assess the problem and begin steps to heighten student interest in school. Teachers, guidance counselors, and parents work together to involve the students in activities that will build self-esteem and academic success, such as the district's televised homework assistance program, personal tutoring, or special responsibilities under a team member's supervision. Referrals to social services are also made as needed.

Children and Grief.   In 1987 alone, students made nearly 5,400 visits to Duval County counselors to talk about losses in their lives. Trained grief counselors are available in two-thirds of the district's schools to directly combat the effects that unresolved grief has on children—inability to concentrate, poor achievement, absenteeism, and aggressive hostility.

Through a cooperative partnership with Hospice of Northeast Florida, a not-for-profit organization that offers support to terminal patients and their families, teachers throughout the district have learned to recognize the effects of grief and how to offer help. Students are referred to the school's designated grief counselor for evaluation and referral to individual and/or group counseling sessions. Support groups for children of divorced parents, children of Navy personnel deployed at sea for months at a time, and classmates who have lost a close friend are examples of school-based efforts to help students face their losses in appropriate ways.

A 1987 comparison of entrance and exit interviews with students showed that nearly 60 percent felt that grief counseling would not take away the hurt, yet 72 percent said they felt better than they expected when they exited the program. Attendance, grades, and disciplinary incidents were tracked for each student, and significant decreases were seen overall for those who received counseling, compared with students who experienced losses before the program began.

Student Options for Success.   Students and parents learn to talk to each other, often for the first time in years, as a result of this three-week program aimed at teens and their families. Guidance counselors conduct the evening sessions that cover such topics as communication skills, anger and impulse control, self-esteem, peer pressure, setting goals, study skills, and resources in the school system. Parents and students attend by mutual agreement, usually at the recommendation of the school counselor. Parents from all walks of life have applauded the program for putting their relationship with their teen into perspective.

Positive Parenting.   Through a six-week series of classes for parents of all school-age children, the Positive Parenting program introduces parents to better methods of working with their children. Evening sessions are taught by school psychologists and social workers and cover such topics as communicating with and motivating children, constructive discipline, and resources in the community and school system. Attendance in the class is voluntary, although referrals are made by school deans, guidance counselors, juvenile court judges, and teachers. A variety of approaches help parents recognize and address behavior problems exhibited by their children in the classroom, including discussion, role-play, videotape, lecture, and homework and practice assignments. Parents have reported that the class not only helped them work with the misbehavior of one child, but also enabled them to prevent similar behavior problems in younger children.

An outgrowth of the Positive Parenting program has been the addition of a staff training component that teaches teachers how to improve the parent conference.

Teachers as Advisors.   Students with academic or behavior problems are identified by teachers and assigned a teacher advisor whose responsibilities included maintaining regular contact with student and parent, tracking students' progress toward promotion, mediating between home and classroom when appropriate, and serving as a liaison for the parents with the school. Implementation of this program varies by school. Stanton College Preparatory School, a district magnet school offering all advanced classes for grades seven through twelve, uses the Teachers as Advisors program to meet weekly with students and stay in touch with each student's response to stress, encouraging a balance in extracurricular activities and serving as the student's personal mentor. Ft. Caroline Elementary pairs troubled children (identified through the Care Team, below) with teachers who volunteer to be a "Care-O-Line", an adult friend at school. The relationship is symbolically begun when the teacher gives her "I ♥ F.C." button to the student. To the student, the button is a symbol of pride, meaning "I love Ft. Caroline." To the teacher, the button is a daily reminder, "I love fragile children."

Skills for Adolescence.   All sixth grade students in Duval County participate in a special curriculum to develop the skills and self-confidence they will need through the teen years. It addresses the primary causes of many of the problems of adolescence: low self-esteem, negative peer pressure, poor family communication, irresponsibility, lack of goals, and poor decision-making skills.

Designed by a team of educators, underwritten by The Lions Club International and The Quest National Center, this comprehensive program provides classroom materials and activities that can be incorporated into language arts, health and social studies curricula, teacher in-service plans, and a family involvement component, including a handbook on surviving adolescence, communication workshops, and numerous homework assignments that get students and parents talking. Although this is in its first year of use, response to the curriculum from teachers and students has been enthusiastic.

Intervention

Care Team.   A sudden outburst of disruptive behavior or an about-face in a child's attitude about school are often the outward signs of an emotional upheaval in a student's life. Two district-level psychologists and one social worker form the core of the Care Team, a resource that teachers, counselors, principals, and parents can call on in an emergency. An immediate and thorough evaluation of the student ensures the most appropriate handling of the situation, freeing the school staff to respond to other student needs. The Care Team makes recommendations regarding discipline of such cases, and works with the parents to find ongoing therapeutic assistance in the community. The Careline telephone number is advertised through school posters, brochures, and bookmarks.

Secondary Dropout Prevention Program.   The Secondary Dropout Prevention Program is organized to intervene in cases where the student is considering leaving school permanently. A team composed of the vice principal, teachers, assistant principal for student services, and a counselor is charged with determining and implementing interventions which address the student's reason for leaving school. Teachers and school staff are trained in identifying at-risk behaviors, including, but not limited to, disciplinary problems, poor attitude, emotional concerns, and poor academic performance. Intervention plans for each student directly address the student's problem, whether it is a need for personal counseling, a vocational program instead of an academic track, a work-study arrangement to meet financial needs, tutoring, recognition, or career guidance. The team also is responsible for follow-up and for documenting the results monthly.

Since the Secondary Dropout Prevention Team concept was instituted in 1981, the dropout rate has declined consistently—a strong indicator of the importance of flexibility in meeting the needs of students.

Competency Development Program.   The Competency Development Program (CDP) is a nongraded program for students who are unable to meet promotion requirements in the standard school environment. As early as fourth grade, students who have been retained more than once, are eligible for exceptional education services, have a history of absenteeism or disruptive behavior, and are older than students at the same grade level may choose to enroll in the CDP track. Students attend one of thirty vocational training programs at the three district vocational training centers, where they learn basic skills required for employment. Students who remain in the CDP program throughout high school earn a certificate of completion. Because it is a voluntary program, students may return to the regular academic program at any time to work toward a high school diploma.

The CDP program is credited in Duval County with "saving" hundreds of students considered at risk for dropping out of school.

SAVE (Selected Alternatives for Vocational Education). Exceptional education students who are at least fourteen years of age and have failed two or more years are targeted for a prevocational training program designed to revive their interest in learning. (Although it is not a requirement for admission, all of the students enrolled have repeatedly violated the Student Code of Conduct.) Work sample kits for twenty-seven vocations are available to the student, to explore what it is like to work as a carpenter, chef, or real estate agent, for example. Each student works through an individualized competency-based program (geared to vocational interests and abilities), moving at his or her own pace, usually for one to two years. The program emphasizes, among other things, developing personal skills, giving students a defined approach to dealing with anger, problem solving, and interviews. At the completion of the program, students have the option to return to the regular ESE classroom or to enroll in a full-time vocational training program.

SAVE programs are being piloted in two junior high schools, and are open to referrals from teachers, guidance counselors, or the district's Child Study Team.

Peer Counseling. This program uses established criteria such as attendance problems, grades, and behavior records to identify potential dropouts. These students are then paired with students who have received peer counseling training and are recommended by their teachers to be a volunteer peer counselor, under the supervision of certified school counselors. The concept of peer counseling is the focus of a summer camp for teens who want to broaden their personal skills. Nearly one hundred area youth are sponsored by parents and local businesses to attend the week-long session filled with discussions, role-play, small group workshops, and recreation.

The peer counseling concept has been endorsed by the School Board and is included in most of the district's secondary schools.

Rotary Challenge.   Five area chapters of Rotary International have been challenged to make a difference in the lives of at-risk students. Each chapter has been paired with a local school, with members individually assigned to students, to get involved in the teens' lives, offering whatever support may be needed to keep them out of trouble and in school, such as by tutoring, serving as a male role model, or offering part-time employment. Although the program is only in its first year and some students have been initially unwilling to accept the Rotarians' help, several volunteers have expressed a growing understanding of the need for their involvement and have reinforced their commitment to find a way to help.

Alcohol and Drug Abuse Programs.   A substance abuse prevention and intervention team, consisting of an administrator, a counselor, teachers, and a parent, has been trained for each of the forty-three secondary public schools in Duval County. Each team is charged with developing and implementing a plan of activities specifically designed to intervene with students in need of alcohol and drug abuse counseling, and to involve students in meaningful prevention efforts. *Heartbeat*, a series of one-act plays written, directed, and performed by a group of students from one area high school affected by the tragic death of four seniors in an automobile crash, is an outgrowth of one team's plan to help students make sense out of their loss. Elementary schools have parades, guest speakers, poster contests, and writing assignments to practice saying "no".

Students with documented behavior patterns suggesting alcohol or substance abuse may be given the following options. Chemically dependent students may be referred to an in-patient or out-patient treatment facility. Students using alcohol or drugs, but who are not chemically dependent, may be referred to the Darnell-Cookman Counseling Center (see below). Two evenings a week parents of substance abusers are obligated to attend a Substance Abuse Counseling Program.

Discipline

Students unable or unwilling to respond to more traditional methods of discipline are given several alternatives. The Duval County alternative school program provides an intervention process for students who are unresponsive or even hostile to initial efforts of the school to control discipline problems.

In-School Suspension Program.   The In-School Suspension Program is an alternative to suspension or other disciplinary action for students committing a class II infraction of the Student Code of Conduct. For a minimum of three days, students are removed from their regular academic program and report to a type of study hall. The school's occupational specialists, counselors, and teachers are assigned to the program to keep the students involved in a day of academic work and counseling. The concept of in-school suspension has been offered in Duval County as an alternative discipline for approximately fifteen years. Since 1982, the use of corporal punishment has dropped nearly 60 percent in favor of the academic benefits of in-school suspension. Although the state of Florida authorizes school principals to administer corporal punishment, we encourage this as a last resort and prefer to encourage the use of alternatives such as in-school suspension and parent conferences as the most appropriate manner of resolving disciplinary problems.

Darnell-Cookman Counseling Center.   The Darnell-Cookman Counseling Center is an alternative to expulsion for Class II and Class III violations of the Student Code of Conduct, offering students the chance for rehabilitation and a fresh start. By enrolling in the center for a minimum of twenty days, students agree to attend group and individual counseling sessions, drug and alcohol counseling, math and language labs, and physical education class, in addition to keeping up with missed classroom assignments from the home school. Students remain in the center until they request to return to the home school and make a commitment to change their behavior.

An average of seven hundred students elect to participate annually in the Darnell-Cookman alternative setting. The heavy emphasis on improving self-esteem and arming students with the ability to take responsibility for their actions has resulted in a 19 percent recidivism rate—a remarkably low figure given the discipline problems exhibited by each student before entering the program.

Monitoring, once again, plays a role in the success of the district's program. After returning to the home school, monthly progress reports are completed by the dean and counselor and shared with the student. They include information about the student's grades, attendance, and any behavioral problems. Copies are sent to the parent and to the alternative school for evaluating the success of the program. Evaluation reports on the majority of students attending the center indicate improved academic performance, improved personal responsibility for their actions, and a significant decline in behavior problems.

John E. Ford Career Center.   The John E. Ford Career Center is designed to provide intervention for students who have a history of disruptive behavior in school, have committed offenses which may warrant expulsion according to the district's Code of Student Conduct, or are status offenders and juvenile justice offenders. For many, it is the last stop in the school system after a stay at the Darnell-Cookman Counseling Center has failed to produce a change in attitude and behavior. Students in grades seven through twelve are enrolled for a minimum of ninety days in a wide range of vocational training programs. At the end of the three-month stay, students who exhibit appropriate behavior may choose to return to their home school or to remain in the center for up to a year upon the counselor's and principal's recommendations.

MAINTAINING BALANCE

Student discipline is a balance of rights and responsibilities. Although not all of Duval County's preventive efforts are new or unique, the environment in which they are conducted enhances their effectiveness. Moreover, because no two students are alike, program parameters are tailored to meet individual problems and levels of misbehavior.

Four elements of the district's approach to student discipline are considered the framework for maintaining balance:

1. Student behavioral expectations are identified, widely communicated, and equitably enforced.

2. Intervention programs encourage the development of acceptable behavior within the system as opposed to removing the student from school through suspension, expulsion, or withdrawal.

3. Programs offer flexibility to encourage sensitivity to crucial differences in students which may affect student behavior.

4. Educators are aware of a frequent relationship between disruptive behavior and recent loss.

To date, the results have been positive. Recognizing the strong link between behavior and academic success, Duval County's declining dropout rate and increasing student achievement are evidence that balance is being maintained in the classroom.

Just ten years ago, district scores on the Stanford Achievement Test (SAT) averaged at the 43rd percentile. Eighty percent of the students of a predominantly black high school flunked the state-required competency test. The number of students leaving school during the year averaged 5.5 percent, with 102 lost to expulsions.

In 1987, SAT scores reached the 56th percentile in communications and the 62nd percentile in math. More than 80 percent of the students at that same high school passed the state tests. Recent SAT scores of black students topped the national average for black students by 31 points. Duval County's advanced placement program (recently recognized as a strong component in keeping bright students interested in school) was one of two in the Southeast to receive an award of excellence from the College Board, with the number of students qualifying for college credit on advanced placement exams rising by 25 percent over the last year alone. National Merit Scholarship semifinalists have doubled in five years (fifteen to thirty), with forty being named in the 1988 school year.

At a time when schools are being asked to take a more active role in the social and moral growth of students, a clear yet flexible approach to student discipline puts students in control of their lives, enables them to take responsibility for their actions, and redirects their behavior to achieve the balance that is essential to student academic achievement.

Coerced Community Service as a School Discipline Strategy

Jackson Toby and Adam Scrupski

The 350-page report to the Congress, *Violent Schools—Safe Schools* (U.S. Department of Health, Education, and Welfare, 1978) contained mountains of data bearing on the causes of violence and vandalism in American public schools and on possible remedies. For instance, thousands of students, teachers, and principals were asked their opinions about countermeasures: "If a school had a problem with personal attacks, theft, and property destruction, what could be done to make it safer?" Interestingly enough, the most frequent response of all three groups—students, teachers, and principals— was some variation of "stricter discipline." But what did respondents mean by "stricter discipline"?

Probably most students and some teachers and principals meant traditional punishments: visiting physically and symbolically unpleasant humiliations on offenders to make them regret their transgressions. This punitive emphasis was actually in place in many schools; 14 percent of the big-city schools and 42 percent of the schools in rural areas used "paddling" in 1976, when the study was conducted. Certainly nineteenth century educator William C. Bagley meant traditional punishments when he recommended to a young teacher to "pile penalty upon penalty for misdemeanors and let the 'sting' of each penalty be double that of its predecessor" (Waller, 1932, p. 308).

However, when teachers and principals today speak of "discipline", they often mean something else. They refer to "effective classroom management" and imply that the art of good classroom management can prevent discipline problems from arising in the first place. In a sense, a teacher who complains about discipline problems in the classroom labels himself or herself as a poor manager.

Yet this newly fashionable way that educators think about discipline does not change the fact that hundreds of thousands of instances of rule violation occur in American schools, some minor, some very serious. What do teachers and principals do about them? For relatively minor infractions, there are reprimands, after-school detention, and in-school suspension. For serious infractions, there are transfers to alternate schools, suspensions, and, very rarely, expulsions. The most frequent response to serious infractions, suspension, has been under suspicion as pointless in light of the classroom management philosophy. If students are chronically truant, what sense is there in suspending them? They obviously don't want to be in school anyway. If students do not apply themselves to schoolwork and apply themselves instead to mischief, doesn't suspension increase their marginal relationship to the curriculum? Suspension seems irrational if the goal is to rehabilitate the offender.

One recent appraisal of school discipline speaks of both suspension and corporal punishment as "blatantly inhuman" disciplinary techniques (Radin, 1988). Another sees suspension as a "backstage" way of dealing with difficult children in urban schools by excluding them (Tropea, 1987). Still another sees suspension as "capital punishment for misdemeanors" (Comerford and Jacobson, 1987). Professional condemnations of suspension provide support for the public suspicion of suspension as the stigmatization of child and family, which of course it is. And in almost every study where parental preferences were investigated, parents preferred less drastic sanctions to suspensions. Even as a response to violent offenses, suspension has fallen into disrepute. After all, suspension turns deviance-prone youth loose in the community—unsupervised; consequently, it may increase the likelihood of further damage to the community. Furthermore, data show racial disproportionality in suspension, thus suggesting a special dysfunction of suspension for minority-group youth most in need of the continuous service of schools.

These appraisals ignore the empirical effects of suspension on suspended students and on the rest of the school community. Although the academic achievement of suspended students may be lowered by their suspensions, it is likely that suspension delivers an effective symbolic message to the offender. The message is that the school, as the official representative of the local community, has temporarily given up on the student. To be suspended is to become a temporary pariah. Who wants that? We hypothesize that most rule violators do not want it and that their parents want it even less. What is at stake for them is not only education but membership in the community, including membership in the peer community.

The community's connection to suspension from school is revealed in the locus of the authority to suspend students. Classroom teachers may reprimand or detain misbehaving pupils, but in most school districts only the principal or his or her surrogate responsible for behavior in the school as a whole may suspend. Thus, principals or their surrogates suspend in cases of failure of teacher-employed sanctions, in cases where the classroom offense is serious enough that the more moderate teacher sanctions are insufficient, or in cases where the offense occurs in the school at large, for example, in corridors or lavatories. Although in practice the school tends to "go it alone" in its administration of suspensions, the community is the ultimate authority in depriving a child of the right to attend school through suspension. In New Jersey, for instance, the board of education must be notified each month of every suspension.

The camouflaging of the community as the ultimate order-maintaining authority in disciplinary suspensions is one reason why suspensions have come to be viewed suspiciously. If those responsible for order in the school could devise some sanction that would represent the community in its demand for conforming behavior, order would be easier to maintain. It will be suggested that "coerced community service," unlike suspension, is more likely to be perceived by students as a community response to misbehavior than ordinary school sanctions, including suspensions.

The outline of the presentation is as follows: First, it will be argued that currently available school sanctions—suspension, in-school suspension, graduated punishment, and alternative school placement—have limited effectiveness as responses to serious student misbehavior. Second, it will be shown that a community-related alternative to suspension that is sufficiently punitive to be effective is needed. Third, a plan for a punitive sanction, coerced community service, will be advanced. The nature of the service and its supervisors will be described, as will the offenses eligible for such service. Finally, obvious objections to coerced community service will be taken up and responded to, including the continuing need for an effective response to serious misbehavior at school.

SCHOOL SANCTIONS FOR STUDENT
MISBEHAVIOR

Disciplinary sanctions have been part of the history and culture of schools from the start of compulsory education. The word *discipline*, almost as familiar a term as *recess* and *graduation*, has traditionally implied punitive consequences for misbehavior. Although *punishment* is not often spoken of explicitly, punishment under other names — *assertive discipline*, for example — has continued to be of interest, for example, in recent schemes of graduated penalties from verbal correction, through time-outs, and then detention. In any case, the concurrent search for alternatives to suspension, the school's ultimate sanction, suggests that assertive discipline is not a very effective solution to school disciplinary problems.

Punishment as a response to student misbehavior has two implications, one for the offender and one for conforming students. For the offender, it constitutes an attempt to stop his misbehavior; getting his "just desserts" demonstrates to him the futility of his deviance.[1] Punishment is intended as a preliminary to the punished individual's return to conformity. For the group, punishment has consequences for the morale of conformists; it protects the normative system of school rules and regulations by making the offender unenviable (Toby, 1964; 1981). Unfortunately, neither of these functions of punitive school discipline has received much research attention.

Robert Slavin (1986) reports that "many studies have demonstrated the effectiveness of certain mild punishments for reducing inappropriate behavior." Slavin is referring to studies in which teachers administer such sanctions as five-minute detentions and "time-outs" as behavior modification strategies operating to inhibit interruptions in the flow of instructional activity. Despite the widespread use of suspension, a thrusting out of the offending student from the school community, and the contemporary controversy surrounding its use, research on the effectiveness of suspension is surprisingly uncommon.

Few studies bear on the issue of whether suspension works as it is supposed to work. Do suspended students take suspension as a joke or do they think twice about engaging in future misbehavior? Thus, of forty-one studies turned up in a computer search of *Psychological Abstracts* using the identifying word *suspension*, only three dealt in any way with the effects of suspension on students. All three were doctoral dissertations that compared in-school and out-of-school suspension (one was a study of attitudes of suspendees; two were studies of suspendees' subsequent offenses). The other thirty-eight dealt with characteristics of suspended students, characteristics of schools that varied in suspension rates, attempts to treat disruptive students psychologically, subjective assessments of alternatives to suspension, and descriptions of such alternatives.

A parallel search of Educational Resources Information Center materials revealed that of one hundred documents turned up by the descriptor *suspension*, only seven dealt with the effects of suspension on students. All seven were attempts to assess the consequences of varieties of in-school suspension for student behavior. At most, the studies compared such phenomena as suspension rates before and after the initiation of innovative programs. None employed a control group and none sustained comparisons beyond a year or two. Of the one hundred studies, about twenty percent dealt with legal issues involved in the disciplining of handicapped students; many viewed suspension as a dependent variable and attempted to identify characteristics of suspendees or characteristics of schools with varying suspension rates, generally and interracially.

The problem at the school level is to locate an effective second line of defense against serious student misbehavior if and when prevention fails. Formerly, suspension was that second line of defense. It was considered demonstrative of the futility of misbehavior and sufficiently protective of the normative system. Some studies show that it is still regarded as appropriate by some constituencies of many public schools. For example, Bordenick (1976) found that the majority of students, teachers, parents, and administrators believed that suspension increased respect for the teacher, that it affected the behavior of other students, and that a prohibition of the use of suspension would limit teacher effectiveness. And Stallworth (1978) found that in a large Michigan city school system suspension was considered a positive diciplinary measure by both teachers and administrators.

However, as a penalty for truancy and class cutting (both serious problems in many schools today), suspension seems to many to constitute overkill. But if suspension is to be deemphasized, what other disciplinary measures are appropriate? Critics of suspension offer two less punitive alternatives, in-school suspension and alternative school placement. Comprehensive research into these two alternatives, however, is rare and sometimes of dubious quality. Thus, Daniel Duke, in a chapter included in this volume, summarizes research conducted by school districts concerning the consequences of their own in-school suspension programs. All but two of these studies used as indicants only teacher, student, or parent *perceptions*; not surprisingly, they reported beneficial consequences of in-school suspension. In such cases, given the district's investment in the plan, Duke's cautious words are, if anything, understatement:"it is likely that many [district-conducted] evaluations tend to portray results in as positive a manner as possible."

It is true that some early studies of in-school suspension treated the success of in-school suspension in terms of objective consequences (disciplinary referrals) and reported dramatic effects. Representative of the earlier studies is one by Harvey and Moosha (1977) of in-school suspension in two Virginia Beach secondary schools. The study reported a marked reduction in total and repeat suspensions during the year that the program was introduced. And Garrett (1981) reported that in thirty-two southern Illinois counties out-of-school suspensions decreased after in-school suspension was instituted, although Garrett was not sure that student *behavior* had improved. Unfortunately, later studies have reported less favorable consequences. Lynch (1983), in a study of an urban school district in California (San Jose), reported no decrease in out-of-school suspensions after in-school suspensions were introduced. And a recent study of two New Jersey districts (Crews, 1984) showed a significant decline in discipline referrals during the first year of in-school suspension but a return in the second year almost to levels that existed before the in-school suspension program was instituted.

One possible inference from these equivocal results is that in-school suspension belongs in a school's panoply of disciplinary sanctions but not for all infractions. Perhaps it is an appropriate response to offenses more serious than those that would bring a reprimand or detention but not for infractions as serious as those acts that would normally bring out-of-school suspension. Indeed, a study conducted by Montgomery County, Maryland, Public Schools (1981) found in-school suspension used mainly for less serious disciplinary offenses; nevertheless, there was a high recidivism rate for students whose first suspension was in school. Lynch (1983) also found in-school suspensions used for less serious offenses, as did Herzog (1980) and Angiolillo (1986). Herzog noted that, once in-school suspensions were available, a higher proportion of students were given in-school suspensions than had previously been given out-of-school suspensions.

Concurrent with the growing use of in-school suspension is another approach to serious discipline cases: transfer to an alternative school. Alternative schools, which at the time of their inception in the 1970s recruited various kinds of nonconformist and even "creative" students, in more recent years seem increasingly to house a more disruptive student clientele. Nevertheless, research on these schools finds their students more appreciative of their alternative school setting than they were of conventional schools and, in most cases, better behaved than they were previously. Thus, a study by Duke and Perry (1978) reported by Duke in this volume found student behavior rarely a major concern in alternative schools.

An early study (Heinle, 1976), which compared eleventh and twelfth grades in an alternative school with classmates in a conventional program, found alternative school students scoring significantly more positively on attitude variables. Achievement score results were mixed, however; the total comparison group scored higher in vocabulary and the alternative twelfth grade group was higher on reading comprehension. Similar findings, favoring alternative schools in attitudinal variables, were found by Smith, Gregory, and Pugh (1981) in a comparison of seven alternative schools with six comprehensive high schools. The researchers found the alternative school students more favorably disposed to their schools (than were the comprehensive schools students) on need satisfaction in the areas of security, social relationships, esteem, and self-actualization. Similarly, Trickett et al. (1985) found New Haven alternative school students manifesting more teacher-student affection, more school satisfaction, a greater tolerance for nontraditional ideologies, and less blame on blacks for discrimination than did students who had volunteered for the same alternative school but had not been chosen for it (the control group).

Gold and Mann (1982) compared volunteer and assigned students in three alternative schools with students at their originally assigned schools. They found that the alternative schools had a beneficial effect on both volunteers and assigned students—but only if they were "buoyant" rather than "beset" (anxious or depressed) students. (However, if the "buoyants" were more likely to be volunteers and the "besets" assignees and if disruptive students were more likely to be assigned to alternative schools rather than to volunteer for them, as seems plausible, the seeming effectiveness of alternative schools as a disciplinary resource may be illusory. Gold and Mann did not report whether buoyant or beset students were more likely to have been assigned.)

On the surface, alternative schools appear to be a good idea for chronically disruptive students whose confirmed deviance requires more individualized treatment and a less crowded setting. Alternative schools are more informally organized than traditional schools. Even if the student-teacher ratio is not much lower than that of the conventional school, the reduced numbers, as has been demonstrated in day care studies, seem to make possible a more relaxed situation, in which teachers can relate more personally to students. Although one recent study reports waning enthusiasm for an alternative school (Cubbage, 1986), others have reported alternative schools in existence for more than ten and in one case fifteen years (Smith, Gregory, and Pugh, 1981).

On the other hand, it is difficult to evaluate the *effectiveness* of alternative schools as a response to serious discipline problems. One consideration has already been mentioned: the mixture of volunteers and assigned students in alternative schools. Another consideration is the proportion of misbehaving students assigned to alternative schools who actually attend them. If the proportion is low, assignment to an alternate school may simply be a covert technique for encouraging students to drop out. The fact is that alternative schools enroll very small proportions of students in public school systems. Why so? Is it only because they are more expensive to operate? Finally, research has not addressed the question of how assigning deviant or eccentric students to alternative schools affects the schools from which they came. One urban New Jersey school administrator suggests that there is something about the history, ethos, structure, and general clientele of a school that ensures a certain number of discipline problems even if the most disruptive students are removed. It is almost as if, once the role of discipline problem has been vacated, candidates arise to fill it as if it had been an advertised position.

In-school suspension and alternative school placement are intra-school sanctions. Though they impose a degree of isolation from the school's regular complement of students—and thus are more stigmatizing than reprimands or detention, neither stigmatizes as much as out-of-school suspension in that students given in-school suspension or assigned to an alternative school remain physically in a school building.

A crucial question that should be asked of both in-school suspension and alternative school programs is: what kind of sanction, if any, stands behind them? What supplementary sanctions compel attendance on the part of assigned students? One early in-school suspension program referred noncompliant assignees to juvenile court. Perhaps the resulting "tough" image was responsible for the decline in discipline referrals it reported (Frith, Lindsey, and Sasser, 1980). The existence or nonexistence of a backup sanction is important not only theoretically but also for research purposes. When studies of in-school suspension and alternative school programs are conducted, do they include the students who don't show up? Those who do not attend regularly?

An effective program to cope with student misbehavior must come to grips with the seriousness of the triggering offenses as well as the question of backup sanctions. The disciplinary response should include a range of sanctions, from scoldings, detention, and in-school suspensions to more severe sanctions designed to discourage the offender's deviant career and to make him unenviable as a role model. In-school suspensions and alternative school placements may have been intended to achieve these objectives, but whether they are perceived as in the same range as out-of-school suspensions, expulsions, and referral to the juvenile court is doubtful. A tougher in-school sanction may make possible less reliance on these out-of-school responses while at the same time expressing strong enough disapproval to deter.

THE PROBLEM OF MAINTAINING ORDER

Sensitivity to children's rights makes suspension of students, even of violent students, less easy than it used to be (U.S. Supreme Court, 1975; Toby, 1980, 1983). Expulsion of students, especially younger students, is rare. And enrollment in alternative schools tends to be quasi-voluntary. From some points of view, schools have become more humane. But there has been a cost.

However undesirable punitive and summary discipline might have been from a human rights standpoint, it helped teachers and principals to maintain an orderly, albeit authoritarian, school environment. It has been argued that schools have loosened up too much, that Constitutional requirements for the protection of children's rights can be met by an on-the-spot inquiry that enables the student to present a defense, if there is one, thus preserving the system of strict discipline by using short suspensions (see chapter by Lufler). However, the actual legal requirements produced by the recent emphasis on children's rights is not the main source of the weakening of school discipline. What weakens the administration of disciplinary action, moderate or severe, are the rational or irrational fears aroused in administrators about possible legal action in defense of children's rights. Though Lufler points out that courts uphold the school more often than not in contested discipline decisions, he also admits that information concerning cases where courts do not uphold the school circulates more pervasively among school personnel than does knowledge of court decisions supporting strict discipline. Perhaps because schools are "domesticated organizations" (Carlson, 1964), school personnel tend to exaggerate the threat of court intervention on behalf of children.

The school's ability to expel or suspend on behalf of the larger community has eroded; many youngsters who formerly would have been extruded from schools are now left in them. For some teachers and principals, this is tantamount to an abdication of discipline. Despite a continuing resort to suspension if not to expulsion in the face of mounting school behavior problems, not all of which require a drastic response, suspensions seem inadequate to the task. Some critics of the public schools have complained that suspension is overused, and, if they are right, it is because, between detention and suspension, schools have precious little in the way of a disciplinary sanction. In order to control their most unruly students, schools need disciplinary options intermediate in severity between after-school detention or in-school suspension and long-term suspension or expulsion. Furthermore, such an intermediate sanction would be more effective if it demonstrated to the misbehaving student that he has offended not just school authorities but the collectivity of community members as well.

SCHOOL-JUVENILE COURT COLLABORATION ON MAINTAINING ORDER

One possibility is for the school to collaborate with a community agency, the juvenile justice system, in dealing with the most serious cases of school crime: youngsters accused of assaulting fellow students or teachers, of the sale or use of drugs in the school building, of extorting money from fellow students, or of major vandalism. In theory they do so now. But juvenile courts, like the schools, lack an intermediate punishment. They must choose between an extremely punitive response, incarceration in a juvenile correctional facility, and lesser penalties such as juvenile probation, sometimes accompanied by "diversion" into rehabilitative programs or fines. The fines are often uncollectible. Overburdened by a large volume of cases, some very serious, the juvenile courts, understandably, tend to avoid incarceration as a response to school misbehavior. As a result, few offenders at school are removed from the community and therefore from the schools. Many return to the school where the offense took place, despite adjudication as delinquent in the juvenile court, with what seems to them a negligible disciplinary response from both the juvenile justice system and from school authorities.

A visible and appropriately powerful disciplinary response would be desirable from the standpoint both of nipping the offender's deviant tendencies in the bud and of deterring *other* youngsters from following his bad example. Can the juvenile justice system and the school district *together* develop an intermediate punishment for serious disciplinary infractions that neither has been able to develop alone?

Suppose that when youngsters are referred to juvenile court, one option considered by the court is to offer adjudicated delinquents the chance to return to school and work off the offense by doing onerous manual labor under supervision of school authorities. Since the offense was committed in school, it might be appropriate for the restitution to occur in school. However, the school would have to have a coerced community service program in place and be willing to accept into it fairly serious offenders. In short, each case would be handled by negotiation between the juvenile court and the school district. In some cases the school might not want to take the youngster; in others the judge might prefer to impose a stiff fine, paid not by the parents of the youngster but by the youngster himself: through the proceeds of weekend and other part-time employment monitored by probation officers attached to the court (National Associaton of Secondary School Principals, 1981). For those youngsters who claim to be unable to find remunerative employment by means of which to fulfill this requirement or who would prefer to be punished by school authorities, the school-based community service option would give the judge an alternative.

Community service as a disciplinary disposition in the school might consist of weekend supervised work within a school building — cleaning, polishing, painting — or of similar service in the local community supervised by school employees. Once coerced community service exists, not all participants need come from those convicted of target offenses in the juvenile court. The school could also offer coerced community service as an alternative to short suspensions in cases that are very serious from the school's point of view, such as defying teacher authority, but which may be treated as less serious in the larger society by the juvenile court.

Although community service may be rehabilitative for some youngsters, it should not be defined as rehabilitation. It is an alternative punishment, presumably less unattractive to wrongdoers than more drastic punishments that could be imposed by the school or by the juvenile court, separately or in collaboration. Even though criminologists may not consider juvenile probation a tough punishment — and it may not be regarded as such by the more hardened young offenders—the empirical question is how most youngsters rank it compared with coerced community service. If it is viewed as worse by most youngsters, it *is* worse—in the sense that community service is preferable. The same reasoning applies to out-of-school suspension. Our tentative hypothesis is that out-of-school suspension is a serious threat to most students and their parents, so much so that a punishment like coerced community service would seem preferable. Suspension is not a paper tiger. Studies of student response to in-school and out-of-school suspensions show a strong preference on the part of offenders for in-school suspension when offered the alternative (Williams, 1982; Clark, 1980).

When a youngster is offered a sentence of a certain number of weekend days of service in lieu of more drastic penalties, failure to fulfill the terms of the community service penalty would result in the imposition of the original penalty, suspension, in cases where it is deemed an appropriate punishment, or in further action by the juvenile justice system, including probation or possibly incarceration, in cases where probation has insufficient sting.

Furthermore, the option of community service as an alternative to other punishment means that, in a sense, youngsters choose servitude. Voluntary choice may have the incidental consequence of making both community service and its alternatives more acceptable both to offenders and to their sympathizers. Nonetheless, the community service is coerced too because, once the community service option is taken, whether in direct negotiation with school authorities or in juvenile court, failure to fulfill the required service results in reinstatement of the avoided penalty, such as suspension from school or probation administered by the juvenile court. Thus, the community service should be considered to be coerced—in somewhat the same way that military service is coerced once the individual has volunteered.

Two activities are needed to support coerced community service:

1. *Work procurement.* Certainly the development of a work program will be a major organizational task, but it will not be insuperable. For example, removing graffiti from the school system offers unending opportunities for hard labor. The useful tasks called to mind are, like cleaning up graffiti, aimed at improving the physical environment—including the built environment, like housing projects, schools, churches, and government buildings. Although the school might seem the logical site for such service—since it is presumably the site of the damage or deviance—other community agencies as a

site for service may demonstrate more thoroughly to the offender the source of school behavioral norms in the community and the community's support for those norms.

2. *Work supervision.* Someone has to supervise the work requirements. A judicial probationary period often merely involves perfunctory checking up by a probation officer. The community service alternative, however, will demand careful minute-to-minute supervision. Failure to follow through would merely increase the perception on the part of the offender that both the school and the juvenile justice system are impotent. Furthermore, where supervision is lacking, there would be insufficient means of ascertaining whether the prescribed task had been performed.

One solution to this problem is to hire college students to supervise "convicted" juveniles on a one-to-one basis. Expensive? Yes, but not as expensive as incarceration. If it costs $15,000 a year to incarcerate a juvenile, it may cost $5,000 a year to supervise him or her in the community at hard labor. Furthermore, since the supervisors would be college students, American society could consider part of the cost a financial-aid program for higher education. Perhaps 50 percent of the juveniles sentenced to hard work in the community would be from minority backgrounds (judging from national statistics on sentences to correctional institutions). Although matching the ethnic background of supervisors with those of offenders would be objectionable on principle, a substantial proportion of the student supervisors would probably come from minority backgrounds even in the absence of matching because a substantial proportion of the community service assignments would be in inner-city schools. Thus, the financial benefits of the program would benefit disproportionately minority college students, who have an especially pressing need for financial aid, rather than more affluent white students.

Presumably, the college students would be positive role models for the offenders—would, in short, help to "rehabilitate" them. However, this would be an incidental benefit. The main objective is to place a credible deterrent in the hands of school and community authorities. Hard labor in the community could not be a credible threat unless the original (and fairly severe) sanctions—suspension or expulsion from school and possible incarceration in juvenile correctional institutions—would be invoked if offenders failed to complete their work assignments. For a variety of reasons—refusal to accept the sentence of hard labor in the community, failure to appear on the job despite a promise to do so, poor work performance, or an offense so violent as to exceed the tolerance of the community — some convicted offenders will continue to be suspended or expelled from school, referred to juvenile court, and, possibly, be incarcerated.

The kernel of the coerced community service idea is sentencing juveniles found guilty of fairly serious school offenses to "hard labor" in the community. The model is an adaptation of the community service sentences in this country, in England and other European countries, and in Australia and New Zealand. As in some of these programs, the offender should be offered a choice between labor in the community and a worse sanction. It is a constrained choice, but even a constrained choice is better than no choice at all.

ELIGIBLE OFFENSES

The new sanctioning policy would be limited to serious offenses because harsh penalties could not realistically be meted out for minor offenses. For example, youngsters could not be sentenced to coerced community service for minor vandalism, such as scratching graffiti on a bathroom wall, because it would be unjust as well as unpopular to utilize expulsion or even suspension for failure to complete the sentence. A harsh penalty for a minor offense would not be supported by school administrators, the juvenile court, or the local community. Therefore, the coerced community service option would be targeted for offenses that the school authorities consider intolerable, including verbal abuse of a teacher, even though such behavior may not normally be referred to the juvenile court. One of the most common school offenses, larceny, would not be sufficiently serious to qualify for the coerced community service program. Aside from the practical consideration that the community will not tolerate severe punishment for nonserious offenses, the deliberate withholding of the community service sanction for larceny offenders would provide a control group whose subsequent behavior could be compared with that of students in the community service program.

THE TOLERANCE LIMIT FOR PUNITIVE SCHOOL SANCTIONS

Would coerced community service increase the level of sanctions over what it is already? After all, school districts try to control their schools, and they utilize suspensions, expulsions, and referrals to the juvenile justice system to do so. Why do they not simply increase the number of suspensions, expulsions, and referrals to the juvenile justice system instead of experimenting with a new form of punishment?

Probably they cannot. Existing punishments are invoked to the extent that they are acceptable in the particular community in which the school is located. For example, schools come up against informal upper limits to the number of suspensions they can make within a school year. If this is so, consider the effect of offering a convicted offender the option of community service for a definite number of weekends:

1. He refuses the option and receives the usual penalty, say, suspension.

2. He accepts the option and carries out the service. If he does this, he will serve a deterrent function provided that other students and especially potential offenders regard coerced community service as undesirable.

3. He initially accepts the option but fails to fulfill the obligations of community service. It is necessary for the school system to invoke the initial penalty, suspension.

In the first and third cases, the school system is forced to "use up" its limited number of deterrent suspensions. In the second case, however, the school system obtains some deterrence without using suspensions. Consequently, the school system continues to have suspension available as a resource to be used with other convicted offenders. No one can predict how frequently case 2 will occur. If it occurs rarely, perhaps because offenders fail to complete the service program even though they initially opt for it, coerced community service will not be a useful resource for coping with school crime. But this is an empirical question that an experiment could explore.

There are other reasons why coerced community service might not prove practical. If either school officials or the student body perceived community service as a light penalty, a slap on the wrist for offenders who deserve real punishment, the community service program would not serve as a deterrent. This is, once again, an empirical question. In the course of an experiment, this question could be explored directly by including on a victimization questionnaire (filled out by students and teachers after the program had been in operation for a sufficient period of time) items pertaining to perceptions of the community service program. If the community's tolerance level for suspensions (and, more rarely, expulsions) is not reached by the number of cases of serious crime for which they would be an appropriate penalty, coerced community service would not be a practical remedy. Although there may be some school systems in this situation, especially school systems with low crime rates, the usual situation in high-crime communities is that there are *more* apprehended offenders than the community would be willing to see suspended.

In the event that the community service option proves so attractive to serious offenders that there are few suspensions and many offenders sentenced to community service, it is also an empirical question how community service compares with suspension as a deterrent. To take a concrete but hypothetical example: If a school had suspended 120 students in the year before the experiment and, during the year of the experiment, suspended 35 students and allowed 85 to be punished by community service instead of suspension, research could determine whether the 85 cases of community service deterred the misbehavior of other students as successfully or more successfully than the suspensions did in the previous year.

CONCLUSION

Punishment is still a naughty word in educational circles. Although such schemes as "assertive discipline," the administration of a schedule of graduated punishments, may be useful as a classroom management tool, what happens on occasions when the "time outs," detentions, and in-school suspensions prove ineffective? Our impression is that the current wisdom in schools of education does not prepare new teachers adequately for this eventuality.

Coerced community service as a punishment is a new version of an old approach: the expression of penitence for misdeeds. Perhaps it will help make schools more orderly and therefore better places in which teachers can teach and students can learn. In addition, considering a negative sanction like coerced community service may be in itself constructive for education professionals. It would help make the investigation of punishment to maintain school discipline intellectually respectable.

NOTES

CHAPTER 1

1. This list of directors was compiled by S.D. Melville of the Educational Testing Service and shared with the author by Walter Hathway of Portland Public Schools. Directors were asked to send any studies conducted within the last five years that examined organizational approaches to student behavior.

CHAPTER 2

1. This section is taken from a more detailed account of the Effective Schools Project (Gottfredson, 1987a).

2. This comparison involved post-tests only. Examination of pretest measures and demographic characteristics suggested that the cohorts were equivalent.

3. Measures of administrative response to misconduct are at best ambiguous measures of student behavior. Measures of disciplinary removals are included here to show that increases in school orderliness measured more directly by reports of students and teachers did not come about simply by removing more troublesome students from school.

4. This section is taken from a more detailed account of these strategies (Gottfredson, 1987b).

CHAPTER 3

1. See also Anderson, 1982; Bacharach, Conley, and Shedd, 1986; Brookover et al., 1979; Cohen, 1983; Coleman, Hoffer, and Kilgore, 1982; Goodlad, 1984; Hawley et al., 1984; Lieberman and Miller, 1984; Lightfoot, 1983; Lipsitz, 1984; MacKenzie, 1983; Purkey and Smith, 1985; Rosenholtz, 1985; Rutter et al., 1979; and Sarason, 1971.

2. These ideas were suggested by Fred Newmann.

3. Case histories such as Wigginton's (1985) description of the origin of the Foxfire program, recent critical studies of secondary school classrooms (e.g., Powell, Farrar, and Cohen, 1985; Sizer, 1984), and ethnographic explorations of classroom teaching and student work (Everhart, 1983; McNeil, 1983) converge to suggest that the classrooms in which authentic learning takes place (i.e., that reflect the criteria enumerated above) are orderly and productive. It is only logical to assume that, except for an incorrigible minority of students, student disorders would be greatly reduced in buildings throughout which students were engaged in work they found meaningful, challenging, and satisfying.

CHAPTER 9

1. The author assumes the responsibility for any errors and omissions in this paper. Helpful comments on an earlier draft were received from James A. Rapp, Ivan B. Gluckman, Oliver C. Moles, Robert A. Kohl, Amy L. Schwartz, Perry A. Zirkel, Michael W. Apple, and Michael R. Olneck. Ann K. Wallace made helpful editorial suggestions, and Claire A. Shaffer supervised the manuscript preparation.

2. 384 U.S. 436 (1966). The court cases cited in this chapter are presented using the standard legal citation format. The volume number is first, followed by the initials that represent the name of the reporting series, the page number of the case, and the year in which it was issued. Legal reporters are available in any law school library.

3. *Engel v. Vitale*, 370 U.S. 421 (1962) (school prayer); *Abington School District v. Schempp*, 374 U.S. 203 (1963) (Bible verses read at the beginning of the school day).

4. *Tinker v. Des Moines Independent Community School District*, 393 U.S. 503 (1969); see also *Bethel v. Fraser*, 478 U.S. 675 (1986) regarding free speech at a student assembly.

5. 420 U.S. 308 (1975).

6. 419 U.S. 563 (1975).

7. *Carey v. Piphus*, 435 U.S. 247 (1978). See also *Smalling v. Epperson*, 438 U.S. 948 (1978).

8. *Ingraham v. Wright*, 430 U.S. 651 (1977).

9. The number of attorneys doubled in number in the United States between 1960 and 1980. (Clark, 1981, p. 94).

10. For a discussion of attitudinal differences between counselors and administrators, see Schwab (1979).

11. Center for Education Statistics (1986a). See also Wright and Moles (1985).

12. For a bibliography source focusing on both elementary and secondary teachers, see Zirkel (1985b).

13. *NOLPE Notes*, published by the National Organization on Legal Problems of Education, has featured a series of articles on impact research that are helpful in setting this research agenda. See, for example, Quigley, Redding, and Zirkel (1986).

14. For background on this topic, see Schimmel and Williams (1985).

CHAPTER 13

1. Our use of the masculine pronoun (instead of the gender-neutral *his or her* or some alternation of the two) reflects less stylistic custom than the tendency for suspendees still to be predominantly male.

REFERENCES

INTRODUCTION

Baker, K. (1985). Research evidence of a school discipline problem. *Phi Delta Kappan, 66,* 482-496.

Center for Education Statistics (1986). Discipline in public secondary schools. Washington, D.C.: U.S. Department of Education.

———. (1987). Public school teacher perspectives on school discipline. Washington, D.C.: U.S. Department of Education.

Edmonds, R. (1979). Some schools work and more can. *Social Policy, 9,* 32.

Gallup, A.M., and Elam, S.M. (1988). The 20th annual Gallup poll of the public's attitudes toward the public schools. *Phi Delta Kappan, 70,* 33-46.

Gallup, G. (1982). The 14th annual Gallup poll of the public's attitudes toward the public schools. *Phi Delta Kappan, 64,* 37-50.

———. (1985). The Gallup youth survey: Violence in the school persists. Princeton, N.J.: The Gallup Organization.

Garibaldi, A. (ed.). (1979). *In-school alternatives to suspension: Conference report.* Washington, D.C.: U.S. Government Printing Office.

Glass, G. (1977). Integrating findings: The meta-analysis of research. In L. Shulman (ed.), *Review of Research in Education.* Itasca, Ill: Peacock.

Gottfredson, G.D. (1987). American education—American delinquency. Unpublished manuscript. Center for Social Organization of Schools, The Johns Hopkins University.

Gottfredson, G.D., and Gottfredson, D.C. (1985) *Victimization in schools.* New York: Plenum.

Johnson, R.E. (1979). *Juvenile delinquency and its origins: An integrated theoretical approach.* New York: Cambridge University Press.

Metropolitan Life survey of former teachers in America (1986, summer). *American Educator, 10,* 36.

Metz, M.H. (1978). *Classrooms and corridors: The crisis of authority in desegregated schools.* Berkeley: University of California Press.

Moles, O.C. (1987). Trends in student misconduct: The 70s and 80s. Unpublished manuscript. Office of Educational Research and Improvement, U.S. Department of Education.

Myers, D.E., Milne, A.M., Baker, K., and Ginsburg, A. (1987). Student discipline and high school performance. *Sociology of Education, 60,* 18-33.

National Institute of Education (1978). *Violent schools—safe schools: The Safe School Study report to the Congress.* Vol. 1. Washington, D.C.: U.S. Government Printing Office.

Safer, D.J. (1982). *School programs for disruptive adolescents.* Baltimore, Md.: University Park Press.

Slavin, R.E. (1984, October). Meta-analysis in education: How has it been used? *Educational Researcher, 13,* 7.

———. (1986). *Educational psychology: Theory into practice.* Englewood Cliffs, N.J.: Prentice-Hall.

Wayne, I., and Rubel, R.J. (1982). Student fear in secondary schools. *The Urban Review, 14* (2), 197-237.

Wayson, W.W., Voss, G.G., Kaeser, S.C., Lasley, T., Pinnell, G.S., and the Phi Delta Kappa Commission on Discipline. (1982). *Handbook for developing schools with good discipline.* Bloomington, Ind.: Phi Delta Kappa.

INTRODUCTION, PART I

Cloward, R.A., and Ohlin, L.E. (1960). *Delinquency and opportunity.* New York: Free Press.

Cohen, A.K. (1955). *Delinquent boys.* Glencoe, Ill: Free Press.

Fullan, M., Miles, M.B., and Taylor, G. (1980). Organization development in schools: The state of the art. *Review of Educational Research, 50,* 121-183.

Hirschi, T. (1969). *Causes of delinquency.* Berkeley, Calif.: University of California Press.

Klausmeier, H.J. (1985). A research strategy for educational improvement. *Educational Researcher, 11*(2), 8-13.

Merton, R.K. (1938). Social structure and anomie. *American Sociological Review, 3*, 672-682.

Purkey, S.C., and Smith, M. (1983). Effective schools: A review. *Elementary School Journal*, March, 427-452.

Sarason, S.B. (1971). *The culture of the school and the problem of change.* Boston: Allyn and Bacon.

Schwartz, A.J. (1988). Principals' leadership behaviors in gang-impacted high schools and their effects on pupil climate. Paper presented at the annual meeting of the American Educational Research Association, New Orleans. (ERIC Document Reproduction Service No. ED 296451)

Weick, K. (1976). Educational organizations as loosely-coupled systems. *Administrative Science Quarterly, 21*, 1-19.

CHAPTER 1

Anderson, S. (1985). The investigation of school climate. In Gilbert R. Austin and Herbert Garber (eds.), *Research on exemplary schools*. New York: Academic Press.

Austin, G.R., and Holowenzak, S.P. (1985). An examination of 10 years of research on exemplary schools. In Gilbert R. Austin and Herbert Garber (eds.), *Research on exemplary schools*. New York: Academic Press.

Bickel, F., and Qualls, R. (1980). The impact of school climate on suspension rates in the Jefferson County Public Schools. *The Urban Review, 12*, 79-86.

Crawford, G., Miskel, C., and Johnson, M.C., (1980). An urban school renewal program: A case analysis. *The Urban Review, 12*, 175-199.

Cuban, L. Effective schools: A friendly but cautionary note. *Phi Delta Kappan, 64*, 695-696.

Cusick, P.A. (1983). *The egalitarian ideal and the American high school.* New York: Longman.

——. (1973). *Inside high school.* New York: Holt, Rinehart and Winston.

Duke, D.L., (1982, October). Leadership functions and instructional effectiveness. *NASSP Bulletin, 66*, 1-12.

——. (1987). School leadership and instructional improvement. New York: Random House.

Duke, D.L., and Meckel, A.M. (1980, October). Student attendance problems and school organization: A case study. *Urban Education, 15,* 325-358.

Duke, D.L., and Perry, C. (1978, Fall). Can alternative schools succeed where Benjamin Spock, Spiro Agnew, and B.F. Skinner have failed? *Adolescence, 13,* 375-392.

Duke, D.L., and Seidman, W. (1983). Are public schools organized to minimize behavior problems? In Daniel L. Duke (ed.) *Helping teachers manage classrooms.* Alexandria, Va.: Association for Supervision and Curriculum Development.

Fiqueira-McDonough, J. (1986). School context, gender, and delinquency. *Journal of Youth and Adolescence, 15,* 79-98.

Gold, M., and Mann, D.W. (1984). *Expelled to a friendlier place.* Ann Arbor: University of Michigan Press.

Gottfredson, D.C. (1986a). *An assessment of a delinquency prevention demonstration with both individual and environmental interventions.* Report No. 361. Baltimore, Md.: Center for Social Organization of Schools, The Johns Hopkins University.

————. (1986b). *Creating effective urban public schools through researcher-practitioner collaboration.* Baltimore, Md.: Center for Social Organization of Schools, The Johns Hopkins University.

Gottfredson, G.D., and Daiger, D.C. (1979). *Disruption in six hundred schools.* Report No. 289. Baltimore, Md.: Center for Social Organization of Schools, The Johns Hopkins University.

Gottfredson, G.D., and Gottfredson, D.C. (1985). *Victimization in schools.* New York: Plenum.

Hollingsworth, E.J., Lufler, H.S., and Clune, W.H. (1984). *School discipline: Order and autonomy.* New York: Praeger.

McPartland, J.M., and McDill, E.L. (1976). *The unique role of schools in the causes of youthful crime.* Report No. 216. Baltimore, Md.: Center for Social Organization of Schools, The Johns Hopkins University.

Metz, M.H. (1978). *Classrooms and corridors: The crisis of authority in desegregated schools.* Berkeley: University of California Press.

National Institute of Education (1978). *Violent Schools—Safe Schools: The Safe School Study report to Congress.* Washington, D.C.: U.S. Government Printing Office.

Natriello, G., Pallas, A.M., and McDill, E.L. (1986, Spring). Taking stock: Reviewing our research agenda on the causes and consequences of dropping out. *Teachers College Record, 87,* 430-440.

Peng, S.S., Fetters, W.B., and Kolstad, A.J. (1981). *High school and beyond: A national longitudinal study for the 1980's.* Washington, D.C.: National Center for Educational Statistics.

Perry, C.L. (1980). *Adolescent behavior and criminogenic conditions in and around the high school.* Ph.D. dissertation, Stanford University.

Purkey, S.C. (1984). *School improvement: An analysis of an urban school district effective schools project.* Madison: Wisconsin Center for Education Research.

Rutter, M., Maughan, B., Mortimore, P., and Ouston, J. (1979). *Fifteen thousand hours.* Cambridge: Harvard University Press.

Safer, D.J. (1982). *School programs for disruptive adolescents.* Baltimore, Md.: University Park Press.

Sarason, S.B. (1971). *The culture of the school and the problem of change.* Boston: Allyn and Bacon.

Stedman, L.C. (1985, October). A new look at the effective schools literature. *Urban Education, 20,* 295-326.

Trickett, E.J., McConahay, J.B., Phillips, D., and Ginter, M.A. (1985). Natural experiments and the educational context: The environment and effects of an alternative inner-city public school on adolescents. *American Journal of Community Psychology, 13,* 617-643.

Wehlage, G.G., and Rutter, R. (1986, Spring). Dropping out: How much do schools contribute to the problem? *Teachers College Record, 87,* 374-392.

Wu, S., Pink, W., Crain, R., and Moles, O. (1982). Student suspension: A critical reappraisal. *The Urban Review, 14,* 245-303.

CHAPTER 2

Bahner, J.M. (1980). Testimony at the oversight hearing on American secondary education. In *Hearings before the Subcommittee on Elementary, Secondary, and Vocational Education, U.S. House of Representatives.* Washington, D.C.: U.S. Government Printing Office.

Berman, P., and McLaughlin, M.W. (1978). *Federal programs supporting educational change*: Vol. 8. *Implementing and sustaining innovations (R-1589/8-HEW).* Santa Monica, Calif.: Rand.

Canter, L., and Canter, M. (1976). *Assertive discipline.* Los Angeles, Calif.: Lee Canter and Associates.

Corcoran, T.B. (1985). Effective secondary schools. In R.M.J. Kyle (ed.), *Reaching for excellence: An effective schools sourcebook.* Washington, D.C.: U.S. Government Printing Office.

Empey, L.T. (1982). *American delinqency: Its meaning and construction* (rev. ed.). Homewood, Ill.: Dorsey Press.

Fullan, M., Miles, M.B., and Taylor, G. (1980). Organization development in schools: The state of the art. *Review of Educational Research, 50,* 121-183.

Glasser, W. (1969). *Schools without failure.* New York: Harper and Row.

Gottfredson, D.C. (1986a) *Creating effective urban public schools through researcher-practitioner collaboration.* Baltimore, Md.: Center for Social Organization of Schools, The Johns Hopkins University.

————. (1986b). An empirical test of school-based environmental and individual interventions to reduce the risk of delinquent behavior. *Criminology, 24,* 705-731.

————. (1986c). *Academy for Community Education: Final report.* Baltimore, Md.: Center for Social Organization of Schools, The Johns Hopkins University.

————. (1987a). An evaluation of an organization development approach to reducing school disorder. *Evaluation Review, 11,* 739-764.

————. (1987b) Changing school structures to benefit high-risk youths. Paper presented at the Symposium on Structural Change in Secondary Education, Madison, Wisconsin.

Gottfredson, D.C., and Cook, M.S. (1986). *Increasinq school relevance and student decision making: Effective strategies for reducing delinquency?* Baltimore, Md.: Center for Social Organization of Schools, The Johns Hopkins University.

Gottfredson, G.D. (1981). Schooling and delinquency. In S.E. Martin, L.B. Sechrest, and R. Redner (eds.), *New directions in the rehabilitation of criminal offenders.* Washington, D.C.: National Academy Press.

————. (1984). A theory-ridden approach to program evaluation: A method for stimulating researcher-implementer collaboration. *American Psychologist, 39,* 1101-1112.

————. (1985). *Effective School Battery: User's manual.* Odessa, Fla.: Psychological Assessment Resources.

Gottfredson, G.D., and Gottfredson, D.C. (1985). *Victimization in schools.* New York: Plenum.

Gottfredson, G.D., Gottfredson, D.C., and Cook, M.S. (eds.) (1983). *The School Action Effectiveness Study: Second interim report.* Report No. 342. Baltimore, Md.: Center for Social Organization of Schools, The Johns Hopkins University. (ERIC No. ED 237 892)

Gottfredson, G.D., Rickert, D.E., Gottfredson, D.C., and Advani, N. (1984). Standards for Program Development Evaluation plans. *Psychological Documents, 14,* 32. (Ms. No. 2668)

Grant, J., and Capell, F. (1983). *Reducinq school crime: A report on the School Team Approach.* San Rafael, Calif.: Social Action Research Center.

Hall, G.E., and Loucks, S.F. (1977). A development model for determining whether the treatment is actually implemented. *American Educational Research Journal, 14,* 263-276.

Hirschi, T. (1969). *Causes of delinquency.* Berkeley: University of California Press.

Johnson, G., Bird, T., and Little, J. (1979). *Delinquency prevention: Theories and strategies.* Washington, D.C.: U.S. Department of Justice, Law Enforcement Assistance Administration, Office of Juvenile Justice and Delinquency Prevention.

Klausmeier, H.J. (1985). A research strategy for educational improvement. *Educational Researcher, 11*(2), 8-13.

Lewin, K. (1951). *Field theory in social science.* New York: Harper.

Miles, M.B. (1981). Mapping the common properties of schools. In R. Lehming and M. Kane (eds.), *Improving schools: Using what we know* (pp. 42-114). Beverly Hills, Calif.: Sage.

National Commission on Excellence in Education (1983). *A nation at risk: The imperative for educational reform* (A Report to the Nation and the Secretary of Education). Washington, D.C.: U.S. Department of Education. (ERIC No. ED 226 006)

Office of Juvenile Justice and Delinquency Prevention (OJJDP) (1980). *Program announcement: Delinquency prevention through alternative education.* Washington, D.C.: Author.

Sarason, S.B. (1971). *The culture of the school and the problem of change.* Boston: Allyn and Bacon.

Slavin, R.E. (1980). Using student team learning (rev. ed.) Baltimore, Md.: Center for Social Organization of Schools, The Johns Hopkins University, The Johns Hopkins Team Learning Project.

Weick, K.E. (1982). Administering education in loosely coupled schools. *Phi Delta Kappan, 63*, 673-676.

CHAPTER 3

Anderson, C.S. (1982). The search for school climate: A review of the research. *Review of Educational Research, 52*, 368-420.

Aries, P. (1962). *Centuries of childhood.* New York: Vintage Books.

Bacharach, S.B., Conley, S.C., and Shedd, J.B. (1986). *Education reform and the American teacher.* Ithaca, N.Y.: Organizational Analysis and Practice.

Barth, R. (1980). *Run school run.* Cambridge: Harvard University Press.

Berman, P., and McLaughlin, M.W. (1977). *Federal programs supporting educational change: Factors affecting implementation and continuation.* Vol. 7. Santa Monica, Calif.: Rand.

Berrueta-Clement, J.R., Schweinhart, L.J., Barnett, W.S., Epstein, A.S., and Weikart, D.P. (1984). *Changed lives.* Ypsilanti, Mich.: High/Scope.

Bowen, E. (1988). Getting tough. *Time, 131*, 52-58.

Boyer, E.L. (1983). *High school: A report on secondary education in America.* New York: Harper and Row.

Brookover, W.B., Beady, C., Flood, F., Schweitzer, J., and Wisenbaker, J. (1979). *School social systems and student achievement: Schools can make a difference.* New York: Praeger.

Cohen, M. (1983). Instructional management and social considerations in effective schools. In A. Odden and L.D. Webb (eds.), *School finance and improvement: Linkage for the 1980's* (Fourth annual Yearbook). Cambridge, Mass.: American Education Finance Association.

Coleman, J.S., Hoffer, T., & Kilgore, S. (1982). *High school achievement: Public, Catholic and private schools compared.* New York: Basic Books.

David, J.L., and Peterson, S.M. (1984). *Can schools improve themselves? A study of school-based improvement programs.* Palo Alto, Calif.: Bay Area Research Group.

Deal, T.E. and Kennedy, A.A. (1982). *Corporate cultures.* Reading, Mass.: Addison-Wesley.

———. (1983). Culture and school performance. *Educational Leadership, 40*, 14-15.

Deming, W.E. (1982). *Quality, productivity. and competitive position.* Cambridge: Massachusetts Institute of Technology, Center for Advanced Engineering Study.

Elmore, R.F. (1978). Organizational models of social program implementation. In D. Mann (ed.), *Making change happen.* New York: Teachers College Press.

Everhart, R. (1983). *Reading, writing and resistance: Adolescence and labor in a junior high school.* London: Routledge and Kegan Paul.

Farrar, E., and Cipollone, A. (1985). *After the signing: The Boston Compact 1982-84,* Report to the Edna McConnell Clark Foundation.

Fullan, M. (1985). Change processes and strategies at the local level. *The Elementary School Journal, 85,* 391-421.

Gaddy, G.D. (1986). *Order and achievement in the American high school.* Madison, Wisconsin Center for Education Research, University of Wisconsin-Madison.

Gallup, A.M. (1985). The 17th annual Gallup Poll of the public's attitudes towards the public schools. *Phi Delta Kappan, 67,* 35-47.

Gersten, R., Carnine, D., and Green, S. (1982). The principal as instructional leader: A second look. *Educational Leadership, 40,* 47-50.

Goodlad, J.I. (1984) *A place called school: Prospects for the future.* New York: McGraw-Hill.

Gottfredson, D.C., (1986). Promising strategies for improving student behavior. Paper prepared for the Conference on Student Discipline Strategies, United States Department of Education, November 6-7, 1986. Washington, D.C.

Gottfredson, G.D., and Gottfredson, D.C. (1985). *Victimization in schools.* New York: Plenum.

Hall, G.E., Hord, S.M., Huling, L.L., Rutherford, W.L., and Stiegelbauer, S.M. (1983). *Leadership variables associated with successful school improvement.* Report no 3164. Austin: Research and Development Center for Teacher Education, University of Texas at Austin.

Hargrove, E.C., Graham, S.G., Ward, L.E., Abernethy V., Cunningham, J., and Vaughn, W.K. (1981). *Regulations and schools: The implementation of equal education for handicapped children.* Nashville, Tenn.: Institute for Public Policy Studies, Vanderbilt University.

Hawley, W.D., and Rosenholtz, S.J. (with Goddstein and T. Hasselbring) (1984). Good schools: What research says about improving student acievement. *Peabody Journal of Education, 61.*

Huberman, A.M., and Miles, M.B. (1984). *Innovation up close*. New York: Plenum.

Kanter, R.M. (1983). *The change masters*. New York: Simon and Shuster.

Katz, M.B. (1968). *The irony of early school reform*. Boston: Beacon.

Kulka, R.A., et al. (1982). Aggression, deviance, and personality adaptation as antecedents and consequences of alienation and involvement in high school. *Journal of Youth and Adolescence, 11*, 273.

Lieberman, A., and Miller, L. (1984). *Teachers, their world and their work*. Alexandria, Va.: Association for Supervision and Curriculum Development.

Lightfoot, S.L. (1983). *The good high school: Portraits of character and culture*. New York: Basc Books.

Lipsitz, J. (1984). *Successful schools for young adolescents*. New Brunswick, N.J.: Transactions Books.

MacKenzie, D.E. (1983). Research for school improvement: An appraisal of some recent trends. *Educational Researcher, 12,*, 5-17.

McNeil, L.M. (1983). Defensive teaching and classroom control. In M.W. Apple and J.L. Weis (eds.), *Ideology and practice in schools*. Philadelphia: Temple University Press.

McPartland, J.M., and McDill, E.L. (1976). *The unique role of schools in the causes of youthful crime*. Report No. 216. Baltimore: Center for Social Organization of Schools, The Johns Hopkins University.

Manasse, A. Lorri (1985). Improving conditions for principal effectiveness: Policy implications of research. *The Elementary School Journal, 85*, 439-463.

Matthews, I. (1987). Greendown community school—West Swindon, UK. Paper prepared for Symposium on Restructuring Secondary Education sponsored by the National Center on Effective Secondary Schools, University of Wisconsin-Madison, School of Education, May 11-12, 1987, Madison.

Metz, M.H. (1978). *Classroom and corridors: The crisis of authority in desegregated secondary schools*. Berkeley: University of California Press.

Miles, M.B., Farrar, E., and Neufeld, B. (1983). Review of effective schools programs II: The extent of adoption of effective schools programs. Paper repared for the National Commission on Excellence in Education, Washington, D.C.

Nasaw, D. (1979). *Schooled to order: A social history of public schooling in the United States*. New York: Oxford University Press.

National Institute of Education (1978). *Violent schools-safe schools: The safe school study report to the U.S. Congress*. Vol. 1. Washington, D.C. U.S. Government Printing Office.

Newman, J. (1980). From past to future: School violence in a broad view. *Contemporary Education, 52*, 7-12.

Newmann, F.M. (1981). Reducing alienation in high schools: Implications of theory. *Harvard Educational Review, 51*, 546-564.

Newmann, F.M., Rutter, R.A., and Smith, M.S. (1985). *Exploratory analysis of high school teacher climate*. Madison: Wisconsin Center for Education Research, University of Wisconsin-Madison.

Ogbu, J.U. (1978). Minority education and caste: The American system in class-cultural perspective. New York: Academic Press.

Olson, L. (1988). Children 'flourish' here. *Education Week, 18*, 1.

O'Toole, J. (1981). *Making America work*. New York: Continuum.

Patterson, J.L., Purkey, S.C., and Parker, J., (1986). *Productive school systems for a nonrational world*. Alexandria, Va.: Association for Supervision and Curriculum Development.

Peters, T.J., and Waterman, R.H. (1982). *In search of excellence*. New York: Harper and Row.

Pink, W.T. (1986). Continuing the struggle to improve urban schools: An effective schools project revisited. Unpublished paper, Kansas City Missouri Public Schools, Kansas City, Mo.

Powell, A.G., Farrar, E., and Cohen, D.K. (1985). *The shopping mall high school*, Boston: Houghton Mifflin.

Purkey, S.C. (1985). School improvement: An analysis of an urban school district effective schools project (doctoral dissertation, University of Wisconsin-Madison, 1984). *Dissertation Abstracts International, 45*, 1926A. (University Microfilms No. 85-15, 575)

Purkey, S.C., and Rutter, R.A. (1987). High school teaching: Teacher practices and beliefs in urban and suburban public schools. *Educational Policy, 1*, 375-393.

Purkey, S.C., Rutter, R.A., and Newmann, F.M. (Winter 1986-87). U.S. high school improvement programs: A profile from the high school and beyond supplemental survey. *Metropolitan Education*, 59-91.

Purkey, S.C., and Smith, M.S. (1985). School reform: The district policy implications of the effective schools literature. *The Elementary School Journal, 85*, 353-389.

Rosenholtz, S.J. (1985). Effective schools: interpreting the evidence. *American Journal of Education*, *93*, 352-388.

Rutter, M. (1980). *Changing youth in a changing society*. Cambridge: Harvard University Press.

Rutter, M., Maughan, B., Mortimore, P., and Ousten, J. (1979). *Fifteen thousand hours*. Cambridge: Harvard University Press.

Sarason, S.B. (1971). *The culture of the school and the problem of change*. Boston: Allyn and Bacon.

Sizer, T.S. (1984). *Horace's compromise: The dilemma of the American high school*. Boston: Houghton Mifflin.

Sprinthall, N.A., and Mosher, R.L. (eds.) (1978). *Value development . . . as the aim of education*. Schenectady, N.Y.: Character Research Press.

Toby, J. (1980). Crime in American public schools. *The Public Interest*, *58*, 18-42.

Wigginton E. (1985). *Sometimes a shining moment: The Foxfire experience*. Garden City, N.Y.: Anchor Press/Doubleday.

Willis, P.E. (1977). *Learning to labor. Lexington, Mass.: D.C. Heath.*

CHAPTER 4

Deal, T.E. (1987). The culture of schools. In L.T. Sheive and M.B. Schoenheit (eds.), *In leadership examining the elusive*. Washington, D.C.: Association for Supervision and Curriculum Development.

Fullan, M. (1982). *The meaning of educational change* (1st ed.). New York: Teachers College, Columbia University.

Furtwengler, W.J. (1978-1987). *Climate effectiveness inventory, School culture inventory, Public image inventory, Student opinion inventory, Inservice choices inventory, Leadership inventory, Burnout assessment inventory, Learner needs, Learner methods, Learner self-image, and Learner behavior*. Nashville, Tenn.: Research and Service Institute.

————. (1985). Implementing strategies for a school effectiveness program. *Phi Delta Kappan*, December, 262-265.

————. (1986). *Reaching success through involvement: Implementation strategy for creating and maintaining effective schools*. Paper presented at the American Education Research Association meetings, San Francisco.

_____. (1987a). Student-faculty retreats as transitional ceremonies in school improvement projects. Paper presented at the American Educational Research Association meetings, Washington, D.C.

_____. (1987b). *School culture inventory.* Nashville, Tenn.: Research and Service Institute.

Furtwengler, W.J., and Farley, B. (1987). Effective school retreats improve secondary schools. *National Association of Secondary School Principals Bulletin,* September, 118-122.

Furtwengler, W., and Konnert, W. (1982). *Improving school discipline.* Boston: Allyn and Bacon.

Lezotte, L.W., and Bancroft, B.A. (1985). Growing use of the effective schools model for school improvement. *Educational Leadership,* June, 23-27.

Purkey, S.C., and Smith, M. (1983). Effective schools: A review. *Elementary School Journal,* March, 427-452.

Schein, E.H. (1986). *Organizational culture and leadership.* San Francisco, Calif: Jossey-Bass.

Schmuck, R.A., and Runkel, P.J. (1984). *The handbook of organization development in schools* (3rd ed.). Palo Alto, Calif.: Mayfield Publishing.

Upton, B. (1986). Measuring school effectiveness using the school culture inventory; a validation study. Doctoral dissertation, Vanderbilt University, Nashville, Tenn.

INTRODUCTION, PART II

Bandura, A. (1977). *Social learning theory.* Englewood Cliffs, N.J.: Prentice-Hall.

Elliott, D.C., Huizinga, D., and Menard, S. (1988). Multiple problem youth: Delinquency, substance use and mental health problems. Boulder: University of Colorado, Institute of Behavioral Science.

Gottfredson, G.D., and Gottfredson, D.C. (1985). *Victimization in schools.* New York: Plenum.

Johnson, G., and Hunter, R. (1985). *Law related education as a delinquency prevention strategy.* Boulder, CO: Center for Action Research.

Metz, M.H. (1978). *Classrooms and corridors: The crisis of authority in desegregated schools.* Berkeley: University of California Press.

National Institute of Education (1978). *Violent schools—safe schools: The safe school study report to the Congress.* Vol. 1. Washington, D.C.: U.S. Government Printing Office.

CHAPTER 6

Anderson, L., and Prawat, R. (1983). A synthesis of research on teaching self-control. *Educational Leadership, 40,* 62-66.

Arlin, M. (1982). Teacher responses to student time differences in mastery learning. *American Journal of Education, 90,* 334-352.

Blumenfeld, P.C., Hamilton, V.L., Wessels, K., and Falkner, D. (1979). Teaching responsibility to first graders. *Theory into Practice, 18*(3), 174-180.

Bongiavanni, A.F. (1979). A review of research on the effects of punishment: Implications for corporal punishment in the schools. In I.A. Hyman and H. Wise (eds.), *Corporal punishment in American education: Research in history, practice, and alternatives.* Philadelphia: Temple University Press.

Bremme, D., and Erickson, F. (1977). Relationships among verbal and non-verbal classroom behaviors. *Theory into Practice, 5,* 153-161.

Brooks, D.M., and Wagenhauser, B. (1980). Completion time as a nonverbal component of teacher attitude. *Elementary School Journal, 81,* 24-27.

Brophy, J.E. (1983). Classroom organization and management. *Elementary School Journal, 83,* 265-286.

Carter, K. (1986). Classroom management as cognitive problem solving: Toward teacher comprehension in teacher education. Paper presented at the annual meeting of the American Educational Research Association, San Francisco.

Carter, K., and Doyle, W. (1986). Teachers' knowledge structures and comprehension processes. In J. Calderhead (ed.), *Exploring Teachers' Thinking.* London: Holt, Rinehart and Winston.

Cartledge, G., and Milburn, J. (1978). The case for teaching social skills in the classroom: A review. *Review of Educational Research, 48,* 133-156.

Charles, C.M. (1981). *Building classroom discipline.* New York:Longman.

Cohen, E.G. (1979). Status equalization in the desegregated school. Paper presented at the annual meeting of the American Educational Research Association, San Francisco.

Cusick, P.A., Martin, W., and Palonsky, S. (1976). Organizational structure and student behaviour in secondary school. *Journal of Curriculum Studies, 8,* 3-14.

Doyle, W. (1978). Are students behaving worse than they used to behave? *Journal of Research and Development in Education, 2*(4), 3-16.

————. (1979). Making managerial decisions in classrooms. In D.L. Duke (ed.), *Classroom management* (78th yearbook of the National Society for the Study of Education, Part 2). Chicago: University of Chicago Press.

————. (1986). Classroom organization and management. In M.C. Wittrock (ed.), *Handbook of research on teaching* (3rd ed.). New York: Macmillan.

Doyle, W., and Carter, K. (1984). Academic tasks in classrooms. *Curriculum Inquiry, 14,* 129-149.

Duer, J.L., and Parke, R.D. (1970). Effects of inconsistent punishment and aggression in children. *Developmental Psychology, 2,* 403-411.

Duke, D.L. (1978). How administrators view the crisis in school discipline. *Phi Delta Kappan, 59,* 325-330.

Elardo, R. (1978). Behavior modification in an elementary school:Problems and issues. *Phi Delta Kappan, 59,* 334-338.

Emmer, E.T. (1984). *Classroom management: Research and implications* (R&D Rep. No. 6178). Austin: University of Texas, R & D Center for Teacher Education.

Emmer, E.T., Evertson, C.M., and Anderson, L.M. (1980). Effective classroom management at the beginning of the school year. *Elementary School Journal, 80,* 219-231.

Emmer, E.T., Sanford, J.P., Clements, B.S., and Martin, J. (1982). *Improving classroom management and organization in junior high schools: An experimental investigation* (R&D Rep. No. 6153). Austin: University of Texas, R&D Center for Teacher Education.

Emmer, E.T., Sanford, J.P., Evertson, C.M., Clements, B.S., and Martin, J. (1981). *The Classroom Management Improvement Study: An experiment in elementary school classrooms* (R&D Rep. No. 6050). Austin: University of Texas, R&D Center for Teacher Education.

Erickson, F., and Mohatt, G. (1982). Cultural organization of participation structures in two classrooms of Indian students. In G. Spindler (ed.), *Doing the ethnography of schooling.* New York: Holt, Rinehart and Winston.

Erickson, F., and Shultz, J. (1981). When is a context? Some issues and methods in the analysis of social competence. In J. L. Green and C. Wallat (eds.), *Ethnography and language in educational settings.* Norwood, N.J.: Ablex.

Felmlee, D., and Eder, D. (1983). Contextual effects in the classroom: The impact of ability groups on group attention. *Sociology of Education, 56,* 77-87.

Garibaldi, A.M. (1979). In-school alternatives to suspension: Trendy educational innovations. *Urban Review, 11*(2), 97-103.

Gump, P.V. (1969). Intra-setting analysis: The third grade classroom as a special but instructive case. In E. Willems and H. Rausch (eds.), *Naturalistic viewpoints in psychological research.* New York: Holt, Rinehart and Winston.

―――. (1982). School settings and their keeping. In D.L. Duke (ed.), *Helping teachers manage classrooms.* Alexandria, Va.: Association for Supervision and Curriculum Development.

Hapkiewicz, W.G. (1975). Research on corporal punishment effectiveness: Contributions and limitations. Paper presented at the annual meeting of the American Educational Research Association, Washington, D.C.

Hargreaves, D.H., Hester, S.K., and Mellor, F.J. (1975). *Deviance in classrooms.* Boston: Routledge and Kegan Paul.

Humphrey, F.M. (1979). "Shh!": A sociolinguistic study of teachers' turn-taking sanctions in primary school lessons. Doctoral dissertation, Georgetown University, Washington, D.C.

Hyman, I.A. (1981). Violence, stress and punitiveness: Educational and social policy implications for the 80s. *Journal of the International Association of Pupil Personnel Workers, 25,* 174-189.

Hyman, I.A., Bilus, F., Dennehy, N., Feldman, G., Flanagan, D., Lovoratano, J., Maital, S., and McDowell, E. (1979). Discipline in American education: An overview and analysis. *Journal of Education, 161*(2), 51-70.

Kounin, J.S. (1970). *Discipline and group management in classrooms.* New York: Holt, Rinehart and Winston.

Kounin, J.S., and Gump, P.V. (1958). The ripple effect in discipline. *Elementary School Journal, 59,* 158-162.

―――. (1974). Signal systems of lesson settings and the task related behavior of preschool children. *Journal of Educational Psychology, 66,* 554-562.

Leeper, M., and Green, D. (1978). *The hidden costs of rewards: New perspectives on the psychology of human motivation.* Hillsdale, N.J.: Lawrence Erlbaum.

Leonard, C.M. (1984). *Evaluation report on "PASS:" Positive Alternatives to Student Suspensions.* Portland, Oreg.: Portland Public Schools, Research and Evaluation Department. (ED 256 772)

McDermott, R.P. (1976). Kids make sense: An ethnographic account of the interactional management of success and failure in one first-grade classroom. Doctoral dissertation, Stanford University, Stanford, Calif.

McLaughlin, T.F. (1976). Self-control in the classroom. *Review of Educational Research, 46,* 631-663.

Metz, M. (1978). *Classrooms and corridors.* Berkeley: University of California Press.

O'Leary, K.D., and O'Leary, S.G. (1977). *Classroom management: The successful use of behavior modification* (2nd ed.). New York: Pergamon.

Parents Union for Public Schools (1982). *Suspended students—Suspended learning: A report on suspensions in the Philadelphia public schools.* Philadelphia: Parents Union for Public Schools. (ED 263 270)

Parke, R.D., and Duer, J.L. (1972). Schedule of punishment and inhibition of aggression in children. *Developmental Psychology, 4,* 266-269.

Phillips, J.S., and Ray, R.S. (1980). Behavioral approaches to children's disorders. *Behavior Modification, 4,* 3-34.

Rose, T.L. (1984). Current uses of corporal punishment in American public schools. *Journal of Educational Psychology, 76,* 427-441.

Sawin, D.B., and Parke, R.D. (1979). Inconsistent discipline or aggression in young boys. *Journal of Experimental Child Psychology, 28,* 525-538.

Short, P.M., and Noblit, G.W. (1985). Missing the mark in in-school suspension: An explanation and proposal. *NASSP Bulletin, 69*(484), 112-116.

Sieber, R.T. (1976). Schooling in the bureaucratic classroom: Socialization and social reproduction in Chestnut Heights. Doctoral dissertation, New York University.

———. (1979). Classmates as workmates: Informal peer activity in the elementary school. *Anthropology and Education Quarterly,* 10, 207-235.

Spaulding, R.L. (1983). Applications of low-inference observation in teacher education. In D.C. Smith (ed.), *Essential knowledge for beginning educators.* Washington, D.C.: American Association of Colleges for Teacher Education.

Stevens, L.B. (1983). *Suspension and corporal punishment of students in the Cleveland public schools, 1981-1982.* Cleveland, Ohio: Cleveland Public Schools, Office of School Monitoring and Community Relations. (ED 263 269)

Thompson, M., Brassell, W., Persons, S., Tucker, R., and Rollins, H. (1974). Contingency management in the schools: How often and how well does it work? *American Educational Research Journal, 11*, 19-28.

Weinstein, C.S. (1979). The physical environment of the school: A review of the research. *Review of Educational Research, 49*, 557-610.

Yinger, R.J. (1980). A study of teacher planning. *Elementary School Journal, 80*, 107-127.

CHAPTER 7

Allen, Rodney Dale (1983). The effect of Assertive Discipline on the number of junior high school disciplinary referrals. *Dissertation Abstracts International, 43*, 2299A. (University Microfilms No. 83-25320)

Atwell, Bobbie McGuire (1982). A study of Teaching Reality Therapy to adolescents for self-management (doctoral dissertation, The University of North Carolina at Greensboro). *Dissertation Abstracts International, 43*, 669A.

Barrett, E.R. (1985). The effects of Assertive Discipline training on pre-service teachers' pupil control ideology, anxiety levels, and teaching concerns (doctoral dissertation, Texas A&M University). *Dissertation Abstracts International, 47*, 64A.

Barrett, E.R., and Curtis, K.F. (1986). The effect of Assertive Discipline Training on student teachers. *Teacher Education and Practice, 3*(1), 53-56.

Bauer, R.L. (1982). A quasi-experimental study of the effects of "Assertive Discipline" (doctoral dissertation, Miami University). *Dissertation Abstracts International, 43*, 25A.

Blume, D.M. (1977). Effects of Active Listening training on verbal responses of University of Florida preservice childhood education teachers (doctoral dissertation, The University of Florida). *Dissertation Abstracts International, 39*, 232A.

Brandon, L.W. (1981). The effect of a Reality Therapy treatment upon students' absenteeism and locus of control of reinforcement (doctoral dissertation, Georgia State University). *Dissertation Abstracts International, 42*, 2380A.

Brannon, J.M. (1977). The impact of teacher stage of concern and level of use of a modified Reality Therapy discipline program on selected student behaviors: A discriminant analysis approach (doctoral dissertation, The University of Mississippi). *Dissertation Abstracts International, 38*, 4037A.

Brophy, J.E., and Putnam, J.G. (1979). Classroom management in the elementary grades. In D. L. Duke (ed.), *Classroom management* (pp. 182-216). Chicago, Ill.: The National Society for the Study of Education.

Browning, B.D. (1978). Effects of Reality Therapy on teacher attitudes, student attitudes, student achievement, and student behavior (doctoral dissertation, North Texas State University). *Dissertation Abstracts International*, *39*, 4010A.

Cady, M.C. (1983). The effects of classroom teachers receiving instruction in Reality Therapy and Adlerian techniques on the attitudes of teachers toward authority in the classroom (doctoral dissertation, University of Maryland). *Dissertation Abstracts International*, *45*, 1679A.

Canter, L. (1976). *Assertive discipline: A take charge approach for today's educator.* Santa Monica, Calif.: Lee Canter and Associates.

————. (1981). *Assertive discipline follow-up guidebook.* Santa Monica, Calif.: Lee Canter and Associates.

Chanow, K.J. (1980). "Teacher Effectiveness Training": An assessment of the changes in self-reported attitudes and student observed attitudes of Junior High School Teachers (doctoral dissertation, St. John's University). *Dissertation Abstracts International*, *41*, 3241A.

Dennehy, M.N. (1981). An assessment of Teacher Effectiveness Training on improving the teacher-student relationship, maintaining classroom discipline and increasing teacher and student capacity for problem solving (doctoral dissertation, Temple University). *Dissertation Abstracts International*, *42*, 609A.

Detmer, W.F. (1974). An evaluation of Gordon's Teacher Effectiveness Training. *Dissertation Abstracts International*, *36*, 809A. (University Microfilms No. 75-16,893)

Dillard, J.W. (1974). An investigation of the effects of Teacher Effectiveness Training on the types of verbal responses and attitude change of preservice teachers (doctoral dissertation, George Peabody College for Teachers). *Dissertation Abstracts International*, *35*, 4282A.

Doyle, W. (1986). Classroom organization and management. In M.C. Wittrock (ed.), *Handbook of research on teaching* (3rd ed.). New York: Macmillan.

Emmer, E.T., Evertson, C.M., and Anderson, L. (1980). Effective classroom management at the beginning of the school year. *Elementary School Journal*, *80*, 219-231.

Ersavas, C.M. (1980). A study of the effect of Assertive Discipline at four elementary schools (doctoral dissertation, United States International University). *Dissertation Abstracts International*, *42*, 473A.

Evertson, C.M., and Emmer, E.T. (1982). Effective management at the beginning of the year in junior high classes. *Journal of Educational Psychology, 74*, 485-498.

Ewing, E. (1980). Teacher Effectiveness Training: An examination of its humanizing effects (doctoral dissertation, California School of Professional Psychology). *Dissertation Abstracts International, 41*, 2755B.

Feather, N.T. (ed.). (1982). *Expectations and actions: Expectancy-value models in psychology.* Hillsdale, N.J.: Lawrence Erlbaum.

Fishbein, M., and Ajzen, I. (1975). *Belief, attitude, intention, and behavior: An introduction to theory and research.* Reading, Mass.: Addison-Wesley.

Gang, M.J. (1974). Empirical validation of a Reality Therapy intervention program in an elementary school classroom (doctoral dissertation, The University of Tennessee). *Dissertation Abstracts International, 35*, 4216A.

Glasser, W. (1969). *Schools without failure.* New York: Harper and Row.

———. (1978). Disorder in our schools: Causes and remedies. *Phi Delta Kappan, 59*, 322-325.

———. (1986). *Control theory in the classroom.* New York: Harper & Row.

Gordon, T. (1974). *Teacher Effectiveness Training.* New York: Peter H. Wyden.

Henderson, C.B. (1982). An analysis of Assertive Discipline training and implementation on inservice elementary teachers' self-concept, locus of control, pupil control ideology and assertive personality characteristics (doctoral dissertation, Indiana University). *Dissertation Abstracts International, 42*, 4797A.

Houston-Slowik, C.A. (1982). The effects of Reality Therapy processes on locus of control and dimensions of self-concept in the school setting of Mexican-American seventh and ninth grade students (doctoral dissertation, University of Houston). *Dissertation Abstracts International, 43*, 2238A.

Huck, Jack Jay. (1975). The effect of teacher participation in Teacher Effectiveness Training on student perceptions of classroom climate in selected secondary classrooms. *Dissertation Abstracts International, 36*, 5134A. (University Microfilms No. 76-4506)

Johnson City Central School District (undated). Report. Johnson City, New York.

Kounin, J.S. (1970). *Discipline and group management in classrooms.* New York: Holt, Rinehart and Winston.

Kounin, J.S., and Doyle, P.H. (1975). Degree of continuity of a lesson's signal system and the task involvement of children. *Journal of Educational Psychology, 67*, 159-164.

Kundtz, M.K. (1981). Assertive Discipline program as a means of developing behavior management skills for classroom teachers. Master's thesis, California State University, Long Beach.

Laseter, J.C. (1981). An investigation into the effect of Teacher Effectiveness Training upon student achievement in reading and mathematics (doctoral dissertation, Georgia State University). *Dissertation Abstracts International, 42*, 937A.

Lynch, Kathryn. W. (1975). A study of the effect of inservice training on teachers in the use of some principles of Reality Therapy upon student achievement of basic mathematical competencies. *Dissertation Abstracts International, 36*, 7978A. (University Microfilm No. 76-13, 340)

McBee, M. (1979). *Evaluation of youth effectiveness training, parent effectiveness training, and affective training workshops* (report). Oklahoma City: Oklahoma City Public Schools.

McCormack, S.L. (1985). Students' off task behavior and Assertive Discipline (time-on-task, classroom management, educational interventions) (doctoral dissertation, University of Oregon). *Dissertation Abstracts International, 46*, 1880A.

Marandola, P., and Imber, S.C. (1979). Glasser's classroom meeting: A humanistic approach to behavior change with preadolescent inner-city learning disabled children. *Journal of Learning Disabilities, 12* (6), 383-387.

Masters, J.R. and Laverty, G.E. (1977). The relationship between changes in attitude and changes in behavior in the schools without failure program. *Journal of Research and Development in Education, 10*(2), 36-49.

Matthews, D.B. (1972). The effects of Reality Therapy on reported self-concept, social-adjustment, reading achievement, and discipline of fourth-graders and fifth-graders in two elementary schools (doctoral dissertation, University of South Carolina). *Dissertation Abstracts International, 33*, 4842A.

Miller, K., and Burch, N. (1979). *Teacher Effectiveness Training instructor guide*. Solana Beach, Calif.: Effectiveness Training.

Moede, L., and Triscari, R. (1985). *Looking at Chapter 2* (final report). Austin, Tex.: Austin Independent School District, Office of Research and Evaluation.

Nummela, Renate M. (1978). The relationship of Teacher Effectiveness Training to pupil self-concept, locus of control, and attitude. *Dissertation Abstracts International, 39*, 6035A. (University Microfilms No. 79-07783)

Parker, Patricia Ross (1984). Effects of secondary-level Assertive Discipline in a Central Texas School District and guidelines to successful assertion and reward strategies. *Dissertation Abstracts International, 45*, 3504A. (University Microfilms No. 85-04730)

Shaddock, J.D. (1972). Relative effectiveness of two communication training models on student teacher classroom behavior. Doctoral dissertation, University of Mississippi.

Sharpe, A.H. (1980). Effects of Assertive Discipline on Title 1 students in the areas of reading and mathematics achievement (doctoral dissertation, Ball State University). *Dissertation Abstracts International, 42*, 1531A.

Smith, S.J. (1983). The effects of Assertive Discipline training on student teachers' self perceptions and classroom management skills (doctoral dissertation, University of South Carolina). *Dissertation Abstracts International, 44*, 269.

Terrell, S.M. (1984). The effects of Assertive Discipline upon selected school discipline variables (alternatives, consequences, school-wide) (doctoral dissertation, Indiana State University). *Dissertation Abstracts International, 46*, 345A.

Thompson, J.L. (1975). The effects of the I-message component of Teacher Effectiveness training (doctoral dissertation, George Peabody College for Teachers). *Dissertation Abstracts International, 36*, 2139A.

Vandercook, R.A. (1983). The impact of the Assertive Discipline model on the Woodworth Elementary School (doctoral dissertation, Central Michigan University). *Dissertation Abstracts International, 22*, 334A.

Walker, J.M. (1983). A study exploring the effects of Teacher Effectiveness Training upon student teacher attitudes and dogmatism (doctoral dissertation, Temple University). *Dissertation Abstracts International, 44*, 2450A.

Ward, L.R. (1983). The effectiveness of "Assertive Discipline" as a means to reduce classroom disruptions (doctoral dissertation, Texas Tech University). *Dissertation Abstracts International, 44*, 2323A.

Webb, M.M. (1983). An evaluation of Assertive Discipline and its degree of effectiveness as perceived by the professional staff in selected school corporations (doctoral dissertation, Indiana University). *Dissertation Abstracts International, 44*, 2324A.

Welch, F.C. (1978). The effect of inservice training in Glasser's techniques of Reality Therapy and class meetings on teacher and student behavior (doctoral dissertation, University of South Carolina). *Dissertation Abstracts International, 39,* 7296 A.

Welch, F.C., and Dolly, J. (1980). A systematic evaluation of Glasser's techniques. *Psychology in the Schools, 17*(1), 385-389.

Wolfgang, C., and Glickman, C. (1986). *Solving discipline problems* (2nd ed.). Boston: Allyn and Bacon.

CHAPTER 8

American Psychological Association (1975). Proceedings for 1974, Resolution on corporal punishment. *American Psychologist, 30,* 605-606.

Bachman, J.G., Johnston, L.D., and O'Malley, P.M. (1984). *Monitoring the future, 1982.* Ann Arbor: University of Michigan.

Baltimore Catechism. (1943). *Father Connell's The new Baltimore catechism,* no. 3, being the text of the official revised edition, 1941, of the Baltimore catechism, no. 2. New York: Benziger Bros.

Barker, R.G., and Gump, P.V. (1964). *Big school, small school.* Stanford, Calif.: Stanford University Press.

Bridges, E.M. (1986). *The incompetent teacher.* Philadelphia: Falmer Press.

Bronfenbrenner, U. (1970). *Two worlds of childhood.* New York: Russell Sage.

Coleman, J.S. (1961). *The adolescent society.* New York: Free Press.

Durkheim, E. (1961). *Moral education.* New York: Free Press.

Englehard, G. (1986). The discovery of educational goals. Paper presented at the annual meeting of the American Education Research Association.

Forness, S., and Sinclair, E. (1984). Avoiding corporal punishment in school: Issues for school counselors. *Elementary School Guidance and Counseling, 8,* 268-276.

Gallup, G.H. (1980). *The international Gallup polls: Public opinion 1978.* Wilmington, Del.: Scholarly Resources.

Gottfredson, G.D., and Gottfredson, D.C. (1985). *Victimization in schools.* New York: Plenum.

Hallinger, P., and Murphy, J. (1985). Defining an organizational mission in schools. Paper presented at the annual meeting of the American Education Research Association.

Harris, L., et al. (1988). *The American Teacher, 1988.* New York: Harris Poll.

Hastings, E.H., and Hauser, P.H. (eds.). (1985). *International index of public opinion.* Westport, Conn.: Greenwood Press.

Holmes, M. (1984). The victory and failure of educational modernism. *Issues in Education, 2.* 23-35.

Klapp, O. (1969). *The collective search for identity.* New York: Holt, Rinehart and Winston.

Krumbholtz, J.D., and Krumbholtz, H.L. (1972). *Changing children's behavior.* Englewood-Cliffs, N.J.: Prentice-Hall.

Office of Educational Research and Improvement, Center for Education Statistics (1987). *Public school teacher perspectives on school discipline.* Washington, D.C.: U.S. Department of Education.

Personal communication. (1988). Gary Gottfredson, Center for the Social Organization of Schools, Baltimore, Md.

Peshkin, A. (1986). *The total world of a fundamentalist Christian school.* Chicago: University of Chicago Press.

Rossman, G.B., Corbett, H.D., and Firestone, W.A. (1985). *Professional cultures, improvement efforts and effectiveness.* Philadelphia: Research for Better Schools.

Rubel, R. (1977). *The unruly school.* Lexington, Mass.: D. C. Heath.

Schrag, F. (1979). The principal as a moral actor. In D.A. Erickson and V.L. Reller, eds., *The Principal in metropolitan schools.* (pp. 208-232). Berkeley: McCutchan.

Skinner, B.F. (1971). *Beyond freedom and dignity.* New York: Bantam.

Slavin, R. (1980). *Using team learning.* Baltimore, Md.: Center for the Study of Schools.

U. S. Supreme Court (1962). *Engel v. Vitale,* 370 U.S. 421.

————. (1980). *Stone v. Graham,* 449 U.S. 39.

van den Haag, E. (1975). *Punishing criminals.* New York: Basic Books.

Vitz, P. (1986). Religion in school textbooks. *The Public Interest, 84,* 79-90.

Wellish, J.B., MacQueen, L., Carriere, R.A., and Duck, G.A. (1978). School management and the organization in successful schools. *Sociology of Education, 51,* 211-227.

Wynne, E.A. (1985). *Chicago area award winning schools: 1984-85.* Chicago: College of Education, University of Illinois at Chicago.

———. (1986). The great tradition in education. *Educational Leadership, 48*, 3-14.

Wynne, E.A., and Hess, M. (1986). Long-terms trends in youth conduct and the revival of traditional value patterns. *Educational Evaluation and Policy Analysis, 8*, 294-308.

Yulish, S.M. (1980). *The search for a civic religion.* Washington, D.C.: University Press of America.

Zabel, R.H. (1981). Behavioral approaches to behavioral management. In G. Brown, R.L. McDowell and J. Smith, eds., *Educating adolescents with behavior disorders.* (pp. 192-212). Columbus, Ohio: Charles Merrill.

INTRODUCTION, PART III

Duke, D.L. (1986). School discipline plans and the quest for order in American schools. In D.P. Tattum (ed.), *Management of disruptive pupil behaviour in schools.* New York: Wiley.

Foster, M.E. (1980). *Resource handbook on discipline codes.* Cambridge, Mass.: Oelgeschlager, Gunn and Hain.

Gluckman, I.B. (1986) Reactions to school-community cooperation strategies session. Paper presented at the student discipline strategies analysis conference of the Office of Educational Research and Improvement, U.S. Department of Education, Washington, D.C.

Grant, J., and Capell, F.J. (1983). Reducing school crime: A report on the school team approach. Executive summary. San Rafael, Calif.: Social Action Research Center.

Jann, R.J., and Hyman, I. (1988). An analysis of state regulations on school discipline and corporal punishment. Paper presented at the annual convention of the National Association of School Psychologists, Chicago.

Rapp, J.A. (1986). Student discipline strategies analysis: Courts and school policies reactions. Paper presented at the student discipline strategies analysis conference of the Office of Educational Research and Improvement, U.S. Department of Education, Washington, D.C.

Rubel, R.J., and Ames, N.L. (1986). *Reducing school crime and student misbehavior: A problem-solving strategy.* Washington, D.C.: U.S. Department of Justice, National Institute of Justice.

Simon, J. (1984). Discipline in the public schools: A dual standard for handicapped and nonhandicapped students? *Journal of Law and Education, 13*, 209-237.

U.S. Department of Education (1986). *The school team approach.* Washington, D.C.: U.S. Department of Education, Alcohol and Drug Abuse Education Program.

CHAPTER 9

Barth, T. (1968). Perception and acceptance of Supreme Court decisions at the state and local levels. *Journal of Public Law, 17,* 308-350.

Bartlett, L. (1985, March). Legal responsibilities of students: Study shows school officials also win court decisions. *NASSP Bulletin, 69,* 39-47.

Becker, T., and Feeley, M. (eds.) (1973). *The impact of Supreme Court decisions.* New York: Oxford University Press.

Bennett, D. (1979). The impact of court ordered desegregation: A defendant's view. In P. Piele (ed.), *Schools and the courts.* Eugene, Oreg.: ERIC Clearinghouse on Educational Management.

Brothers, W.R. (1975, January). Procedural due process: What is it? *NASSP Bulletin, 59,* 1-8.

Center for Education Statistics (1986a). Discipline in public secondary schools. Washington, D.C.: U.S. Department of Education.

―――. (1986b). School discipline policies and practices. Washington, D.C.: U.S. Department of Education.

―――. (1987). Public school teacher perspectives on school discipline. Washington, D.C.: U.S. Department of Education.

Clark, D. (1981). Adjudication to administration: A statistical analysis of federal district courts in the twentieth century. *Southern California Law Review, 55,* 65-152.

Classroom discipline (1984). Testimony before the Senate Subcommittee on Education, Arts and Humanities, Senate Hearing 98-820. Washington, D.C.: U.S. Government Printing Office.

Cuban, L. (1975). *Hobson v. Hansen*: A study in organizational response. *Educational Administration Quarterly, 2,* 15-37.

Dolbeare, K. (1967). The public views the Supreme Court. In H. Jacob (ed.), *Law, politics, and the federal courts* (pp. 194-212). Boston: Little, Brown and Company.

Dolbeare, K., and Hammond, P. (1971). *The school prayer decisions: From court policy to local practice.* Chicago: University of Chicago Press.

Fleming, M. (1970). Court survival in the litigation explosion. *Judicature, 54,* 109-113.

Flygare, T. (1986, October). Is *Tinker* dead? *Phi Delta Kappan, 68*, 165-166.

Galanter, M. (1983). Reading the landscape of disputes: What we know and don't know (and think we know) about our allegedly contentious and litigious society. *UCLA Law Review, 31*, 4-71.

————. (1986). The day after the litigation explosion. *Maryland Law Review, 46*, 3-39.

Glazer, N. (1975). Towards an imperial judiciary. *The Public Interest, 41*, 104-108.

Gluckman, I., and Zirkel, P. (1983, September). It's the law: Is the proverbial pendulum swinging? *NASSP Bulletin, 67*, 126-128.

Graham, F. (1970). *The self-inflicted wound.* New York: Macmillan.

Grossman, J., and Sarat, A. (1975). Litigation in the federal courts: A comparative perspective. *Law and Society Review, 9*, 321-346.

Hazard, W. (1976). The law and schooling: Some observations and questions. *Education and Urban Society, 8*, 417-440.

Hillman, S. (1985). Knowledge of legally sanctioned discipline procedures by school personnel. Paper presented at the annual meeting of the American Educational Research Association, Chicago.

Hollingsworth, E.J., Lufler, H., Jr., and Clune, W., III. (1984). *School discipline: Order and autonomy.* New York: Praeger.

Horowitz, D. (1977). *The courts and social policies.* Washington, D.C.: The Brookings Institution.

Kessel, J. (1966). Public perception of the Supreme Court. *Midwest Journal of Political Science, 10*, 167-191.

Kirp, D. (1976). Proceduralism and bureaucracy: Due process in the school setting. *Stanford Law Review, 28*, 841-876.

Lempert, R. (1978). Exploring changes in the "dispute settlement function" of trial courts. *Law and Society Review, 13*, 91-138.

Lufler, H., Jr. (1979). Unintended impact of Supreme Court school discipline decisions. In M. A. McGhehey (ed.), *Contemporary legal issues in education* (pp. 102-110). Topeka, Kans.: National Organization on Legal Problems of Education.

————. (1982). Past court cases and future school discipline. *Education and Urban Society, 14*, 169-184.

Menacker, J. (Spring 1982). The courts are not killing our children. *Public Interest, 67*, 131-139.

Menacker, J., and Pascarella, E. (1983, February). How aware are educators of Supreme Court decisions that affect them? *Phi Delta Kappan, 64,* 424-426.

Muir, W.K., Jr. (1967). *Prayer in the public schools, law and attitude change.* Chicago: University of Chicago Press.

Nolte, M.C. (1975a, March). The Supreme Court's new rules for due process and how (somehow) schools must make them work. *American School Board Journal, 162,* 47-49.

_____. (1975b, May). How to survive the Supreme Court's momentous new strictures on school people. *American School Board Journal, 162,* 50-53.

Ogletree, E., and Garrett, W. (1984). Teachers' knowledge of school law. *Chicago Principals Reporter, 6,* 32-43.

Quigley, E., Redding, A.C., and Zirkel, P.A. (1986, June). Empirical research relating to school law: Impact studies in special education. *NOLPE Notes, 21,* 2-7.

Rodgers, H., Jr., and Bullock, C., III. (1976). *Coercion to compliance.* Lexington, Mass.: D.C. Heath.

Rodham, H. (1973). Children under the law. *Harvard Educational Review, 43,* 487-514.

Sametz, L., and McLoughlin, C. (1985). *Educators, children and the law.* Springfield, Ill.: Charles C. Thomas.

Sarat, A., and Felstiner, W.L.F. (1986). Law and strategy in the divorce lawyer's office, *Law and Society Review, 20,* 93-134.

Sawyer, K. (1983). The right to safe schools: A newly recognized inalienable right. *Pacific Law Journal, 14,* 1309-1341.

Scheingold, S. (1974). *The politics of rights.* New Haven, Conn.: Yale University Press.

Schimmel, D., and Williams, R. (1985, December/January). Does due process interfere with school discipline? *The High School Journal, 68,* 47-51.

Schwab, J. (1979). The perceptions of Pennsylvania principals and counselors on the issues of student rights. Doctoral dissertation, Walden University.

Sorauf, F. (1976). *The wall of separation.* Princeton, N.J.: Princeton University Press.

Teitelbaum, L. (1983). School discipline procedures: Some empirical findings and some theoretical questions. *Indiana Law Journal, 58,* 547-596.

Wasby, S. (1970). *The impact of the United States Supreme Court.* Homewood, Ill.: Dorsey Press.

Wilkinson, J.H., III. (1976). *Goss v. Lopez*: The supreme Court as school superintendent. In P. Kurland (ed.), *1975 Supreme Court Review* (pp. 25-75). Chicago: University of Chicago Press.

Wright, D., and Moles, O. (1985). Legal issues in educational order: Principals' perceptions of school discipline policies and practices. Paper presented at the annual conference of the American Educational Research Association.

Yudof, M. (1979). Procedural fairness and substantive justice: Due process, bureaucracy, and the public schools. In J. Newitt (ed.), *Future trends in education policy.* Lexington, Mass.: D.C. Heath.

———. (1986, July). Educational research relating to school law: An appraisal. *NOLPE Notes, 21,* 1-3.

Zirkel, P.A. (1977). A checklist based on Supreme Court decisions affecting education. *School Law Journal, 7,* 199-208.

———. (1978, April). A test on Supreme Court decisions affecting education. *Phi Delta Kappan, 59,* 521-522.

———. (1985a, April). The minor suit award *Phi Delta Kappan, 66,* 576-577.

———. (1985b, July). Educational research relating to school law: Educators' knowledge of school law. *NOLPE Notes, 20,* 3-5.

CHAPTER 10

American Association of School Administrators (1981). *Reporting: Violence, vandalism, and other incidents in schools.* Alexandria, Va.: American Association of School Administrators.

Benton, A.E. (1971). *Dissent and disruption in the schools.* Dayton, Ohio: Institute for Development of Educational Activities, Inc.

Berleman, W.C. (1980). *Reports of the national juvenile justice assessment centers: Juvenile delinquency prevention experiments, a review and analysis.* Washington, D.C.: U.S. Government Printing Office.

Blauvelt, P.D. (1977). They're holding the children hostage. *Nations Schools Report.* Washington, D.C.: Capitol Publications.

———. (1981). *Effective strategies for school security.* Reston, Va.: National Association of Secondary School Principals.

————. (1984). *Interface: Schools and police cooperation.* Austin, Tex.: National Alliance for Safe Schools.

Campbell, W. (1982). *Street gangs.* San Diego, Calif.: San Diego Police Department.

DeJong, W. (1986). Project DARE evaluation results. Unpublished manuscript. Washington, D.C.: National Institute of Justice, U. S. Department of Justice.

District of Columbia Public Schools and the Metropolitan Police Department (1984). *Youth awareness program.* Washington, D.C.: D.C. Public Schools.

Fox, S.L., and Shuck, L.E. (1964). *Relationship of law enforcement agencies and school districts in selected counties of California.* Ann Arbor, Mich.: University Microfilms, Inc.

Gallup, G. (1974-1985). Sixth (through seventeenth) annual Gallup Poll of the public's attitudes toward education. *Phi Delta Kappan, 56-67.*

Gottfredson, G.D. (1983). *The School Action Effectiveness Study: Interim summary of the alternative education evaluation.* Baltimore, Md.: Center for Social Organization of Schools, The Johns Hopkins University.

Grant, J. (1981). The school team approach: Issues in school change. Symposium conducted at the annual meeting of the American Educational Research Association, Los Angeles, California.

————. (1983). Reducing school crime: A report on the school team approach—executive summary. Unpublished manuscript. Washington, D.C.: National Institute for Juvenile Justice and Delinquency Prevention, U.S. Department of Justice.

Gutierrez, R.R. (1984). *South San Francisco Police Department School-Liaison Program.* South San Francisco, Calif.: South San Francisco Police Department.

Hyman, I.A. (1980). Why discipline's a many-splintered thing. *PTA Today, 6* (2), 5-7.

Illinois Criminal Justice Information Authority (1986). *Juvenile justice information policies in Illinois.* Springfield, Ill.: Illinois Criminal Justice Information Authority.

Jacobs, N., Gruber, D., and Chayet, E. (1986). *A school program to evaluate and control drug abuse.* New York, N.Y.: John Jay College of Criminal Justice.

Johnson, G., and Hunter, R. (1986). *Law-related education as a delinquency prevention strategy: A three-year evaluation of the impact of LRE on students.* Boulder, Colo.: Center for Action Research.

Los Angeles County Public Schools (1980). *Strategies for reducing violence and vandalism.* Downey, Calif.: Los Angeles County Public Schools.

May, M.R. (1979). *A descriptive view of security services in selected school districts by geographic region and student population.* Ann Arbor, Mich.: University Microfilms, Inc.

Mayer, G.R., et al. (1983). *Constructive discipline: Building a climate for learning.* Los Angeles, Calif.: Los Angeles County Schools.

Milwaukee Public Schools (1985). Resolution by Director Cullen regarding the possibility of utilizing metal detectors in the schools. Unpublished manuscript. Milwaukee, Wisc.: Milwaukee Public Schools.

_____. (1986). *Comprehensive plan for dealing with students who have committed serious criminal offenses and for improving school discipline.* Milwaukee, Wisc.: Milwaukee Public Schools.

Milwaukee, Wisconsin, Police Department (1983). Gangs: Can you read the signs? Unpublished material. Milwaukee, Wisc.: Gang Crimes Unit of the Milwaukee Police Department.

Mourning, G. (1987). Gangs and gang indicia. Unpublished material. Milwaukee, Wisc.: Milwaukee Public Schools.

Murray, R.E. (1980). *The effectiveness of intrusion alarm systems in reducing school-related crime and vandalism in an inner-city school district.* Ann Arbor, Mich.: University Microfilms, Inc.

National Alliance for Safe Schools (1978). *Checklist for school crisis contingency plans.* Austin, Tex.: National Alliance for Safe Schools.

_____. (1984). *Guide for creating school safety plans.* Austin, Tex.: National Alliance for Safe Schools.

_____. (1985). *National directory: Public school security operations.* Austin, Tex.: National Alliance for Safe Schools.

National Institute of Education (1978). *Violent schools — safe schools, the safe schools report to congress.* Washington, D.C.: U.S. Government Printing Office.

National Institute of Justice (1988). Safer schools — better students. Unpublished proposal to the Program Effectiveness Panel of the National Diffusion Network of the U.S. Department of Education.

National School Safety Center (1986). *School discipline notebook.* Sacramento, Calif.: National School Safety Center.

Nugent, D.M. (1980). An incident-based reporting system for crime and disruptive behavior in Louisiana public schools. Unpublished material. Baton Rouge: Louisiana State Department of Education, Bureau of Curriculum and In-Service, and the Staff Development Office of Discipline.

Nyre, G.E. (1985). *Final evaluation report, 1984-85: Project DARE* (Drug Abuse Resistance Education). Los Angeles, Calif.: Evaluation and Training Institute.

Office of Juvenile Justice and Delinquency Prevention (1979). *Delinquency prevention: Theories and strategies.* Washington, D.C.: U.S. Government Printing Office.

———. (1983). *School Programs.* Rockville, Md.: National Criminal Justice Reference Service.

Patterson, L.B. (1977). How to work with law enforcement agencies to improve conditions in the school. *NASSP Bulletin, 61,* 85-97.

Pursuit, D.G., Gerletti, J.D., Brown, R.M., Jr., and Ward, S. (eds.) (1986). *Police programs for preventing crime and delinquency.* Springfield, Ill.: Charles C. Thomas.

Rubel, R.J. (1977). *The unruly school: Disorders, disruptions, and crimes.* Lexington, Mass.: D.C. Heath.

———. (comp.) (1984). *Checklist: Contingency plans.* Austin, Tex.: National Alliance for Safe Schools.

———. (1986a). *Safer Schools—Better Students* program grant extension application. Unpublished material. Washington, D.C.: National Institute of Justice.

———. (1986b). Twelfth quarterly report of the *Safer Schools—Better Students* program. Unpublished material. Washington, D.C.: National Institute of Justice.

Rubel, R.J., and Ames, N. (1986). *Reducing school crime and student misbehavior: A problem solving strategy.* Washington, D.C.: U.S. Department of Justice, National Institute of Justice.

Sampson, R.J., Castellano, T.C., and Laub, J.H. (1981). *Analysis of national crime victimization survey data to study serious delinquent behavior: Monograph five—Juvenile criminal behavior and its relation to neighborhood characteristics.* Washington, D.C.: U.S. Government Printing Office.

Shepard, G.H., and James, J. (1967). Police: Do they belong in the schools? *American Education, 3,* 2-4.

Social Action Research Center (1983). Reducing school crime: A guide to program interventions. Unpublished material. Washington, D.C.: National Institute for Juvenile Justice and Delinquency Prevention, U.S. Department of Justice.

Spergel, I.A. (1985). Youth gang activity and the Chicago public schools. Unpublished material. Springfield: Illinois State Board of Education in Collaboration with the Chicago Public Schools.

Surratt, J.E. (1974). *A survey and analysis of special police services in large public school districts of the United States.* Ann Arbor, Mich.: University Microfilms, Inc.

Tremper, C.R. (1985). *School crime and student misbehavior: final evaluation report, executive summary.* San Francisco, Calif: The URSA Institute.

U.S. Congress, Senate Subcommittee to Investigate Juvenile Delinquency (1975). *Our nation's schools—A report card: 'A' in school violence and vandalism.* Washington, D.C.: U.S. Government Printing Office.

U.S. Department of Justice, Community Relations Service (1979). *School security: Guidelines for maintaining safety in school desegregation.* Washington, D.C.: U.S. Government Printing Office.

U.S. Department of Justice, Office of Juvenile Justice and Delinquency Prevention (1979). *Delinquency prevention: Theories and strategies.* Washington, D.C.: U.S. Government Printing Office.

Vestermark, S.D. (1971). *Responses to collective violence in threat or act.* Vol. I. Springfield, Va.: National Technical Information Service, Collective Violence in Educational Institutions.

Vestermark, S.D., and Blauvelt, P.D. (1978). *Controlling crime in schools: A complete security handbook for administrators.* West Nyack, N.Y.: Parker Prentice-Hall.

Williams, A.S. (1984). Crowd control guidelines. Unpublished manuscript. Clarksville, Tenn.: Austin Peay State University.

Wisconsin Juvenile Officers' Association, Police/School Liaison Program Development (1981). *Policy guidelines.* Mequon: Wisconsin Juvenile Officers' Association.

CHAPTER 11

Classroom Management and Discipline Program (1987). *Youth-school-community resources: A guide to resources for youth and families in Texas.* San Marcos, Tex.: Author.

Guetzloe, E. (1986). *Teenage suicide*. San Marcos, Tex.: Classroom Management and Discipline Program.

Lambert, L.M., Wilbur, F.P., and Young, M.J. (1987). *National directory of school-college partnerships: Current models and practices*. Washington, D.C.: American Association for Higher Education.

CHAPTER 13

Angiolillo, E.W. (1986). A descriptive study of in-school suspension programs in Pennsylvania secondary schools (doctoral dissertation, Temple University). *Dissertation Abstracts International, 47*, 2809 A.

Bordenick, F.G. (1976). A study of attitudes towards the use and value of suspension in the urban public school (doctoral dissertation, University of Pittsburgh). *Dissertation Abstracts International, 37*, 2596 A.

Carlson, R. (1964). Environmental constraints and organizational consequences. In D.E. Griffiths (ed.), *Behavioral science and educational administration: The sixty-third yearbook of the National Society for the Study of Education*, Part II (pp. 262-276). Chicago: University of Chicago Press.

Clark, W.H. (1980). The effectiveness of supervised discipline centers as an alternative to suspensions in two public secondary schools in Prince George's County, Maryland (doctoral dissertation, University of Southern California). *Dissertation Abstracts International, 42*, 1399 A.

Comerford, D.J., III, and Jacobson, M.G. (1987). Capital punishment for misdemeanors: the use of suspension at four suburban junior high schools and viable alternatives that could work, an ethnographic study. Paper presented at the annual meeting of the American Educational Research Association, Washington, D.C.

Crews, J. (1984). In-school suspension: An effective disciplinary alternative (doctoral dissertation, Rutgers University). *Dissertation Abstracts International, 45*, 2474 A.

Cubbage, D.D. (1986). Hamilton traditional alternative junior high school: A model for fundamental education (doctoral dissertation, University of Kansas). *Dissertation Abstracts International, 48*, 262 A.

Duke, D.L., and Perry, C. (1978). Can alternative schools succeed where Benjamin Spock, Spiro Agnew, and B.F. Skinner have failed? *Adolescence, 13*, 375-393.

Frith, G.H., Lindsey, J.D., and Sasser, J.L. (1980). An alternative approach to school suspension: The Dothan model. *Phi Delta Kappan, 61*, 637-638.

Garrett, J.P. (1981). In-school suspension programs in Southern Illinois high schools (doctoral dissertation, Southern Illinois University). *Dissertation Abstracts International, 42,* 2097 A.

Gold, M., and Mann, D.W. (1982). Alternative schools for troublesome secondary students. *The Urban Review, 14,* 305-317.

Harvey, D.L., and Moosha, W.G. (1977). In-school suspension: Does it work? *NASSP Bulletin, 61,* 14-17.

Heinle, F.W. (1976). Evaluation of an alternative school program: Affective change and cognitive achievements of eleventh and twelfth grade students (doctoral dissertation, University of Southern California). *Dissertation Abstracts International 37,* 5564 A.

Herzog, M.R. (1980). An analysis of data and student opinion regarding two alternatives for reducing aberrant student behavior at Niles East High School (doctoral dissertation, Vanderbilt University, George Peabody College for Teachers). *Dissertation Abstracts International, 42,* 3977 A.

Lynch, A. (1983). A comparative study of three groups of junior high school students to evaluate the effects of different methods of suspension: In-school suspension without schoolwork, in-school suspension with schoolwork, and out-of-school suspension (doctoral dissertation, University of San Francisco). *Dissertation Abstracts International, 45,* 465 A.

Montgomery County Public Schools (1981). A preliminary report of the pilot in-school suspension program, 1980081. Rockville, Md.: Montgomery County Department of Educational Accountability.

National Association of Secondary School Principals (1981). Some alternatives to school discipline: Parental liability and restitution. A legal memorandum. Washington, D.C.

Radin, N. (1988). Alternatives to suspension and corporal punishment. *Urban Education, 22,* 476-495.

Slavin, R.E. (1986). *Educational psychology: Theory into practice.* Englewood Cliffs, N.J.: Prentice-Hall.

Smith, G.R., Gregory, T.B., and Pugh, R.D. (1981). Meeting student needs: Evidence for the superiority of alternative schools. *Phi Delta Kappan, 62,* 561-564.

Stallworth, R.L. (1978). The effect of suspension as a disciplinary technique in the classroom of the 1970's (doctoral dissertation, University of Michigan), *Dissertation Abstracts International, 38,* 3871 A.

Toby, J. (1964). Is punishment necessary? *Journal of Criminal Law, Criminology and Police Science. 55,* 332-337.

REFERENCES

_____. (1980). Crime in American public schools. *The Public Interest,* *58,* 18-42.

_____. (1981). Deterrence without punishment. *Criminology, 19,* 195-209.

_____. (1983). Violence in school. In M. Tonry and N. Morris (eds.), *Crime and justice: An annual review of research,* Vol. IV (pp. 1-47). Chicago: University of Chicago Press.

Trickett, E.J., McConahay, J.B., Phillips, D., and Ginter, M.A. (1985). Natural experiments and the educational context: The environment and effects of an alternative inner-city public school on adolescents. *American Journal of Community Psychology, 13,* 617-643.

Tropea, J.L. (1987). Bureaucratic order and special children: Urban schools, 1950's-1960's. *History of Education Quarterly, 27,* 339-361.

U.S. Department of Health, Education, and Welfare (1978). *Violent schools— safe schools: The safe school study report to the Congress.* Washington, D.C.: U.S. Government Printing Office.

U.S. Supreme Court (1975). *Goss v. Lopez,* 419 U.S. 565.

Waller, W. (1932). *The sociology of teaching.* New York: John Wiley and Sons.

Williams, A. (1982). Comparative analysis of traditional suspension and a confluent school suspension program (doctoral dissertation, University of California, Santa Barbara). *Dissertation Abstracts International, 44,* 616 A.

CONTRIBUTORS

Amy Aussiker is a doctoral candidate in the Department of Educational Psychology at the University of Texas in Austin, Texas.

Walter Doyle is a professor in the College of Education at the University of Arizona, Tucson, Arizona.

Daniel L. Duke is chairman and professor in the Department of Educational Leadership and Policy Studies, Curry School of Education, University of Virginia in Charlottesville, Virginia.

Margaret E. Dunn is Director of the Classroom Management and Discipline Program in the School of Education at Southwest Texas State University, San Marcos, Texas.

Edmund T. Emmer is a professor of educational psychology at the University of Texas in Austin, Texas.

Willis J. Furtwengler is a professor of education at Peabody College, Vanderbilt University in Nashville, Tennessee.

Denise C. Gottfredson is a professor in the Institute of Criminal Justice and Criminology at the University of Maryland in College Park, Maryland.

Victor Herbert is the former Executive Director, Division of High Schools, New York City Public Schools.

Henry S. Lufler, Jr. is the Assistant Dean in the School of Education at the University of Wisconsin-Madison.

Oliver C. Moles is an Education Research Analyst in the Office of Research, Office of Educational Research and Improvement in the U.S. Department of Education, Washington, D.C.

Stewart C. Purkey is a professor of education at Lawrence University, Appleton, Wisconsin.

Robert J. Rubel is Director of the National Alliance for Safe Schools in Bethesda, Maryland.

Herb A. Sang is the former superintendent of the Duval County Public Schools, Jacksonville, Florida. He is currently superintendent, Jefferson County Board of Education, Birmingham, Alabama.

Adam Scrupski is a professor of education and Director of the Teacher Education Programs at Rutgers University, New Brunswick, New Jersey.

Scott D. Thomson is the former Executive Director of the National Association of Secondary School Principals located in Reston, Virginia. He is currently Executive Secretary, National Policy Board for Educational Administration.

Jackson Toby is a professor of sociology and Director of the Institute for Criminological Research at Rutgers University, New Brunswick, New Jersey.

Edward A. Wynne is a professor in the College of Education, University of Illinois at Chicago.

INDEX